LEARNING INNOVATION AND
THE FUTURE OF HIGHER EDUCATION

TECH.EDU : A Hopkins Series on Education and Technology

LEARNING INNOVATION and the FUTURE of HIGHER EDUCATION

JOSHUA KIM *and* EDWARD MALONEY

 JOHNS HOPKINS UNIVERSITY PRESS | *Baltimore*

Printed in the United States of America on acid-free paper
9 8 7 6 5 4 3 2 1

Johns Hopkins University Press
2715 North Charles Street
Baltimore, Maryland 21218-4363
www.press.jhu.edu

Library of Congress Cataloging-in-Publication Data

Names: Kim, Joshua, 1969– author. | Maloney, Edward, 1968– author.
Title: Learning innovation and the future of higher education / Joshua Kim
    and Edward Maloney.
Description: Baltimore : Johns Hopkins University Press, 2020. | Series: Tech.edu:
    A Hopkins series on education and technology | Includes bibliographical
    references and index.
Identifiers: LCCN 2019020737 | ISBN 9781421436630 (hardcover) |
    ISBN 1421436639 (hardcover) | ISBN 9781421436647 (ebook) |
    ISBN 1421436647 (ebook)
Subjects: LCSH: Education, Higher—Computer-assisted instruction. |
    Education, Higher—Effect of technological innovations on. | Education,
    Higher—Aims and objectives. | Educational change.
Classification: LCC LB2395.7 .K54 2020 | DDC 378.0785—dc23
LC record available at https://lccn.loc.gov/2019020737

A catalog record for this book is available from the British Library.

*Special discounts are available for bulk purchases of this book. For more information,
please contact Special Sales at specialsales@press.jhu.edu.*

Johns Hopkins University Press uses environmentally friendly book materials,
including recycled text paper that is composed of at least 30 percent post-consumer
waste, whenever possible.

For Julie
For Kirsten

CONTENTS

Preface   ix

Acknowledgments   xi

INTRODUCTION: A Turn to Learning   1

1   Foundations of the Learning Revolution   21

2   Institutional Change   53

3   Reclaiming Innovation from Disruption   85

4   The Scholarship of Learning   110

5   Leading the Revolution   141

EPILOGUE: The Future of Learning Innovation   176

Notes   193

Index   205

We wrote this book to open up a conversation about how colleges and universities might evolve their institutions to better align teaching practices with the emerging science of learning. The financial and demographic pressures endemic to higher education today will not be going away. Likely, these pressures will only grow more severe. How institutions cope with the structural challenges they face, including both rising costs (for students) and economic sustainability (for schools), while also making significant advances in student learning, is what the study of learning innovation is all about.

Writing this book was both easy and hard. Easy because both of us are fully immersed in a community of learning innovators, both at our own institutions and across the field of higher education. Hard because the ideas that we are grappling with—including our argument that we are in the midst of a postsecondary turn to learning and our vision for the creation of a new interdisciplinary academic field of learning innovation—are both nascent and contestable.

In this book, we try to say some new things—and hopefully some true things—about how learning in higher education is changing. US higher education, however, is not one thing. It is some 4,300 (depending on how one counts) different things. Telling any story about how learning is changing across all of these idiosyncratic places is likely a fool's errand. Arguing for the creation of a new academic discipline, something that almost all of our colleagues across academia warned us against attempting, may also be considered unwise.

Added to the difficulties of writing a book about learning are the growing number of fine books and articles on higher education, on learning, or on both. These are books and articles that we feel guilty for not referencing but were forced to ignore, either because we were trying to write a concise book of ideas or because they came out after our manuscript was complete.

For us, writing this book has been a source of energy and inspiration. Carving out space in our overloaded professional and personal lives to engage in scholarship has been profoundly rewarding. In fact, the act of reorienting our identities from those of academic administrators to scholars has been so rewarding that we spend much of the book recommending this path to others in the learning innovation community. We hope that at least some readers will enjoy even a tiny fraction of the pleasure in reading this book that we have experienced in its writing.

ACKNOWLEDGMENTS

Acknowledging the contributions of all of the people who have shaped our thinking on learning innovation would require a book twice the length that you are currently holding. In thanking some for contributing their ideas and stories to this book, we fear that many who have helped to shape our understanding of how learning is changing in higher education will go unrecognized.

First, we'd like to thank those who generously agreed to participate in a series of in-depth interviews in 2017 and 2018. These colleagues are Derek Bruff, Amy Collier, Adam Croom, Kristen Eshleman, Peter Felten, Adam Finkelstein, Jennifer Frederick, John Fritz, PB Garrett, Jim Groom, Jill Leafstedt, Phillip Long, Shawn Miller, Mark Nemec, Matthew Rascoff, Catherine Ross, Romy Ruukel, Lucas Swineford, and Laura Winer.

Much of this work owes its existence to shared conversations we've had with colleagues deeply immersed in the work of learning innovation, first at the Roundtable on Academic Transformation at Georgetown University and later at the many HAIL (Harvesting Academic Innovation for Learners) symposia. This book was made richer because of the thoughtful insights of Bryan Alexander, Kelvin Bentley, Michael Berman, MJ Bishop, David Cormier, James DeVaney, Peter Eckel, Julie Goff, Michael Feldstein, Phil Hill, Sean Hobson, Harrison Keller, Allison Dulin Salisbury, Daniel Seaton, David Soo, Peter Stokes, and Elliott Visconsi.

Eddie would like to thank his colleagues at Georgetown University, including those at the Center for New Designs in Learning and Scholarship (CNDLS) and within the Program in Learning, Design, and Technology (LDT). Many conversations over the years with Josh Burgher, Molly Chehak, Maggie Debelius, Sharon Koehler, Anna Kruse, Joselyn Schultz Lewis, Kim Luciano, Elizabeth McWilliams, Daryl Nardick, John Rakestraw, Marie Selvanadin, Elizabeth Stephen, Kathryn Temple,

Matthew Tinkcom, and Yianna Vovides contributed immensely to the ideas that shape this book. He would also like to thank Morris Beja, Kelly Marsh, Dominic Pettman, and James Phelan for their friendship and patience as he's tried to explain the often esoteric connections he sees between the work of narrative and critical theory with learning innovation. Many of the ideas at the core of Eddie's contribution to this book have evolved through discussion, at times disagreement, and always in collaboration with Randy Bass, with whom he has been fortunate to have worked and, more importantly, been friends with for the past 20 years. Finally, he would like to thank two colleagues he has been lucky enough to have as thought partners and friends throughout his time at Georgetown, Frank Ambrosio and Ricardo Ortiz.

Launching a new degree program is a daunting task, and the first two cohorts of the LDT entered with a sense of discovery and innovation. Talking with them in class and in conversations in and around the halls have informed many of the concepts at the core of this text. The success of CNDLS and the LDT is due in no small part to the support and leadership of both the provost and the dean of the Graduate School of Arts and Sciences at Georgetown.

Josh would like to thank his colleagues at the Dartmouth Center for the Advancement of Learning and the Learning Design and Technology team for teaching him most everything that he knows about learning. Among the educators that Josh would like to acknowledge for contributing ideas and expertise that have shaped his thinking on learning innovation are: Malcolm Brown, Alan Cattier, Erin DeSilva, Michael Goudzwaard, Anthony Helm, Richard Katz, and Ray Schroeder. InsideHigherEd.com (IHE) has provided Josh with a platform to connect with the learning innovation community for over a decade. The cofounders and editors of IHE, Scott Jaschik and Doug Lederman, were early believers that out of a blog could emerge a book. Josh will always be deeply indebted to Scott and Doug for their patience and guidance as he developed his alternative-academic voice.

We are both grateful to Greg Britton, editorial director of Johns Hopkins University Press, for his skillful and patient guidance as this book evolved from proposal to finished manuscript. We hope this is the first book of many we will collaborate on together. We would also like to thank Joanne Haines for her painstaking and thoughtful copyediting.

Finally, we'd like to say thank you to our families.

Josh's work on this book coincided with his kids, Alexi and Madeleine, leaving home and going off to college. The sort of learning environments that we want to create in higher education for all of our kids was much on Josh's mind as he worked on cowriting this book. Josh would also like to recognize all four of his parents for the wisdom and support that each continues to provide. Lastly, Josh would like to say thank you to his wife, Dr. Julie Kim, as without her love and partnership this book would have never come into the world.

Unlike Josh, Eddie's kids, Eamon and Tess, are still a few years away from college. Writing a book about a future of higher education that may (or may not) be true when they do finally attend school was, too, always on his mind. He's grateful for their patience through many nights and weekends of writing. He owes much of his passion for learning to his mother, his father, his stepmother, and his uncle, who all showed him the importance of higher education and higher education institutions, each in their own way. Finally, his contribution to this book would not have been possible without the amazing patience, love, and support his wife, Kirsten Maloney, has given him. Besides being incredibly lucky, he is forever grateful.

LEARNING INNOVATION AND
THE FUTURE OF HIGHER EDUCATION

A Turn to Learning

IN 2017, Georgetown University launched a new master's degree program called Learning, Design, and Technology (LDT). This is a program with which we are both intimately familiar, with one of us (Eddie) serving as the founding director and professor and the other (Josh) as a senior scholar in the program. When it launched, the LDT joined a growing group of master's degree programs offering training and credentialing in fields such as instructional design, learning analytics, and technology innovation. While there are many excellent graduate programs in the United States in these areas of study,[1] the LDT has a unique focus. The program not only trains students in these core areas, but it situates these fields in relationship to the history (and future) of higher education. In doing so, the program design reflects the conviction that the work of design, innovation, and learning is different in higher education than it is in areas such as elementary and secondary school, the corporate world, government, or nonprofits. By making higher education the center of the work, the context of the university becomes the laboratory in which the teaching, learning, and applied study is carried out. Aside from this particular context, perhaps the most distinct aspect of the LDT is that it is the first graduate program for future higher education learning professionals that was conceived of and designed by the faculty and staff in a center for teaching and learning (CTL), Georgetown

University's Center for New Designs in Learning and Scholarship (CNDLS). While the LDT's academic home is the Graduate School of Arts and Sciences at Georgetown University, it was not developed in the traditional manner by an existing academic department or within a school of education. It is an experiment in institutional innovation.

The Georgetown program was created out of a recognition that to respond to the changing landscape of higher education, we must teach people to do the work of higher education in new and different ways. The next generation of professionals who will conceive of and run institution-wide learning initiatives needs to be responsive to a complex set of intersecting concepts, practices, and models unique to higher education. This approach requires the integration of fields of study and practice that are not usually brought together in graduate programs, and it recognizes that the faculty and experts who are most closely connected to this thinking and teaching—the faculty who are best able to help train the next generation of academic learning leaders—often work within learning organizations, the centers that collaborate with partners across institutions to drive learning transformation.

That one of us leads a campus learning organization that is shepherding a master's degree to train future learning professionals is, we think, illustrative of the times. Our friends and colleagues in the learning community who helped inspire this book may not be running their own graduate programs in their own learning organizations—as far as we know, CNDLS is the only CTL that has some of its faculty involved in designing and implementing a graduate program—but this may change. Even if CNDLS is an outlier now, those in higher education are more likely than not to be involved in leading some institutional-scale learning initiative at their college or university. Learning professionals working in campus learning organizations such as CTLs, online learning units, and academic computing departments are likely to see the learning initiatives and programs they are running as responses to local institutional needs and goals. We have come to believe, however, that new learning programs and initiatives—along with the new and reorganized learning centers and units that have emerged over the past few years—need to be understood as part of a larger and more coherent higher education story.

We believe that we are in the midst of a higher education–wide shift. This larger trend is animating much of the specific and idiosyncratic campus changes that we and our colleagues at other colleges and universities are both creating and navigating. How did we get here?

The Sky Is Falling

In 2012, higher education in the United States was under attack. Steadily rising costs and a growing disconnect between the demands of employers on the one hand, and higher education's perceived role (and lack of direct success) in training future employees on the other, created a climate ripe for criticism. The function of higher education to teach students to be productive members of society, not to mention healthy and happy lifelong learners, was in question. New technologies that leveraged digital media and global connectivity, particularly massive open online courses (MOOCs), suggested to some that there might be better ways to train our traditional students, not to mention educate the millions of other students throughout the world looking for access to advanced content and expertise. Vocal critics of postsecondary education argued that alternative models of training and credentialing would soon disrupt the well-established role colleges and universities had long played in our society. In a now well-worn claim, Sebastian Thrun, founder of Udacity, one of the first MOOC providers, imagined a world in fifty years in which there were only ten institutions of higher education,[2] down from the estimated 28,000 currently.[3] The future was, at the very least, unclear.

For institutions built on long-held traditions—and the stability those traditions provided—this was a scary time. The year 2012 marks an inflection point in higher education, and MOOCs were the catalyst that made it happen. The promise and threat of MOOCs forced colleges and universities to ask questions—some for the first time—about higher education's well-established approaches to teaching and learning. This moment forced higher education to consider the efficacy of overnight solutions, such as MOOCs, to educate a diverse group of students with a complex set of goals and aspirations. While the anxiety of 2012 may seem excessive in hindsight, the questions and challenges raised continue to resonate and inform much of the work higher education has undertaken to think about its future.

This book marks this moment in higher education. We track not only from where we've come but to where we hope higher education will go. We do so by recognizing that the very real questions that surfaced in 2012 have not been answered and thankfully are not going away. What has happened since 2012, however, has been a fuller realization of what we are calling "a turn to learning." As we discuss in chapter 1, this turn to learning has long been in the making. Where and when it started is up for some debate, but it highlights an ongoing shift from the traditional delivery of education—often called "the banking model of education" after Paulo Freire's well-known characterization—to a more active, engaged learning. The pedagogical changes ushered in by new student-centered models as well as new digital technologies, inclusive pedagogy, global networks, and ubiquitous information access have changed not only *what* needs to be taught but *how* best to teach. While we focus primarily on the impact of digital technologies and innovations on learning in this book, we believe this analysis opens up a discussion of a full range of approaches to teaching and learning.

How faculty in colleges and universities teach and students learn has not only evolved because of the rise of new pedagogical approaches and new digital technologies but also because of a complex, evolving expectation about the role of higher education in developing the skills for lifelong learning and professional adaptability. The role of the faculty member as the primary—and often sole—conduit to learning for students is morphing, and many colleges and universities are creating new structures to meet these ever growing needs. How we teach and how we learn are changing, and we would argue both *need* to change. Whether those changes should be in radical ways, as some have argued, or in constant, steady ways, as others have suggested, remains to be seen. There may be no one single successful approach but rather a multitude of models that continually challenge the traditional models of teaching and learning that have marked the history of higher education.

Given that teaching students to learn is a shared activity throughout higher education, we find it curious that how universities go about understanding and designing for student learning is so little understood or documented itself. There is a growing body of scholarly and popular literature on how people learn. This scholarship, however, is not matched by a parallel scholarship on how universities advance learning. Recent books such as *Make It Stick: The Science of Successful Learning* (2014) and *How We Learn: The Surprising Truth about When, Where, and Why It Happens* (2014) have explored recent advances in learning science for a nonspecialist audience. Little work has been done, however, to examine how advances in the science of learning translate into organizational changes across higher education.

There are also many wonderful books exploring how individual professors may align their teaching practices with the findings of learning science, including Ken Bain's *What the Best College Teachers Do* (2004) and James Lang's *Small Teaching: Everyday Lessons from the Science of Learning* (2016). Books aimed at guiding instructors on research-based pedagogical practices for effective design and instruction of online and blended courses are too numerous to mention. The past few years have seen many excellent books on the future of higher education, as well. The postsecondary learning community eagerly consumes books such as Cathy Davidson's *The New Education: How to Revolutionize the University to Prepare Students for a World in Flux* (2017), Kevin Carey's *The End of College: Creating the Future of Learning and the University of Everywhere* (2016), Michael M. Crow's coauthored *Designing the New American University* (2015), and Joseph E. Aoun's *Robot-Proof: Higher Education in the Age of Artificial Intelligence* (2017). Where these books are read and how their lessons are applied are important considerations for us and for readers of this book. The place in the academy where these books are brought into conversation with each other, where they are read critically and in relationship to the other literature on higher education change, is often less obvious. According to the many learning professionals we interviewed for this book, it is not as clear how the scholarship of higher education is helping to inform and change higher education writ large.

How then do universities change to improve student learning? This seemingly simple question has few good answers. The amount that we know about how learning works is significant and growing every day. The literature on the scholarship of teaching and learning is both theoretically grounded and empirically robust. We have no shortage of knowledge about how learning works and how this knowledge can be applied to advance teaching. What we lack is an understanding of the conditions in which learning science propagates through institutions to change organizational structures and teaching practices. We know that universities can adapt to align their policies and curricula with learning science. Beyond anecdotes and social media, we don't know how or why they do so. Nor do we have a deep understanding of what steps higher education leaders should take to match how the students at their schools learn with the research on how these students might learn best. We do not have a comprehensive understanding of how theories of design, technology, innovation, and analytics are challenging our fundamental assumptions about teaching and learning in higher education. These are the central questions of what we are calling "learning innovation."

Defining Learning Innovation

In this book, we define learning innovation as the interplay between the complex set of practices, methods, and designs that are part of the attempts by higher education to improve teaching and student learning. The practices not only bring together learning science, applied educational technologies, and learning analytics, but they do so within the framework of the institutional structures, policies, investments, and strategic leadership that enable this work. In this respect, learning innovation is as much about innovations in teaching and learning (in the classroom, course, or curriculum) as it is about sustainable innovations at the institutional level. The pairing of "learning" and "innovation" brings together an array of ideas, concepts, theories, arguments, and data into a synthetic field of inquiry. We explore the innovation half of the phrase in greater detail in chapter 3. For the time being, when we use the word "innovation," we mean an intentional and aspirational investment in change to improve practices. These practices occur along a continuum from individual faculty transformations to institutional reforms.

The learning side of this pairing carries with it the full range of research questions that constitute fields such as learning science and educational technology but also those fields related to the study of higher education. The scholarship of learning innovation concerns itself with unpacking the causes and consequences of how universities change in response to advances in the science of learning. Learning innovation relocates the unit of analysis of the conditions that support or inhibit student learning from that of the individual student to the scale of the institution and to everywhere in between. Largely this book leaves to the side a full treatment of the components of the study of learning. We use the word "learning" as a shorthand for this complex interplay of ideas, methods, and theories that underpin and explain how our colleges and universities structure the learning experience. Our choice to forgo in-depth discussions of the attributes that make up the larger academic study of how people learn has largely been driven by the goals of this book. The turn to learning we are marking stems in part from a focus on making institutional changes and investments in student learning across all of higher education. We think this trend deserves the attention that can only come with the dedicated scholarship possible in the creation of interdisciplinary fields. In making this argument, we chose to address the full implications of the term "learning innovation," with the assumption that most of our readers will come to the book with good knowledge of areas such as learning science, design theory, educational technology, learning analytics, and pedagogical theory. There are many excellent books about how people learn. There are few, if any, books about how universities are changing in response to innovations in learning.

A Tenuous Shift?

While we argue that learning innovation is part of a turn to learning, we also worry about the fragility of this shift. As practitioners situated within schools undergoing both rapid and profound change in how teaching and learning are constructed, our perspective is that the gains made during this turn to learning have not yet solidified. The feeling of impermanence in the turn to learning may be a function of a lack of long-range commitments and strategic priorities in which this shift has occurred. Few college presidents or provosts would announce publicly that their school's current practices about teaching and learning do not fully align with the science of learning. Institutional rankings and status do not benefit from candid admissions about shortcomings in pedagogy. No college or university, on the other hand, is shy in claiming excellence in teaching and learning.

Many of the factors that we suspect have contributed to this turn to learning, such as the growth of online education and experiments in massive open online courses, have been motivated by factors outside of the goal of advancing student learning. It is not clear if the emergence of centers for innovation will persist as the campus leaders who championed these new organizational structures move on to other positions or retire. Other changes, such as campus reorganizations that combined previously disparate campus resources and services related to student learning into a single campus unit, may have more staying power. It's an open question, however, if even these newly constituted units (such as integrated centers for teaching and learning) will succeed in maintaining a mandate (and funding) for experimentation and risk-taking.

Part of our motivation for writing this book is to argue for the need to sustain the gains from the turn to learning in which we have both participated. As we discovered in our research for this book, a common reason given by our peers at a range of institutions for the focus on learning innovation is what we might call "the magical provost." In a few instances, the magical provost is replaced by the charismatic president. Our read of the postsecondary landscape indicates that charismatic presidents who prioritize learning innovation are a bit rarer than the magical provost. Most often, the magical provost is the one who can knock down bureaucratic barriers and find the funding for new organizations and initiatives aimed at dramatic improvements in student learning. The reliance on the magical provost to catalyze campus learning innovation is a dual-edged sword, as provosts (and in particular activist provosts) don't seem to stick around very long. Rather than relying on visionary campus leaders, we are arguing that the work of learning innovation needs to find a more solid organizational and intellectual footing within the academy. Learning innovations must become provost independent if this turn to learning is to survive the next funding crisis or the next educational fad.

The Challenge of Learning Innovation

We wrote this book not only to mark this turn to learning but also to acknowledge the work our colleagues at learning organizations across higher education have found themselves undertaking to nurture this turn. The learning innovation they are helping to lead might be happening under a host of synonyms and parallel titles, from academic innovation to learning transformation to entrepreneurial learning. At Georgetown, this work is happening in a complex, intersecting partnership between the LDT, CNDLS, and the Red House, an incubator for academic innovation and equity. At Dartmouth, learning innovations are embedded in collaborations that the Dartmouth Center for the Advancement of Learning has with faculty and a range of centers and units across the institution—collaborations designed to explore new instructional models within an intimate liberal arts tradition of teaching and learning.

The learning innovation initiatives that those reading this book are leading on their own campuses are likely equal parts energizing and terrifying. Energizing because teaching and learning in higher education are changing at a terrific pace. The confluence of advances in learning science with the emergence of new learning technologies, techniques, and models has brought more change to teaching and learning in the last seven years than perhaps the previous seventy. Terrifying because those charged with leading new campus learning innovation initiatives—be they the institution-wide adoption of new learning technologies and programs or the creation of new online or residential programs—are likely the first on their campuses to attempt this work. To work in the field of postsecondary learning in the last few years is to work without a map and perhaps without a net.

Many readers will be like us, either inhabiting a role that has some relatively short history or, in many cases, the first to hold a newly created job title. Whatever the history of these positions is at individual schools, people in these roles will likely find themselves running learning programs and learning initiatives that are wholly new to their institutions. The dizzying pace of innovations in learning across higher education has outpaced the professional—and we argue, scholarly—foundations that support and inform this work. It is common to hear from those leading learning innovation efforts that they feel "professionally at sea," a displacement that is neither productive nor sustainable. As we discuss in chapter 4, the professional associations and organizations that developed around earlier eras of educator development, educational technologies, and online learning have been unable to evolve quickly enough to meet the needs of those leading institution-wide learning innovation efforts.

As the work of these professionals demonstrates, learning innovation is as much about leading organizational change as it is about pedagogy and technology. Those of us who have found ourselves in new roles leading learning innovation have found it difficult to find a home within the existing structures of professional associations because the work of learning innovation crosses job titles and organizational categories. It is not that the learning innovation community is absent from the existing professional associations, it is more that we are spread across a range of previously established communities of practice. As we explore in chapter 2, the learning innovation community is fragmented across a variety of centers for teaching excellence, online learning, academic computing, and educational technology, as well as other professional associations and organizations. Lacking a coherent set of frameworks and methods—and with little consistency in training or background or career paths—those of us engaged in the work of institutional learning innovation can easily feel isolated and unsure of our next steps.

Some within this developing learning innovation community have tried to overcome the limitations of existing associations and organizations by either reforming professional groups in which they have long been affiliated or building new more grassroots learning innovation organizations. This book is, in part, an argument against exclusively following this approach. Rather than understanding our roles in leading learning innovation efforts on our campuses through a professional lens, we argue in chapter 4 for a reconception of this work as an emergent interdisciplinary field of study. We firmly believe that these times call for a breaching of the barriers that separate higher education services and operations from the scholarship of higher education. The old divides between those who "administer" higher education and those who "teach" in higher education will only serve to inhibit meaningful change across our institutions, and specifically in areas related to learning.

We argue that those of us committed to innovating learning on our campuses need to find ways to transform the learning organizations we are connected with—whether they are CTLs or academic computing units or online learning divisions—into something entirely new, equal parts academic department and support unit. Starting in the early twentieth century, there have been growing distinctions (and divides) between academic and administrative units, between faculty and staff. Administrative units focused on service to the institution and cocurricular activities (student affairs, student formation), whereas academic units had primary responsibilities around teaching and scholarship. This is changing. Nowhere in higher education are the academic/administrative and faculty/staff barriers breaking down more quickly than in areas related to learning. The service work that learning professionals engage in when they collaborate with faculty on course and program design is complemented, reinforced, and reinvigorated by scholarship and teaching. This hybrid approach also means that in addition to the service work that learning organizations provide to their institutions, they will also need to prioritize a new scholarship of learning innovation. This reorientation of the work from a professional activity to an applied scholarly endeavor will also require us to rethink how tomorrow's scholar-practitioners of learning innovation are trained and if the current practice of recruiting into this work from professional training programs and traditional academic disciplines will suffice.

Those of us developing, managing, and leading learning initiatives toward a scholarship of learning innovation have to piece together research from many different fields in order to guide our efforts (see chapter 3). For this work to have lasting impact, learning professionals need to engage in scholarship ourselves to study how universities are changing to align with learning science and to take advantage of new technologies and methods. The idea that the work of learning professionals is that of a scholar-practitioner—and that the intellectual work of understanding how universities change to advance learning should be undertaken in an interdisciplinary field of our own making—will require something of a mind shift. The separation of the intellectual work from the administrative/service work of the university is deeply ingrained and mirrored in the organizational structures of our institutions. Faculty work in departments and schools. Staff work in centers and units. Faculty have academic freedom and retain the rights to their own intellectual property. Staff are not generally protected by the conventions of academic freedom, and their output (including intellectual output) is often owned by the institution in which they work, a problem we explore further in chapter 4. The primary loyalty of professors is to the discipline in which they trained, as career advancement and recognition hinge on peer review from disciplinary colleagues across institutions. Administrative staff, conversely, are primarily tied to the institutions in which they are employed—with career advancement hinging on service and contribution to the institution. For faculty whose primary roles are teaching courses and conducting research, service work tends to be valued far less than their teaching and research. For staff, service to the institution, at the organizational and institutional levels, is their primary activity.

If the turn to learning is happening as we suggest, the cultural orientations and organizational structures of the modern university, ones where faculty/staff lines are clearly demarcated, are lagging behind the new realities of how learning is now constructed. Learning professionals in nonfaculty roles engage in a mix of service, support, scholarship, and teaching. We are already doing this work. It is also true that the intellectual (and sometimes teaching) work of nonfaculty educators most commonly goes unrecognized in determining the career progression and professional achievements of nonfaculty educators. Scholarship must be undertaken on top of and around regular administrative service and support responsibilities. Teaching is not part of the regular job but layered on top of these customary accountabilities. This can make efforts to integrate the range of service and support tasks that learning professionals undertake with the desire to build a portfolio of scholarship and teaching feel like an impossible task.

What is lost when a university fails to make space for scholar-practitioners within its campus learning organizations is the institution's ability to evolve its core educational practices. Teaching methods are best thought of as continuous disciplined experiments. Teaching practices should evolve with the research on how people learn and with the tools educators have at their disposal. The rapid shift that higher education is experiencing toward the digitization of teaching, with learning increasingly mediated through online platforms rather than residential classrooms, is only accelerating the need for colleges and universities to adapt their educational practices.

There are some very serious implications of these distinctions that fundamentally affect the challenges facing higher education. It is well recognized that the rising cost of higher education is often attributed (rightly or wrongly) to growing administrative costs. The functions of administrative units are often seen as separate from the fundamental functions of colleges and universities. The new reality we explore throughout this book suggests that a more productive approach to both cost and impact would be better served if faculty and administration saw their roles as diametrically linked. Administrative units necessarily play a greater role in the mission of teaching and learning today, just as faculty have deep expertise that should help inform how colleges and universities function. The dynamic we are exploring here, then, is at the intersection of this relationship, where faculty and professional staff inform the work of each other to strengthen the entire learning experience for students.

How universities should combine existing and new methods of teaching are not immediately obvious. There is no easily discoverable algorithm to guide the development of educational practices. Improving student learning outcomes at any end of the spectrum, from reducing attrition to cultivating wisdom, is a wicked problem. Deciding where to adopt new teaching methods and new educational practices in support of advancing learning is immensely challenging. Added to this difficulty in advancing learning are the financial challenges that higher education faces as a result of public policy choices (state-level disinvestment), demographic headwinds, a highly educated (and therefore expensive) staff and faculty, and new postsecondary competitors. Institutional investments to advance student learning are difficult to make in an environment of scarcity and fragility.

If what we are arguing is true, the work of learning professionals in the future will be less about implementing techniques, methods, and technologies to improve student learning outcomes. The low-hanging fruit of making low-cost changes to teaching practices to encourage active and student-centered learning may soon reach a point across higher education where it's mostly been harvested. Online degree programs that quickly enroll new students in order to meet unmet market demand have been created at many institutions. The shift away from lecture-only residential courses to blended teaching methods and the reconfiguration of fixed-seat classrooms to flexible learning spaces have enough momentum to continue. But these do not go far enough to address the challenges of teaching twenty-first-century students. Learning professionals will need to discover ways to advance learning science and learning technologies within the new financial, demographic, and competitive realities of higher education. Learning innovation no longer means only improving learning outcomes but rather doing so within an environment of largely unprecedented economic constraints and competition. The work of learning innovation will need to focus not only on individual learners, or even entire programs and degrees, but on contributing directly to institutional resiliency.

The Learning Innovation Conversation

In researching this book, we spoke with colleagues from across the United States, from a variety of institutional types, from public to private, from two-year to research institutions. We found that our peers and colleagues leading learning innovation initiatives on their campuses also have a hunger for a different sort of conversation about the future of higher education. Like us, they are motivated to participate in the large-scale structural changes at their schools that will lead to sustainable and nonincremental advances in student learning. Also like us, they are challenged by traditional academic norms that divide scholarship and teaching on learning innovation from the day-to-day work of leading learning innovation efforts. For those building careers in learning outside of traditional faculty roles, career advancement requires one to take on expanding responsibilities around management (more direct reports) and budget authority. Few learning professionals were originally motivated to build a career in higher education, however, based on a desire to manage people or budgets. There are few career paths for learning professionals in which institutional influence aligns with contributions to teaching, scholarship, and service. Institution-wide learning initiatives that should be critically studied in order to develop generalizable conclusions go largely unstudied. As a result, each college or university that attempts a new learning innovation—be it a new online program or a course redesign initiative—does so *de novo*. Both learning professionals and the institutions in which they work will lose out as long as the scholar-practitioner divide is maintained.

In the pages that follow, we develop our ideas for a new type of learning career and a new type of learning organization. We make this argument through the lens of learning innovation—both as a practice and as a newly emergent interdisciplinary field. We hope our colleagues across the multitude of nontraditional academic roles who work to advance student learning find their contributions represented in these pages. One of the challenges in writing about how learning is changing in higher education is the sheer diversity and variability of programs, projects, and initiatives. Our aim in this book is not to catalog or critique even a representative portion of learning innovations. Rather, our goal is to lay the foundation for the critical study of learning innovation.

We hope that those reading this book will find at least some of our arguments about learning innovation valuable. We make the case for understanding the turn to learning in higher education, the importance of creating new forms of learning organizations and new pathways for nonfaculty learning careers, the limits of professional organizations and social media, and the need to establish a new interdisciplinary field of learning innovation. While this is a book built around a series of arguments related to learning, its success or failure does not hinge on their persuasiveness. Rather, we believe its success or failure will be based on whether we have initiated a different sort of conversation about learning innovation. The intellectual space to discuss how universities are changing to advance learning—which we believe this book plays a part in creating—is one that encourages, indeed depends upon, dialogue, debate, and disagreement. The measure of the success of any disciplinary or interdisciplinary field is not the answers that it provides but the questions that it asks. We have been lacking a shared intellectual space in which learning innovations can be evaluated, debated, and critically examined. When discussions of learning innovation occur, they are too often ahistorical, decontextualized, and data impoverished. The norms of knowledge creation that govern scholarly investigation in established academic disciplines are inconsistently applied to critical evaluations of institutional learning innovation. This book is our attempt to situate the question of how universities change to advance student learning, as well as the work of leading institution-wide learning innovation initiatives, on a more solid scholarly foundation.

Our Audience

The book is intended to provide a useful mirror back to the work of those in centers for teaching and learning, academic computing units, online learning divisions, and other departments, divisions, and centers where the focus is on advancing learning. These colleagues go by many titles, including instructional and learning designer, educational technologist, and learning analytics specialist. What unites this group is not where they work on campus, or what their job title may be, but rather the work that they do to create environments and opportunities to advance student learning. In some instances, these colleagues are also professors (or instructors) engaged in teaching as well as scholarship and administrative tasks. In most cases, however, our peers in the learning innovation world are collaborators and partners with the more traditional campus educators and leaders: professors, chairs, deans, and provosts.

The learning professionals that we write for and about occupy liminal roles in the educational mission of the institution. They work in the gray areas between faculty and administrator. They are educators, yet their primary job responsibilities on campus do not include teaching two or three classes a semester. They are staff, as almost none are eligible for tenure, and yet their internal motivations and academic training often closely resemble those of their faculty colleagues. Sometimes known as alternative academics (or alt-acs), this is a group of educators seeking to establish both their credibility and their roles within the institutions that they work. We hope that this group of colleagues sees their work reflected with accuracy and empathy in the pages to follow.

A second group with whom we'd like this book to gain some traction is those in higher education leadership. Throughout this book, we offer ideas to support and diffuse learning innovation. The gatekeepers that enable the move from ideas to action are the deans, provosts (including vice and assistant provosts), presidents, and even board members and trustees. So much of the work of learning innovation depends on the ability of learning professionals to gain and keep executive sponsorship. The more that higher education leaders feel that learning investments are strategic investments, ones that align with institutional goals around differentiation and long-term viability, the more they will support proactive investments in learning. We hope that university leaders will be curious about the learning innovations that we discuss at numerous colleges and universities and be motivated to make the difficult strategic and resource tradeoffs necessary to ensure that learning is a strategic institutional priority.

The third audience that we have in mind for this book is those doing the teaching—the professors. One of the areas of potential opportunity to advance student learning that we identify in the book is the tradition around faculty autonomy and shared governance. Rather than seeing the independent role of faculty as an impediment to positive learning advances, we believe this attribute to be essential for a sustained and sustainable turn to learning. In direct opposition to those enamored by the potential of disruptive innovation on our campuses, we view the practices of tenure and accountability to one's academic discipline as a bulwark of learning innovation. Part of our call to build the status and resources available to learning is to invest in professors. The faculty workforce is increasingly made up of contingent professors with tenuous job security. This situation is antithetical to the goals of advancing student learning. This book is intended to support a range of faculty, from those who are tenured (or on the tenure track) to the visiting and adjunct instructors who make up an increasing proportion of all post-secondary educators.

How We Approached Writing about Learning Innovation

Our goal for this book is to contribute to a larger conversation around learning innovation in higher education. This is a conversation in which we have been active participants and one that has grown more intense and consequential over the past few years. This conversation takes place within our institutions, at professional conferences, and across various social media platforms. Where this conversation is occurring too little is in classrooms and books. The contours, challenges, and lessons of learning innovation are not being taught to either graduate students or undergraduates to the degree they should. The dissertations are mostly not being written. The result is that while conversations on learning innovation feel immediate and vital, they are likely to be ephemeral. As we discuss in chapter 4, blog posts and tweets are excellent for community building and ideation but poor vehicles for sustained engagement. Conference discussions help us bring best practices and new ideas back to our campuses, but their value is restricted to those with the opportunities to attend professional events.

The advantage that we had in researching this book is that the world of higher education learning innovation is small and highly networked. We have gotten to know many of the people leading learning innovation efforts at their institutions. Happily, some of our closest colleagues have also been promoted into leadership roles, most commonly as provosts, but in at least one case as a university president. We have been able to leverage these deep networks to engage in in-depth conversations with colleagues and peers. In almost every case, we knew our interviewees well and had therefore developed a level of trust that we think contributed to high levels of openness and transparency.

The community of peers for whom we developed and rehearsed the ideas for this book consists of three primary networks of learning innovators. The first network represents colleagues from a series of small gatherings that we have both facilitated and participated in over the past three years. The first gathering took place at Georgetown University in May 2016, in which we gathered thirty colleagues for what we called the Leadership Roundtable on Academic Transformation, Digital Learning, and Design. This initial meeting was followed by a slightly larger convening named Harvesting Academic Innovation for Learners, or HAIL. The first HAIL meeting occurred in January 2017 with a follow-up in September of that same year, and it included many of the same participants as the original Georgetown meeting, a number of whom we also interviewed for this book.

The second network that we drew upon for in-depth conversations was colleagues that we have met through participation in the edX consortium. We have more to say about the role of edX and MOOCs in chapter 1. For our purposes here, it is important to recognize that this consortium has played an important role in the turn to learning at our institutions and at those of other members of the organization. While at the time it was little understood or anticipated, the lasting impact of the MOOC craze of 2012 may be the establishment of deep cross-institutional relationships among educators leading learning innovation initiatives. In some cases these learning professionals owe their innovation-centric roles to the MOOC bubble. Massive open online courses may have failed to "disrupt" higher education, but they did a wonderful job of creating new communities of practice devoted to learning innovation.

The third set of networks that we drew upon to develop the ideas expressed in this book was more diverse. These were colleagues we have met through professional associations such as the EDUCAUSE Learning Initiative, the Professional and Organizational Development (POD) Network in Higher Education, the University Professional and Continuing Education Association (UPCEA), and the Online Learning Consortium (OLC). We also participate in a set of peer networks, such as the Association of Jesuit Colleges and Universities (AJCU) and the Ivy Plus consortium. It is through these professional associations and networks that we first understood that learning innovation was emerging as a central strategic focus across institutions. And it is through these groups that we also began to formulate our ideas about the need to move the conversation of learning innovation beyond professional associations and institutional member organizations and on to a more academic and scholarly foundation.

The Chapters Ahead

The book is organized into five chapters and an epilogue. In chapter 1, "Foundations of the Learning Revolution," we ground our arguments that higher education is currently at an inflection point by exploring and integrating the major trends related to changes in teaching and learning into a single narrative of change. Chapter 2, "Institutional Change," explores the relationship between institutional change and learning science via case studies from a number of universities. In chapter 3, "Reclaiming Innovation from Disruption," we offer a set of alternative frameworks in order to understand how universities evolve to align with advances in learning science. Chapter 4, "The Scholarship of Learning," builds an argument for centering discussions on organizational changes to advance student learning within a more traditional academic/scholarly framework, in addition to the professional association networks and social media platforms where this work is mostly located. Chapter 5, "Leading the Revolution," suggests ways in which advances in learning innovation may be instantiated through concrete organizational changes and initiatives. Finally, in the epilogue we offer advice for people engaged in this work and provide some thoughts about where the scholarship of learning innovation should proceed from here.

As we have suggested, we think the work of learning innovation is challenging many of our long-standing assumptions about teaching, learning, and the role of higher education. We hope the chapters that follow help to keep a conversation going for a long time to come.

ONE

Foundations of the Learning Revolution

IN OCTOBER 2016 the University of Michigan announced that it was creating a new campus organization called the Office of Academic Innovation.[1] In the press release about this new office, Provost Martha Pollack proclaimed that the "Office of Academic Innovation is charged with creating a culture of innovation in learning."[2] In a letter to all University of Michigan faculty, President Mark Schlissel wrote that the new office would "examine how teaching can be enhanced by ubiquitous access to digital content, by unprecedented opportunities for connection, and by an explosion of data about learners, educators, and their interactions."[3]

The launch of Michigan's Office of Academic Innovation is not unique. Many schools have invested recently in centers, offices, and people dedicated to academic innovation, including the schools where we each work: Dartmouth and Georgetown. The Office of Academic Innovation at Michigan and others like it serve as examples of a much larger story of a dynamic, changing system of higher education. This is the latest chapter in the story of the turn to learning, and it's the story we hope to tell in this book. Unfortunately, as we will see, this story has been overshadowed by the widely held idea that higher education is in "crisis" and that only "disruptive innovation" will fix what ails the system. This book is an attempt to highlight this story of innovation and learning happening across higher education and to bring back into focus the importance of colleges and universities investing in this work of learning at both the individual and institutional levels.

As with all big changes, recognizing that one is living through a historic shift is difficult. It often takes the benefits of hindsight to identify and make sense of times of profound change. We believe future scholars of higher education will look back on the early twenty-first century as an inflection point in higher education. Much like we look back today on Charles William Eliot's (1834–1926) presidency of Harvard University and his reforms that created the modern comprehensive research university, we will come to understand today's turn to learning as every bit as profound as the nineteenth-century introduction of admissions standards, electives, and specialized graduate training.

While it's had a presence in the press, the turn to learning has been largely missed—by both those inside and outside of higher education— or dismissed as simply an anxious response to the disruptive momentum under way. As such, the causes and effects of the turn to learning have not been fully explored. Even more importantly, the possible lasting impact of all the various learning initiatives occurring at almost every school has not been well examined. The moment of change we are unpacking places at risk the work of those within institutions to build capacities and structures to advance student learning. This risk is a peril of a particular kind of institutional ephemerality. Campus organizations dedicated to investing in learning innovation are in their early stages of development. The next provost to come to campus may have different priorities. The next financial crisis may eliminate whatever resources are available to advance learning. The next challenge to higher education's role in society may turn heads in a direction other than teaching and learning. The tenuous nature of this recent turn to learning is concerning, but just as tenure, departments, and graduate training have become part of the DNA of colleges and universities in the United States, we believe an active investment in learning innovation is vital to the future success of higher education.

For anyone working in higher education in the early part of this century, it can seem that the challenging economic times for our colleges and universities is the only story that matters. One of the reasons we wrote this book is to provide a competing and perhaps even complementary narrative. The structural, economic, demographic, and competitive challenges that the higher education sector now must face are real. The improvements that individual colleges and universities are now making to advance learning are equally real. The problem is that the steps that colleges and universities are taking to improve student learning have largely been dismissed as not radical enough. The institutional initiatives that touch on learning are seen as disconnected, as too little, too late. They have not been understood as part of a larger trend that describes how higher education is changing.

This is not a narrative told only by those on the outside of higher education. Many who play roles helping to lead their institutions forward are struggling with how best to respond to the pressures of new platforms, models, and innovators in the learning space traditionally occupied by higher education. At a 2018 HAIL (Harvesting Academic Innovation for Learning) meeting, participants were asked whether, in response to these growing external pressures, higher education needed to be radically disrupted or whether it needed to change incrementally. The learning professionals in attendance were then asked to stand and physically position themselves at one end of the room or the other (or somewhere in between) to indicate how strongly they felt about the type of change higher education needed to make to maintain its relevance. While the room was fairly well spread out between both ends of the spectrum, a large plurality of the passionate educators believed strongly in radical disruption as the only way for higher education to move forward.

It would probably come as a surprise to anyone who went to college in the 1980s and 1990s (as we did) that a college education, when looked at through the lens of student learning, is dramatically better today than in the past. The entire student learning experience has been radically recentered, from one of passive participation to one of active engagement. Learning today is no longer seen as a transfer of information but rather a lifelong pursuit, supported by both the curricular and cocurricular structures and functions of colleges and universities. Still, one is much more likely to hear about the amenities arms race of fancy residence halls, lazy rivers, and climbing walls than of advances in teaching and learning. How often does the conversation in the popular press about the changes in higher education turn to the positive stories of courses designed around the learning research? How often do we hear about the astounding numbers of classrooms that have been renovated to promote active learning? When online learning is discussed, it is mostly positioned purely as a new delivery mechanism (or worse, revenue stream) rather than as a catalyst to improve teaching and learning across the institution. Seldom discussed is the impact online education is having on residential learning through the introduction of learning design ideas and instructional design professionals on our campuses. Nor has the shift toward student-centered active learning principles in large-enrollment/gateway courses across many institutions been recognized beyond a limited number of higher education insiders. Each story of learning innovation at colleges and universities tends to be described as a one-off occurrence, rather than part of a larger system-wide story of how higher education is changing.

Once considered radical, innovative theories of learning such as student-centered classrooms and experiential education are recognized more and more as mainstream activities fundamental to the success of our students. In his influential book *Robot-Proof: Higher Education in the Age of Artificial Intelligence*, Joseph Aoun argues not only for the value of experiential learning but also for the recentering from traditional information transfer to activities that support the literacies (data, technological, and human) and capacities (systems thinking, entrepreneurship, cultural agility, and critical thinking) necessary to serve our students well as they continually adapt to radically new economic and professional realities. Even before Aoun's call to action, these literacies and capacities have arguably become more and more a part of how higher education trains its students precisely because of its recent turn to learning. We cannot teach our students to adapt to these new literacies and capacities without new models of learning innovation.

There is a great deal to explore at this moment in time, and far more than we give justice to in this book alone. To begin to understand the current investment in learning innovation, however, let's look at five trends we believe reflect and inform the turn to learning:

1. The diffusion of learning science: active learning and student-centered design principles
2. The ubiquitous learning management system
3. The growth of online education
4. The impact of the massive open online course (MOOC) bubble
5. New learning innovation organizations, including new models for centers for teaching and learning

Taken separately, none of these trends might be understood as a significant inflection point in teaching and learning in higher education. Taken together, these trends aggregate and interact to result in a nonlinear advancement in how students are learning. While we plan to spend some time discussing what we see as the advances occurring at both Dartmouth and Georgetown, in doing research for this book we learned that these trends are happening throughout the country at institutions of all types, resources, and missions.

The Diffusion of Learning Science: Active Learning and Student-Centered Design Principles

Among critics of higher education, it is not uncommon to hear an observation that if a student from the late nineteenth century (or even fifteenth century) traveled in time to the twenty-first century, they would feel entirely at home in a typical college classroom. This joke may have been true for most of the twentieth century, and it was partially true when we were in college in the 1980s. But it is no longer true today. Although traditional sage-on-the-stage lectures consisting of professors orating for sixty or ninety minutes while students diligently take notes still occurs across American campuses, this model of teaching is increasingly rare or at the very least frowned upon in most parts of higher education.

Today, most colleges and universities are implementing (or at least experimenting with) new methods of course design and teaching. This shift, like many of the changes in the postsecondary turn to learning, has been so widespread and measured that its impact on the system of higher education has been rendered almost invisible. One of the main factors driving the turn to learning in higher education has been the growth in the scholarship of teaching and learning (SoTL), as well as the scholarly output and impact around the science of learning.[4] The National Research Council's 1999 monograph titled *How People Learn: Brain, Mind, Experience, and School*[5] served to synthesize a large body of research in cognitive and developmental psychology, neuroscience, and educational psychology. The book provided the empirical foundations for the efficacy of pedagogical approaches based on principles of active and experiential learning. The authors of *How People Learn* put forth three main domains where teaching practices should align with learning science. The first is in recognizing that teaching must be contextualized to the preconceptions that students bring to the classroom. As the authors note, if students' "initial understanding is not engaged, they may fail to grasp new concepts and information presented in the classroom, or they may learn them for purposes of a test but revert to their preconceptions outside the classroom." And they go on to emphasize that factual knowledge must be accompanied by the development of a robust set of conceptual frameworks. These conceptual frameworks enable students to "organize information into meaningful patterns and store it hierarchically in memory to facilitate retrieval for problem-solving."[6] An approach that puts weight on integrating factual information with the development of conceptual frameworks allows students to transfer learning across domains and challenges. *How People Learn* concluded that the teaching of metacognitive skills should be integrated across the curriculum. The goal of education should be to encourage students to think about how they are thinking. Opportunities for reflection and application should be structured into the design of teaching strategies.

How People Learn is but one example of an outpouring of scholarship in the science of learning in the past two decades that has had an impact outside of the learning science community. The book aimed to translate findings in cognitive science and neuroscience in order to change how we teach and learn. The field of learning science is multidisciplinary and broad, encompassing disciplines as diverse as cognitive science, educational psychology, computer science, anthropology, sociology, information sciences, neurosciences, education, design studies, instructional design, and other fields. Much of this work appears in the International Society of the Learning Sciences's publication the *Journal of the Learning Sciences*, the premier peer-reviewed journal in the field. While much of learning science has significantly affected college teaching and learning, arguably the biggest impact on these activities in higher education has come from SoTL.[7]

In 1990, Ernest L. Boyer published his influential book *Scholarship Reconsidered: Priorities of the Professoriate*.[8] This book differed from previous scholarship of teaching and learning because its focus was on higher education, as opposed to K–12, and its findings were intended to be generalizable across disciplines even as they were generated by practitioners within specific disciplines. While there existed some investigation into effective teaching practices within traditional academic disciplines before 1990—particularly in the field of writing and composition—SoTL research attempted to deepen this work and give it meaning for disciplinary practitioners. A primary aim of early SoTL researchers was to elevate the scholarship of teaching to equal status among the professoriate as that of other forms of scholarship. Boyer sought to move beyond the existing "teaching vs. research" dyad to offer an alternative model where both activities were integral, inseparable, and ideally of equal status within the academy.

In their 1997 book *Scholarship Assessed: Evaluation of the Professoriate*,[9] Charles Glassick, Mary Huber, and Gene Maeroff build on Boyer's research to identify how SoTL fits within the traditional model of scholarship. They argue that all research has six components: (1) clear goals, (2) adequate preparation, (3) appropriate methods, (4) significant results, (5) effective presentation, and (6) reflective critique. The value of SoTL as a field of scholarly endeavor, according to *Scholarship Assessed*, should be judged against these criteria, just as with any other field of scholarship. In 2004, the International Society for the Scholarship of Teaching and Learning (ISSOTL) was formed by a committee of sixty-seven scholars from several countries to ratify these principles.[10] This organization publishes *Teaching & Learning Inquiry*, a journal whose mission it is to provide "insightful research, theory, commentary, and other scholarly works that document or facilitate investigations of teaching and learning in higher education."[11] Over the past twenty-plus years, we have seen a significant increase in the number of peer-reviewed SoTL publications, including the *International Journal for the Scholarship of Teaching and Learning, Journal of the Scholarship of Teaching and Learning, Active Learning in Higher Education, College Teaching, Teaching in Higher Education, Academic Exchange Quarterly, New Directions for Teaching and Learning,* and *Journal on Excellence for College Teaching.* This is only a subset of the journals focusing on SoTL, with many more covering teaching and learning within specific academic disciplines.

A full and adequate discussion of the origins, reach, and impact of the multidisciplinary field of learning sciences and the research domain of SoTL is beyond the scope of this book. What is important to recognize is that the recent fascination with learning across higher education rests on decades of scholarship and practice based on research in learning science and on the scholarship of teaching and learning. Much of the contemporary language around "transformation" in postsecondary education is based on the principles of student-centered and active learning that has deep roots in three decades of research and practice. The foundational ideas of learning science and SoTL are built, of course, on the earlier work of educational reform and the scholarship of learning dating back to John Dewey (1859–1952), Maria Montessori (1870–1952), Jean Piaget (1896–1980), Carl Rogers (1902–1987), Paulo Freire (1921–1997), and Herbert Simon (1916–2001), among many others. These thinkers and their ideas about student-centered learning and theories of educational constructivism have long been central to scholars of education. The intellectual history and critical methodological insights of learning theory constitute the core curriculum of both undergraduate training in education and advanced graduate studies in instructional design. What is different now is that the theoretical and empirical findings of learning science are beginning to have an impact on teaching practices *across* higher education. Where learning science was once isolated to departments of cognitive and brain science or in schools of education, this research is now making its way to the classroom practices of faculty independent from those fields. The theories, methods, and findings of learning science, particularly through the scholarship of teaching and learning, have begun to spread outside of our schools of education.

Until recently, it was unusual for faculty and graduate students in traditional disciplines to receive any training in learning science. Graduate school in the traditional programs is conceived and structured as a mechanism in which tomorrow's scholars are socialized into the discipline. It is true that many graduate students teach or act as teaching assistants during their studies—and that some programs, such as Syracuse University's Writing Program, have well-established pedagogical support for graduate student teacher training. Time spent beyond the minimum required to fulfill one's teaching duties in graduate school, however, was more often than not seen as potentially distracting from the core purpose of graduate work, which was to develop a research agenda that would eventually lead to a tenure-track position or, as is often the case in the STEM fields, a postdoc or series of postdocs. All that is starting to change. Graduate students are increasingly able to take advantage of opportunities to incorporate the theories, methods, and practices of learning science and SoTL into their teaching responsibilities. As we learned in researching this book, the demand among graduate students for training in learning science and SoTL has been met by a growing supply of opportunities. Centers for teaching and learning (CTLs) have begun to offer workshops, programs, and resources targeted to the needs of future faculty. Departments are supplementing campus-wide training with disciplinary-specific training for future teachers in the profession.

These changes are not isolated to graduate students gaining new access to pedagogical training. A recent (2017) nationwide survey of faculty use of technology for teaching and learning indicated that 73 percent of professors are incorporating both face-to-face and online components in their classes.[12] Only 15 percent of faculty reported that their courses were "exclusively" face-to-face, while 12 percent indicated that their courses were entirely online. In the same survey, fully 86 percent of faculty reported that the courses they teach were either already blended or they were exploring these methods for future courses. Alternatively, only 14 percent of surveyed faculty reported no plans to adopt blended learning techniques in their teaching.

Why have individual faculty members moved to incorporate methods of blended learning into their teaching? One answer to this question can be found in institutional initiatives and programs in course redesign that have grown in scope and ambition, and which are often run by CTLs or other campus units (such as academic computing). These programs for course redesign, however, only account for a small proportion of all experiments in active and student-centered learning that are occurring in college courses. Most efforts to move away from traditional lectures—often by incorporating hands-on learning during class time by shifting information transfer tasks to digital formats that students can access outside of class hours—are being undertaken by faculty because of a growing understanding of the changing dynamic of learning. Faculty increasingly realize that their role as the source of information has been changing for decades. Adapting to this new reality means changing the interactions that occur between faculty and students, placing more emphasis on what to do with the information that is readily available on the internet. This shift away from traditional passive learning/sage-on-the-stage teaching has had a profound impact on student learning, driven in no small part by the growing body of empirical evidence about effective teaching in SoTL literature.

Perhaps the most important catalyst for the move away from the traditional lecture and toward blended teaching methods has been the diffusion of institutional programs in course redesign. Some of the most well-known programs in accelerating course redesign have emerged from the work of Carol Twigg and the National Center for Academic Transformation (NCAT). Founded by Twigg in 1999 with an $8.8 million grant from the Pew Charitable Trusts, NCAT's original Program in Course Redesign was designed to collaborate with universities to improve student success rates in foundational large-enrollment courses while simultaneously reducing costs. Of the original thirty institutions that NCAT first worked with on course redesign, twenty-five showed significant increases in student learning. This program, which touched 50,000 students annually in its initial iteration between 1999 and 2004, was able to use principles of course redesign to lower course dropout rates (from 10 to 20 percent on average), while also reducing instructional costs.[13] Since its inception, NCAT has worked with a diverse range of colleges and universities to redesign 253 courses that enroll 250,000 annually. Among these course redesigns, 72 percent showed improvements in student learning outcomes over traditional lecture-based courses.[14]

Both Dartmouth's Center for the Advancement of Learning (DCAL) and Georgetown's Center for New Designs in Learning and Scholarship (CNDLS) offer support to faculty and graduate students to engage in similar work. Programs include a teaching workshop series, a learning community, a syllabus design workshop, and many other opportunities for training, mentoring, and developing communities of practice. In our experience, faculty today are much more likely than at any time in the past to have both an interest and some background in learning science and SoTL. Core concepts of constructivism, student-centered learning, and active learning are familiar to recent cohorts of postsecondary educators. Interest in research-based pedagogical methods is no longer confined to faculty in schools or departments of education.

The Ubiquitous Learning Management System

New pedagogical models and theories have been slowly changing how colleges and universities approach teaching and learning, but arguably the greatest impact on learning in the past twenty-five years has been the ubiquity of digital and online technologies. Unpacking the role of technology in both driving and inhibiting learning innovation is problematic. Tracing that history requires that we first identify what we mean by technology. The printed book is by any measure the most significant technology for learning yet invented. For some scholars of education, it is the nineteenth-century invention of the chalkboard that gave us our longest lasting and most influential educational technology.[15] For the turn to learning that we are marking, the learning technology that might have had the greatest impact in higher education (beyond the internet, in which all modern learning technologies sit) is the most reviled of them all, the learning management system (LMS).

To claim that the LMS is an enabling technology in learning innovation will strike many readers as strange, for it does not enjoy a good reputation in higher education. Phil Hill, a well-known educational technology analyst, has memorably characterized the LMS as the "minivan of education," writing that "everyone has them and needs them, but there's a certain shame having one in the driveway."[16] The LMS has come under sustained and withering critique from a range of progressive educators and learning technologists. In a 2014 talk entitled "Beyond the LMS," noted independent scholar and ed-tech critic Audrey Watters argues, "The learning management system has shaped a generation's view of education technology, and I'd contend, shaped it for the worst. It has shaped what many people think ed-tech looks like, how it works, whose needs it suits, what it can do, and why it would do so. The learning management system reflects the technological desires of administrators—it's right there in the phrase. 'Management.' It does not reflect the needs of teachers and learners."[17]

Watters points out how the mandated use of the LMS curtails the availability and control of educational materials. Once students complete a course or graduate, they may lose access to digital materials that are posted on the LMS course website. Instructors also lose access to all the work that they have done to develop their LMS course sites if they leave the institution—including syllabi, handouts, and student rosters. What is worse, in Watters's and many other critics' estimations, including ours, is the sublimation of student learning to the administrative functions embedded in the LMS. These administrative functions include the sharing of the course roster between the student information system and the LMS, a capability that makes it possible to record and share individual student grades. As Watters writes, "[The LMS] wasn't about student learning. It was about administration. Course enrollment. Scheduling. Grades." For critics of the LMS, the core functions of the technology were designed primarily for administrative control rather than as a platform to support learning. At worst, the LMS privileges the bookkeeping elements of teaching—the recording of attendance, participation, grades, and so on. At best, the LMS promotes content over learning.

Today, the LMS is ubiquitous. The learning management system is part of a higher education technology industry that by some estimates is valued at $30 billion per year.[18] How can the LMS, a technology so reviled by scholars of educational technology, be understood as a catalyzing force in higher education's turn to learning? Are the critics of the LMS wrong? Our answer is no, but with some caveats. No, the critics of the LMS are not wrong. By itself, the LMS is a problematic technology that reinforces many of the least effective parts of the faculty-student engagement. As Watters and others point out, the LMS is built on fundamentally flawed assumptions about learning. Critics rightly observe that colleges and universities often see the LMS as standing in for all learning technologies, thus enabling them to avoid investing in a variety of technology-enhanced learning innovations.

Despite these and many other problems, the LMS has helped enable a much broader set of transformations across higher education, transformations that have had the effect of driving learning innovation. This enabling function is less a result of the specific features or capabilities of the LMS than of the ubiquity of the adoption of these platforms. The ubiquitous LMS has enabled faculty to teach with technology without knowing how to create HTML web pages. In the twenty years since the LMS started to become widely adopted, it has ceased to be thought of by either professors or students as a new technology. Instead, the LMS has become part of the educational landscape. No different and often no more exciting than an overhead projector. The minivan of educational technology indeed.

Perhaps the best that can be said about the LMS is that it works well as a platform in which faculty (alone or working with an instructional designer) can manage the digital components of an online, blended, or residential course. With some effort, these can be effective instructional platforms for teachers and learning platforms for students. Research-based practices for active learning, such as the creation of learning outcomes and the availability of frequent low-stakes assessments, have been diffused throughout postsecondary education at a scale that was previously not possible without the simple and ubiquitous LMS. The conventional wisdom of those who study educational technologies is that the LMS, with its emphasis on administrative functions such as assignments and grading over a more constructivist and social model of learning, has impeded educational innovation. We would suggest, however, that the LMS, despite (or maybe because of) its many flaws, has been a critical element in the turn to learning.

The Growth of Online Education

The LMS has a problematic relationship to learning innovation, but the relationship between improvements in residential learning and the growth of online education is one of the great underreported stories in higher education. Online education (from hybrid to fully online) is fast becoming the new normal in higher education. This shift is important to our story because the practice of incorporating the principles of learning science and SoTL often originates among practitioners of online education. Faculty at traditional residential institutions have been increasingly exposed to the principles of learning design through their participation in online teaching. Colleges and universities have rapidly expanded their capacities in instructional design to support new online programs.

How big a factor does online education play in the larger system of higher education? In 2015, more than 6 million students, just under 30 percent of all students, were enrolled in one or more online (distance) courses. Of these, about half were taking exclusively online courses, with none of their coursework consisting of residential/face-to-face learning. The other half were enrolled in a combination of residential and online courses. Over 80 percent of these online students were undergraduates.[19] In contrast to popular perceptions, the online learning population is not concentrated within the for-profit higher education sector. Fully two-thirds of online learners attend public institutions. A 2015 analysis of

4,836 degree-granting institutions in the United States found that 3,354 (69.3 percent) participated in online learning programs.[20] Most students learning online, however, attend one of a relatively small number of schools, with almost half of all online students enrolled in 5 percent of institutions. The top forty-seven schools delivering large-scale online programs represent less than 1 percent of all colleges and universities, yet they enroll 23 percent (1.4 million) of all distance enrollments. The other way to look at these numbers is that many schools have small distance learning programs. The 2017 *Changing Landscape of Online Education (CHLOE)* report found that only 24 percent of online learning programs were in large centralized units. A much larger proportion, 47 percent, were small decentralized units distributed across academic departments.[21]

Many incumbent institutions initially resisted the move from residential to online learning. This resistance was generally based on the assumption that online courses are a poor substitute for face-to-face interactions. Faculty often express concerns about the lack in an online course of nonverbal and other visual cues that they consider crucial in connecting with students in face-to-face environments.[22] A 2016 survey found that only 19 percent of faculty agree or strongly agree that "for-credit online courses can achieve student learning outcomes that are at least equivalent to those of in-person courses." The percent of full-time faculty who strongly disagreed with that statement was 25 percent.[23] Among faculty who have taught an online course, 32 percent agreed that students could achieve learning outcomes in an online course that are at least equal to residential courses. This compares to 13 percent of faculty who have never taught online.[24]

As online learning programs continue to grow in both the number of colleges and universities offering programs and the number of students learning online, we expect that faculty attitudes toward online learning will continue to evolve. It seems likely that how faculty think about the quality of online education will begin to align with the research on the effectiveness of online learning. Among the most well-known research in this space is a 2009 meta-analysis and review of online learning studies by the Department of Education.[25] This study found no significant difference in student learning outcomes between residential and online learning modalities. Subsequent research on the effectiveness of online education is voluminous and exhaustive, with the vast majority of empirical findings lending support to the comparative effectiveness of online education. A 2015 analysis found that "92% of all distance and online education studies find that distance and online education is at least as effective, if not better, than traditional education."[26] The differentiating factor for educational quality is not whether the course is residential or online. Instead, quality is a function of the degree to which the structure of the course aligns with pedagogical strategies that emphasize active and experiential learning. It is perhaps ironic that the growth of online education, a trend that caused so much worry within academia about its potentially negative impact on the quality of instruction, has ultimately been one of the prime catalysts for innovation in learning across the entirety of higher education.

The Impact of the MOOC Bubble

Any discussion of a postsecondary learning renaissance must address the complicated role MOOCs play in our narrative. Massive open online courses have often served as a lightning rod for the catalyzing changes brought about by learning innovation. In part, this is due to recognition that MOOCs on their own offer little in terms of actual innovation. In fact, it is entirely arguable that the MOOC platform—as a relatively traditional LMS—reinforces passive modes of learning rather than the more active, student-centered approaches discussed earlier in this chapter. Instead, the benefits of MOOCs are almost exclusively tied to two aspects of the *introduction* of the technology and not to the technology itself. The first is the role that MOOCs played in recentering the conversation at colleges and universities on learning. If these open online courses with their massive enrollments could teach an entire generation of students at scale, providing them access to the best faculty and best material, what role would residential education have going forward? Would all residential colleges go the way of the print newspaper or the railroad, maintaining only a small presence in the industries they once dominated? The introduction of MOOCs encouraged, cajoled, and forced many schools to try to address these questions.

The second benefit occurred in the culture and organizational structures of the colleges and universities that have participated in the open online learning movement. These advances have remained all but invisible to those outside of the institutions in which they are occurring. The MOOC narrative has therefore been confined to one of either higher education disruption or a failure of those signing up for open online courses to complete the coursework. Neither of these narratives captures the real impact of open online courses. The case of MOOCs is a perfect example of this Trojan horse method of organizational change. Few learning professionals took seriously the outsized promises that MOOCs would disrupt higher education. When *New York Times* columnist Thomas Friedman wrote about "the college education revolution" in May 2012,[27] and the *Times* named 2012 "The Year of the MOOC,"[28] those in the field knew we had reached the "peak of inflated expectations" of the MOOC hype cycle (figure 1).[29] This hype, however, would prove helpful in enabling us to meet our goals of opening

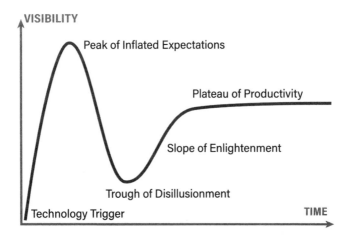

Figure 1. Gartner Research's Hype Cycle
Courtesy of Jeremy Kemp, Wikimedia Commons, accessed December 20, 2018, https://commons.wikimedia.org/wiki/File:Gartner_Hype_Cycle.svg. The underlying concept was conceived by Gartner, Inc.

up a conversation about learning science on our campuses and bringing resources to learning innovation.

The MOOC story does not start with the 2012 founding of Coursera by then Stanford University computer science professors Daphne Koller and Andrew Ng with $16 million in venture capital funding. Nor does it start with edX, a nonprofit consortium founded with an initial $30 million contribution (each) from Harvard University and MIT. In reality, the MOOC story dates back to 2008 and a series of pedagogical experiments run by Canadian academics George Siemens (then of Athabasca University) and Stephen Downes of the National Research Council.[30] That course, Connectivism and Connective Knowledge (CCK08), resulted in educational researchers Bryan Alexander and Dave Cormier to each independently label the experiment as a "massive open online course."[31] This online course was not the first to be opened up to learners outside of the institution in which it was taught. Rather, this was the first course to enroll significant numbers of free online learners (2,200), in addition to the twenty-five tuition-paying students in extended education at the University of Manitoba.[32]

What distinguishes early experiments in MOOCs from the dominance later of the large platform providers of Coursera and edX is that early open online courses represented explicit rejection of traditional pedagogical practices. The Siemens-Downes MOOC and other open online courses developed by Jim Groom (then of the University of Mary Washington) were based on principles of connectivist pedagogy. Open online courses developed from this connectivist pedagogical model, which Downes designated "cMOOCs," prioritized learner-created content and organic network development over a faculty expert/information transmission and assessment model. A cMOOC is collaboratively developed between the facilitator and the learner. In a cMOOC, all participants are responsible for aggregating and remixing content occurring across multiple online platforms. This approach to open networked learning is in contrast to xMOOCs, where faculty develop the curriculum and learners interact with content, discussions, and assessments within the open online platform.

Before 2011, the pedagogical experiments of cMOOCs were of great interest to learning scientists and other education researchers, but they had done little to ignite the system-wide postsecondary renaissance in learning innovation. This changed in 2011 when Stanford's Sebastian Thrun and Peter Norvig opened their course, CS221: An Introduction to Artificial Intelligence, to the world. In short order, 160,000 learners had signed up for the course, causing a media sensation in the world of educational technology. In a September 2012 *Wired* magazine article titled "The Stanford Education Experiment Could Change Higher Learning Forever," one student enrolled in CS221 described the course as the "online Woodstock of the digital era."[33] The success of CS221 caused Thrun to found Udacity (a mash-up of "audacity" and "university") and leave his faculty position at Stanford. He famously said, "Having done this, I can't teach at Stanford again. You can take the blue pill and go back to your classroom and lecture to your twenty students, but I've taken the red pill and I've seen Wonderland."[34] At the peak of MOOC mania, Friedman wrote, "I can see a day soon where you'll create your college degree by taking the best online courses from the best professors from around the world—some computing from Stanford, some entrepreneurship from Wharton, some ethics from Brandeis, some literature from Edinburgh—paying only the nominal fee for the certificates of completion. It will change teaching, learning, and the pathway to employment."[35]

In 2012, the Gates Foundation gave $1 million to MIT to develop an open online course in computer science,[36] following up a year later with a $3 million grant.[37] At the height of MOOC mania, the board of visitors that oversees the University of Virginia attempted to oust respected president Teresa Sullivan, frustrated that she was moving too slowly in bringing MOOCs to UVA.[38] While Sullivan eventually was able to keep her job, university leaders from around the country were put on notice that it would be inadvisable to be on the wrong side of the open online learning revolution.

Following the founding of Coursera and edX, a series of intensive discussions across many universities ensued, each debating the wisdom of joining the open online education movement. The rapid growth of

Coursera and edX, funded by a combination of venture capital dollars (Coursera) and university and foundation investments (edX), increased the attractiveness of MOOCs for many institutions. Among university leaders there was a strong aversion to being viewed as out of touch with the latest technological and educational trends. Leaders of public institutions saw MOOCs as a possible antidote to what William Bowen and William Baumol call the cost disease[39] found in higher education and supported experiments in open online education as aligned with efforts to improve postsecondary productivity.

Readers of this book will be well aware of the fall of MOOCs from the peak of inflated expectations to the trough of disillusionment (see figure 1). This fall came quickly, as early as 2013, when Thrun himself had become disillusioned with the idea that MOOCs could replace traditional universities. In an interview with *Fast Company*, Thrun observed, "We were on the front pages of newspapers and magazines, and at the same time, I was realizing, we don't educate people as others wished, or as I wished. We have a lousy product."[40]

Claims that MOOCs would revolutionize education were increasingly ridiculed both inside and outside higher education. In April 2013, the entire faculty of the San José State University Department of Philosophy wrote an open letter to Michael Sandel, the Harvard professor who developed the edX JusticeX open online course. The San José faculty decried efforts by their university to replace courses taught by existing faculty with Sandel's MOOC. During that same year, San José State was forced to abandon a partnership with Udacity when more than half of enrolled students failed their final exams.[41]

By 2017 MOOC mania was dead. An analysis on Google Trends shows that searches for "MOOCs" in the United States peaked in October 2013. By 2017 there was only a quarter as many searches on Google for "MOOC."[42] Articles about MOOCs have taken on headlines such as "MOOCs Are Dead. Long Live Online Higher Education" and "MOOCs Are 'Dead.' What's Next? Uh-oh."[43] Contrary to reports of the death of MOOCs, the actual number of open online courses and of learners enrolled in these courses has continued to grow. A December 2016 analysis by ClassCentral reported that to date 58 million

MOOC learners are taking 6,850 courses at over 700 universities.[44] Coursera remains the largest provider of open online courses, with over 23 million unique users aggregated on their platform. In 2018, edX boasted a learner base of 15 million individuals. Maybe even more telling is the fact that both Coursera and edX have stopped using the term "MOOC" to describe their online courses.

The irony that it took MOOCs to generate extensive conversations about learning science was not lost on the instructional design, CTL, and online learning communities. A persistent and valid criticism of the academics behind the MOOC platform providers—centered in the Stanford (Coursera and Udacity) orbit and at MIT and Harvard (edX)—has been that they have ignored the decades of scholarship and practices within traditional online learning and learning science discussed previously. The educators who led the development of these early MOOC platforms were engineers and computer scientists, and their approach to platform development and course design reflected these disciplinary backgrounds. Long-established research-based practices on the necessity of student knowledge construction and educator presence were largely ignored by the early champions of MOOCs. Practices in online teaching that had been honed for years by theory and experience were co-opted by the purveyors of MOOC platforms, with little recognition of the contributions of the practitioners of traditional online learning.

In the case of edX and Coursera, the failure to recognize that MOOCs are part of an effort to bring innovative practices to teaching and learning was perhaps most egregious. The founding members of the edX consortium and Coursera university partners had little experience with online education. The institutions that edX and Coursera courted so vigorously to offer MOOCs on their platforms were, at least in some cases, the least prepared to do so with an eye toward improving student learning. Many had little experience with online learning and lacked both the institutional capabilities and campus cultures that might lead to higher quality open online courses.

The first edX and Coursera courses were decidedly content heavy, built around the personas of superstar faculty. This approach is the exact opposite of the state of practice in online education, where course designs are learner centric. MOOCs never did, and never were going to, revolutionize higher education. Nor are practices that bring open educational materials to online learning new to MOOCs. What was different about edX, Coursera, and the other open online learning platform providers is that they brought internet scale to the traditional (legacy) providers of higher education.

Efforts to leverage the low costs and scale of the web to provide learners with learning materials preceded MOOCs. Thrun credits Khan Academy, which started in 2006, with the inspiration for taking the original artificial intelligence course online. MITx can also trace part of its lineage to MIT OpenCourseWare (MIT OCW), the effort that started in 2001 to make all of the digital material used in MIT courses free and open to any learner. What MOOCs did was take the familiar construct of a course, one that is designed and taught by a professor and that students experience as a cohort during a specified time, and match this traditional form of instruction with the scale of a no-cost internet-mediated experience. The innovation of the first MOOCs was not about pedagogy or even technology; they were about size.

Those learning professionals who never bought into the MOOC disruption narrative and were charged with implementing MOOCs have been able to leverage these initiatives to build institutional capacity for learning innovation. MOOCs have, in some cases, subsidized the investment toward meeting longstanding goals to build capacity in instructional design, educational media, analytics, and assessment. At the same time, MOOCs provided a window for campus-wide conversations about developments in learning science and the potential to leverage digital technology to improve learning in residential courses.

Perhaps the longest-lasting benefit of MOOCs in advancing residential learning has been the space that open online education has created for cross-campus and cross-institutional discussions of learning science. It is hard to overstate the shift that MOOC mania enabled by bringing conversations about SoTL from the margins of the academy to the center. Interest among campus leaders and large numbers of faculty in the latest research on how people learn may end up being short-lived, lasting only as long as university communities gather to debate the merits and problems of MOOC participation. MOOCs forced higher education to confront the challenge of disruption and in many respects to make the turn to learning much more prominently than had previously been the case.

New Learning Organizations

The turn to learning enabled and encouraged by many of the trends we have discussed so far has not happened in isolation. The past few years have seen a rise in a particular institutional structure established for the primary purpose of challenging long-standing institutional assumptions about how colleges work. As we mentioned earlier, Michigan's Office of Academic Innovation is an example of the many new divisions, units, centers, programs, and organizations dedicated to transforming learning at their institutions. It is joined by the University System of Maryland's William E. Kirwan Center for Academic Innovation, Davidson College's Digital Learning Research and Design, UC Berkeley's Academic Innovation Studio, George Washington University's Libraries and Academic Innovation, Cornell University's Center for Teaching Innovation, Boston University's Digital Learning & Innovation, the Sandbox Collaborative at Southern New Hampshire University, and both CNDLS and the Red House at Georgetown, to name but a few.

Duke University's Learning Innovation is a new, integrated unit that combined the previously separate Center for Instructional Technology and Online Duke in 2017. Matthew Rascoff, Associate Vice Provost for Digital Education and Innovation at Duke, observed, "Our new name puts learning first. Our strategy is to help Duke students learn more, and to enable more people to learn from Duke. 'Innovation' for us means transformation that helps Duke achieve its educational mission."[45] And the new organization's role is designed to serve four main functions:

- Partner with Duke faculty to support new approaches to student-centered learning and active learning.
- Build and curate an ecosystem of education technology tools that support learning.

- Support online learning opportunities that prioritize increasing flexibility for Duke students while also experimenting with ways to reach the university's extended community of alumni and prospective students.
- Create a research and development lab that will explore bleeding-edge projects while also partnering with faculty to gather data, publish research, and seek grants and sponsored research opportunities.[46]

These four elements of the mission of Duke's Learning Innovation are similar to the goals of other innovations and organizations that have emerged across higher education. These organizations operate both at the system and the institutional level in order to underpin change across campus. Given how new these organizations are, their direct impact on making deep and sustained advances in student learning may perhaps be too early to assess, but their effect on institutional investment in developing an ecosystem of learning innovation is important to understand.

Units such as Duke's demonstrate a growing recognition that learning innovation requires engagement, reflection, action, and dissemination. As we discuss later, disruptive change in industries outside of higher education can happen at a rapid pace by offering alternatives for small pieces of the whole. At campuses that have made investments like Duke's, change comes by seeing the role of these centers not simply as support organizations but rather as integrative units that work to understand the complex, local learning environment. These offices become important spaces for studying and building scholarship around the work of teaching and learning. At the same time that new organizations for learning innovation are opening their doors, existing campus learning organizations have been undergoing profound transformations in their roles and responsibilities. Centers for teaching and learning have expanded their missions to encompass digital and experiential learning programs that move beyond the classroom. While maintaining the traditional CTL portfolio of responsibilities around faculty and graduate student development, course redesign, and a community of practice for campus educators, CTLs have also taken on new roles as change agents for learning innovation.

Examples of CTLs that have recently expanded into integrated campus-wide learning organizations include Yale's Poorvu Center for Teaching and Learning, Columbia's Center for Teaching and Learning, Cornell's Center for Teaching Innovation, and the Office of the Vice Provost for Teaching and Learning at Stanford University. In cases where the CTLs have grown to explicitly encompass learning innovation as part of their core mission, that growth is often accomplished by integrating online and blended teaching services into the center's portfolio. This integration of leadership in digital learning operations looks different at each CTL, but it usually includes the hiring or reassignment of professionals such as instructional designers and media educators into the center's staff.

The recently integrated Poorvu Center for Teaching and Learning at Yale University is indicative of the growing prominence of the CTL on many campuses. At Yale, the traditional faculty development work of the CTL has been combined with a digital education team, providing faculty a single point of entry for an array of teaching and course development tasks. Before 2014 the various teaching- and learning-related services were distributed across a range of organizations and groups. The Yale CTL bundles the core faculty and student services that support learning at the university. These services include support for teaching (grants, workshops, and consulting), student tutoring (including writing labs and tutoring), and technology (the learning management system, online learning, video and media, classroom technologies, and technology pilots). In situating technology and media-enabled education services within the CTL, Yale is aligning the center's expertise in learning research and assessment with capabilities in blended and online course development.

At Georgetown, the Center for New Designs in Learning and Scholarship has long held learning innovation as a core function. Since 2013, however, this work has expanded in partnership with the newly created Red House to explore the full spectrum of assumptions, traditions, and structures that both enable and resist learning on campus. CNDLS has become part of a dynamic partnership of pedagogical experimentation and innovation designed to ask questions about how to best serve students in the changing social, cultural, and economic landscape they will enter upon graduation. Together, the two units try to help the university understand how to create the conditions for students to become lifelong learners adapted and adaptable to the ever-changing realities of work in the twenty-first century.

These short descriptions of changes that have occurred in CTLs reflect a more widespread trend across centers for teaching and learning. A 2015 Gates Foundation study titled *Leading Academic Change: An Early Market Scan of Leading-Edge Postsecondary Academic Innovation Centers* attempted to provide some empirical grounding to postsecondary trends.[47] This study, conducted by MJ Bishop (director of the Kirwan Center for Academic Innovation at the University System of Maryland) and Anne Keehn (president of Quantum Thinking and formerly a senior fellow at the Gates Foundation), surveyed 163 heads of campus teaching and learning organizations. The survey revealed that six in ten centers had experienced changes in their mission in the previous two years or were expecting changes in the next two years. Among the emerging priorities identified by CTL heads and faculty were online and blended course design as well as leveraging educational technology platforms for instruction. The report notes, "Centers for teaching and learning are clearly evolving at the same time, often providing the underlying structure necessary to support academic change more broadly. These centers' missions are shifting from a reactive 'faculty development' focus to a more proactive 'teaching and learning transformation' focus."[48]

Leading Academic Change supports the claim that the responsibilities and impact of CTLs are growing and that learning innovation is at the heart of this shift. Further research needs to be done before any definitive conclusions on CTL changes across higher education can be made. For our discussion about a turn to learning in higher education, however, it is enough that a critical mass of CTLs has enlarged their missions to combine traditional faculty development tasks with those of learning innovation.

What About . . . ?

In this chapter, we have attempted to explain the foundational trends, themes, and developments that have collectively created the conditions for postsecondary learning innovation. In an industry as large, diverse, and fragmented as higher education, it is not possible to articulate each of the explanatory variables behind a system-wide movement to improve learning. Across the some 4,300 degree-granting postsecondary institutions in the United States will be 4,300 different stories of how each institution innovates in learning. In choosing to focus on the developments of learning science, educational technologies, and traditional and open online technologies, we ignore other events and activities that may be equally salient.

Many will argue that the growth of learning analytics, and the vast amount of educational and demographic data on which analytics depends, should be included in any narrative of advancement in student learning. Although we agree that learning analytics hold great potential to enable both institutions and educators to make data-driven decisions to improve teaching, to date the promise of analytics has exceeded its impact. Excitement about the use of data in education is not the same thing as impact. While some institutions have made impressive strides in the use of analytics to improve teaching and identify at-risk students— the University of Maryland, Baltimore County, and Southern New Hampshire University are two examples—our research suggests these schools remain in the minority. Future editions of this book will likely include the penetration and diffusion of analytics across higher education as a critical factor in advancing student learning.

Similarly, while we are as excited by the potential of experiential learning and competency-based education (CBE) as any educators, the actual growth of experiential learning and CBE has been limited to unique programs, such as the one at Northeastern University detailed by Aoun, or niche programs aimed at nontraditional students. Likewise, it may turn out that alternative credentials, such as edX's MicroMasters programs, may have a significant impact on reordering the postsecondary educational economy. Today, however, even the most successful alternative credentialing programs remain in the experimental stage—reaching a small number of students as compared to those enrolled in traditional programs.

Nor have we included here more buzzworthy advances in educational technology. At some point in the future, we may find that adaptive learning platforms offer students a superior learning experience over traditional instructor-led courses. Technologies like adaptive learning platforms will be introduced across higher education, but they will thankfully not replace professors anytime soon. Instead, we foresee that these platforms will serve as complementary technologies, aiding experienced and skilled educators in their teaching. As with learning analytics, we hope that adaptive learning platforms improve quickly as artificial intelligence improves. Although we are reluctant to make any technology-first predictions, we do expect that adaptive learning technologies will evolve into a tool that educators and students will be able to utilize in the quest to advance learning.

Next Steps

Many people in higher education will find it strange we are claiming to be in the midst of a renaissance regarding student learning and faculty teaching during a time of profound crisis across the sector. This postsecondary crisis hinges on the twin trends of rising educational costs and diminishing institutional resilience. Just as the growing cost of attending college has outstripped all other sectors, including health care, the ability of many institutions to survive has been called into question. Student debt now exceeds $1 trillion, with Americans owing more for higher education loans than they do for auto loans or credit cards. Costs for attending public institutions have risen faster than for private schools, owing in part to cutbacks in state funding. However, the number of private tuition-dependent colleges that are experiencing existential financial crises due to challenging demographics and rising costs appears to be increasing as well.

In telling our turn-to-learning story, we may be underplaying the larger story of the higher education crisis that swamps all possible investments in learning innovation. Focusing on a sampling of schools in the detailed interviews we completed for our book research may also mean we are missing what is occurring in the classrooms at many other institutions. Our belief in the efficacy of learning science, new technologies, and new campus organizational changes may be misplaced in an era of adjunctification and cost disease. The real story of higher education might be more understood as a tale of increasing inequality and stratification—of the rich getting richer. As we describe the changes that we interpret as a higher education turn to learning, it would be wise to keep in mind that what we might be describing is further evidence of a society-wide concentration of privilege.

Of course, there is an excellent case to be made that learning has always been at the center of the mission and practices of many institutions, and any turn to learning we are seeing is restricted to those schools that have historically prioritized faculty research ahead of teaching. One example of a set of learner-centric institutions comes from work of the late Loren Pope and the organization Colleges That Change Lives (CTCL), which carries on Pope's work. CTCL is beloved by high school guidance counselors across the nation for its list of colleges and universities dedicated to small classes, engaged teaching faculty, and rigorous learning. There are currently forty-four schools on the CTCL list of colleges that change lives.[49] Colleges such as Antioch, Centre, Juniata, Marlboro, McDaniel, Reed, Wabash, and Wheaton, to name a few. The CTCL list is only one tiny subset of learner-centric colleges and universities. There is a good chance that anyone reading this book will point to the institution that they attended or where they now work as one with a long-term commitment to advancing learning. We acknowledge that the turn to learning is most important for colleges and universities that until recently placed advancing student learning as one priority in a series of priorities. We see the turn to learning as a trend that is pushing big improvements in learning within many institutions. In short, we think that a significant number of schools now have the potential to provide for high-quality student learning in a way that only a smaller number of institutions had in the past.

Another critique to our argument that the turn to learning is a relatively new phenomenon is that many of the forces we highlight are not at all new to higher education. Colleagues in centers for teaching and learning and in divisions of academic computing have been collaborating with faculty for many years. There is a long history within the CTL community of organizational change work to promote research-based teaching practices. The first CTL, the Center for Research on Learning and Teaching, was launched at the University of Michigan (Ann Arbor) in 1962. Part of our turn-to-learning story, however, is about the recent growth of CTLs. Many schools have undergone organizational changes that resulted in previously dispersed services around teaching and learning moving into the centers. What we view as a new development, the growing strategic importance of the CTL, is likely to be old news on many campuses.

A third objection might go beyond scope or timing, instead pointing to a much more fundamental flaw in our turn-to-learning argument. That flaw is that our evidence of a recent move to put the advancement of student learning at the center of postsecondary education points only to inputs and says nothing about outcomes. It would be reasonable to ask if the higher education learning renaissance we believe we are participating in has resulted in improvements along dimensions such as retention or graduation rates. Wouldn't it make sense that if colleges and universities are aligning their institutional practices with learning research, we would see an improvement in the dismal rates of college completion in the United States? The current six-year graduation rate of 56 percent for all four-year degree-granting institutions has shown almost no improvement in over a decade.[50] If there is indeed a turn to learning going on in higher education, it may mirror economist Robert Solow's famous quote about the impact of computers on productivity showing up everywhere except in the statistics. Learning might be improving everywhere, except in the statistics.

Our contention that higher education is undergoing dramatic improvements when it comes to teaching and learning runs directly counter to the findings in Richard Arum and Josipa Roksa's 2011 book *Academically Adrift: Limited Learning on College Campuses*. This research, which relied on a combination of results from the Collegiate Learning Assessment and surveys of 2,300 undergraduates at twenty-four institutions, concluded that US colleges do a poor job of prioritizing student learning. Among the main findings of the book were the results that 45 percent of students failed to demonstrate significant gains in learning in their first two years of school, and 36 percent did not significantly improve in measures of learning in four years. Of those students who did show gains in learning, these gains were small. In explaining why students seem to be learning so little, Arum and Roksa argue that the primary culprit is a distinct lack of rigor. A third of the students examined in *Academically Adrift* did not take courses with forty or more pages of assigned reading a week. Half of all the students were not enrolled in courses that required any significant amount of critical writing. More worrying, the average college student studied only twelve to fourteen hours a week, with much of that studying occurring in groups. *Academically Adrift* came out the year before we date higher education's inflection point, but it is hard to imagine that any of the trends we have discussed would fully ameliorate the problems that the book exposed. While the Collegiate Learning Assessment has been criticized as a valid measure of the change in student learning,[51] and the overall conclusions of *Academically Adrift* have also been disputed,[52] we don't believe that the book's main arguments (even if true) invalidate our claims of a turn to learning. Nor do we think that low and stagnant six-year graduation rates invalidate our conclusions.

The impact of the learning innovations that we highlight may end up being apparent in future research findings, but most likely only if these future studies take a very long view. The turn to learning that we observe is mostly about improving the ability of learners to learn. We view this as a long-run upgrading of human capital; learning is a skill that is hard to measure in either short-term assessments or summary statistics, such as graduation rates. Those rates may be mostly a function of the stressors or supports in students' lives, such as adequate funding to attend school or robust mentoring to get students through inevitable rough spots, while navigating active-learning environments may be difficult for some students.

Despite these and other possible criticisms, we think that the turn to learning is real, influential, and lasting. But we may be wrong. What we are posing is a research question. We are hoping to start a conversation. As we discuss in the next chapters, it is important to frame the question of how universities are changing to advance learning as one of scholarship. The discourse on learning innovation is today occurring primarily as a professional discussion, one carried out in the context of professional associations and social media. We hope this book energizes a debate about how postsecondary learning innovation may be understood now and into the future.

TWO

Institutional Change

THE MODERN HISTORY of higher education in the United States can be traced back to a number of key moments in the nineteenth and early twentieth centuries. As we noted in the previous chapter, perhaps the most important was Charles William Eliot's introduction of many elements we now associate with the modern comprehensive research university—electives, professional schools, research, and new methods for measuring student success.[1] Since then the teaching and learning environment has existed as a relatively straightforward dynamic between the resources (buildings, tools, library) of the institution and the knowledge and expertise of the faculty member. Students were often passive participants in this exchange, there to soak up the information transferred by the faculty member, all within the institutional setting.

Of course, this traditional dynamic had some challenges. The formal teaching that was attached to grades and credits and degrees occurred in classrooms and labs where faculty had little control over the learning environment. The design of the physical classroom—with its seating design and arrangement of assistive teaching technologies, such as blackboards, classroom computers, projectors, and screens—was more often than not outside of the professor's control. With the exception of specialized labs, the tools they had were limited to what was provided.

Faculty taught in the classroom that they were assigned. Despite the profound impact tools such as the blackboard have had on student learning, the role of the institution in shaping learning often went un- (or at least under-) examined.[2]

The corollary is also true. For most of the history of college teaching in the United States, it was the professor alone who designed the course, taught the course, and evaluated the success of the course. This model followed much of the accepted pedagogy of higher education at the time. Faculty are experts in their field, and their job is to transfer knowledge to students. Of course, it never was as simple or stark as we are suggesting. Some faculty were required to use exams and textbooks and even lecture materials from a department-approved list. Other faculty had complete discretion in how their courses were designed and taught. Student course evaluations have always had varying degrees of impact on tenure and promotion, but the use of these student evaluations as guides for continuous improvement were largely left up to the discretion of the professor. This relative autonomy in the classroom has long been an important part of the traditions of academic freedom and shared governance. With a few exceptions, the faculty were responsible for the implementation of the educational mission—including the curriculum and the assessment of student learning and achievement—while the administration was responsible for setting the stage in which that educational mission was undertaken.

Importantly, however, higher education has never been static. Despite claims to the contrary from those advocating for radical disruption, higher education has always changed in response to the needs of the larger society (albeit slowly at times). As the institutional context changed, so too did the ways faculty taught. In the 1950s, for example, when colleges and universities grew in response to the GI Bill, small tutorials and seminars were often replaced by large lectures. More students meant greater demands for efficiency. Small classrooms were replaced by large lecture halls, and faculty were asked to adapt to new modes of teaching that responded to the changing institutional context. And they did this much on their own. As experts in their fields, faculty adapted their pedagogy to meet the needs of the institutions and the students without a great deal of support from the institutions themselves.

Teaching and learning have become more complex in the past two decades. This complexity has been driven in part by the different trends we mentioned in the previous chapter—the growth of online and blended learning, the increased use of educational technologies, and the growing body of research on the impact of different pedagogical approaches—as well as a more prominent focus on improving student learning and retention across higher education as a whole. Retention and graduation rates, in particular, have important economic outcomes for colleges and universities in terms of both tuition and (dwindling) public dollars; they also affect recruitment, yield, and rankings and reflect the fundamental responsibility to support student success. Retention rates are at least partly a function of the quality of teaching and learning to the extent that students are able to succeed in their courses and maintain momentum toward graduation. A school's brand, and therefore its ability to recruit and enroll students, is at least partially built on its reputation for excellence in teaching. Many schools have realized more and more that a focus on student learning is necessary for their ongoing success, not to mention survival. This adaptation to the new teaching and learning environment is one implication of the turn to learning we introduced in the previous chapter.

Because of these complex, intersecting forces, the individual-craftsperson model of teaching and learning is what is changing most rapidly across higher education. In big and small ways, teaching and learning are moving from almost exclusively the domain of the professor to involving collaboration with other educators. No longer is this support simply the availability of physical resources;[3] it now includes introducing faculty to new pedagogical approaches, helping the institutions rethink how classrooms are designed, and working with faculty to navigate the complex dynamic of new technologies that both inform and enhance student learning.

Pedagogical approaches such as shifting the class from face-to-face to hybrid often require understanding and employing the vast array of learning technologies available today, which in turn has practical and financial implications that are continually changing and challenge the long-standing dynamic that has driven teaching throughout much of higher education. It is in the involvement of the institution in the domain of learning—no longer as passive context but as active participant—where the study of learning innovation begins. This institutional involvement may be indirect, such as the work that faculty developers do in centers for teaching and learning to create materials and workshops for professors who are interested in improving their pedagogies. Or it may be more direct, such as through the hiring of instructional designers to collaborate with professors on course design and instruction in online, blended, or residential courses. In both cases, support for learning innovation has increasingly moved beyond the traditional dynamic between faculty and students and requires greater resources from the institution.

Learning Innovation at Dartmouth and Georgetown

Over the past six years, each of us has witnessed this support for learning innovation on our campuses and at the many campuses we have visited. One fundamental question that drives this book is whether our experience of this turn to learning is idiosyncratic or generalizable across the postsecondary ecosystem. We think the answer is increasingly clear. A focus on learning innovation is not occurring only at a small number of elite institutions. Instead, the methods and practices that underpin learning innovation are emerging as part of the fabric of higher education. Colleges and universities across a wide spectrum of institutional types, we believe, are making significant changes in how support for teaching and learning is structured. These changes go back two decades, but they have been accelerating in the past half-dozen years.

Advances in teaching and learning are perhaps reflected most visibly in how campus centers for teaching and learning (CTLs) are changing. Learning organizations first established themselves in higher education with the creation of the Center for Research on Learning and Teaching at the University of Michigan in 1962. At Georgetown, the Center for New Designs in Learning and Scholarship (CNDLS) was founded in 2000, while the Dartmouth Center for the Advancement of Learning (DCAL) began in 2004. Since the mid-2000s, we have seen a rapid rise of CTLs throughout the country, and new ones are still being created today. There has always been a great deal of variation in the roles these centers have played on the campuses in which they were established as well. At some schools, CTLs have had a robust presence— with comparatively large staffs and responsibility for strategic campus-wide initiatives related to teaching and learning. At other schools, CTLs have been relatively small operations, with small staffs and limited levels of institutional investment. CTLs are also only one form of campus organizations devoted to advancing learning. Learning professionals are distributed around academic computing units, online and continuing education departments, and other centers and institutes.

The growth in the breadth and scope of learning innovation activities at Dartmouth and Georgetown has not been one of linear progression but rather one of discontinuous and at times rapid change. We suspect that our peers at learning organizations across the postsecondary land-scape are, like us, still trying to catch their breath. Even with the addition of all the new campus-wide initiatives that learning organizations have taken on, the core activities to which these units are responsible have continued to be maintained. In the case of CTLs, these core activities include the creation and running of workshops and institutes, individual- and department-level consulting, and nurturing campus-wide educator communities of practice.

Centers for teaching and learning are perhaps best understood as mission-driven organizations. They not only encompass a commitment to implementing the scholarship of learning into the practices of teaching but also enable the faculty (and future faculty) with which they collaborate to reach the teaching and learning goals these partners set. As part of their mission to serve both educators and learners, CTLs (including those at Dartmouth and Georgetown) have deeply invested in providing their campuses with resources, consulting, and communities of practice around issues such as syllabus and course design, developing learning goals and assignments, and creating effective classroom discussions, among many others. The core activities of CTLs have, at many institutions, started to take on social justice and well-being activities in recent years, supporting the educational missions of their institutions with attention to topics such as diversity, implicit bias, equity, inclusiveness, and the physical and mental health of their students. Driven by a belief that students learn better when their social and emotional needs are (at minimum) acknowledged, CTLs continue to evolve to meet students where they are in order to help them thrive.

The programming and services that the CTLs at Dartmouth and Georgetown engaged in prior to the moment we are marking, were—and remain—central to the operations and identity of their respective organizations. More and more, however, these core services provided by educational developers within CTLs have been complemented by an entirely new set of learning innovation initiatives. In this respect, the traditional work of the CTL has continued, with new initiatives designed to push experimentation and innovation in teaching and learning—often mediated through new technologies—layered on top of existing responsibilities. We have seen this pattern repeat with our colleagues at CTLs across higher education and extend to learning organizations outside of teaching and learning centers. The specifics of new learning innovation initiatives that academic computing units and online and continuing education divisions have taken on in recent years will vary by institution and circumstance. Since 2012, the year that MOOC mania catalyzed our turn to learning, the action within learning organizations has been intense.

What follows are brief descriptions of how learning innovation came to be prioritized at Dartmouth and Georgetown, and particularly within the CTLs in which we are situated. The descriptions of how our institutions have evolved to both inform and respond to the turn to learning are more illustrative than complete and serve as an introduction to the case studies of Boston University, CSU Channel Islands, and Davidson College, all of which are detailed later in this chapter. The specifics of new initiatives, programs, and metrics is more the stuff of annual reports than a book about how learning is changing in higher education. Rather than go into such specific detail, we instead describe the trends related to learning innovation that are now occurring at our schools and try to relate these shifts to larger trends we suspect are playing out across higher education.

The Integration of Educational Development and Instructional Design

One challenge CTLs often face is the integration of what can appear to be distinctly different types of activities. This integration has happened as centers traditionally invested in helping faculty with the practice of teaching (faculty development) have had to adopt new approaches to design (instructional and learning[4]) and production (media and application) in order to meet the changes in teaching we have been discussing. While there are exceptions, the overall trajectory of educational development had been on a parallel path with the development of the instructional design professions, organizations, and communities of practice. Traditionally, educational developers worked in CTLs and had their primary professional affiliations through groups such as the POD (Professional and Organizational Development) Network. Instructional designers, on the other hand, traditionally worked in academic computing and online education units and were members of professional associations such as EDUCAUSE and the Online Learning Consortium. While the barriers between educational developers and instructional designers were never impermeable, the two professions have historically had distinct educational paths, areas of focus, organizational and professional structures, and cultures.

From 2012 onward, the organizational distinctions between educational-developer and instructional-designer practices have rapidly eroded. At some institutions, such as Georgetown, the campus instructional design professionals have always been located in the CTL. Since its founding in 2000, CNDLS has followed the integrated-CTL model, in which instructional design services along with educational technology and assessment services are delivered by the teaching and learning center. Over the last six years, however, CNDLS has increased its instructional design and multimedia capacities in response to the growing presence of open online courses and technology. The recruitment of instructional designers, web developers, media educators, and graphic designers was made necessary by the growing portfolio of digital, blended, and online learning initiatives and projects that CNDLS spearheaded. Prominent among these initiatives was Georgetown's 2013 Initiative on Technology-Enhanced Learning (ITEL). ITEL was part of Georgetown's commitment to exploring boundary-pushing experiments in teaching and learning while facilitating the widespread adoption of promising tools and approaches both on campus and online. The range of projects and programs that fell under ITEL—and other initiatives run by CNDLS—has continued to increase the demand for instructional design and educational media services from across the institution. From 2012 onward, digital learning has become integral to the full range of learning programs—residential, blended, or fully online—that Georgetown offers. In effect, what started as an initiative to experiment with technology-enhanced learning has been transformed into part of the daily operations of the institution and regular services that CNDLS offers the campus community.

At Dartmouth, the work of DCAL has continued to be organizationally separate from the unit where the learning design team is based, which is within Information, Technology & Consulting (ITC). This organizational separation between the CTL and the instructional design unit (separate reporting lines, budgets, etc.) no longer aligns with realities of the work. In 2014 DCAL launched the campus-wide Digital Learning Initiative (DLI), followed in 2016 by the institution-wide Experiential Learning Initiative (ELI). Both of these initiatives were designed to provide campus-wide coordination, leadership, and funding for projects and experiments evolving the college's core residential practices to incorporate digital and experiential elements. The DLI and ELI funded a large number of diverse projects with Dartmouth faculty and nonfaculty (including cocurricular) activities. What they all had in common was that almost every project that was coordinated or funded by the DLI and ELI required a learning designer to design and run it. In the eyes of the partners and stakeholders for these learning initiatives, the educational developers in DCAL and the learning designers from the ITC unit seemed like a single team. Indeed, it was often a surprise to faculty (and sometimes college leadership) that the learning designers were not part of DCAL, or that DCAL and the learning design unit were organizationally separate. The development of blended residential (flipped) courses, nondegree online programs, and full degree-granting low-residency master's programs all require the contributions of instructional designers and media educators. This increasing emphasis on online programming has meant the work of DCAL to provide ongoing educational development (such as planning workshops and institutes or nurturing communities of practice) is more and more deeply integrated with (and inseparable from) the instructional design and media creation work required for digital learning projects.

In Georgetown's case, the combined work of educational developers and instructional designers occurred in the context of an integrated CTL model. At Dartmouth, this combined work occurred across organizational structures. The integrated CTL is one model in which learning innovation can proceed, but it is not the only (or necessary) way to structure this work. Just as many institutions have recently moved to the integrated CTL model—including schools such as Boston University, Cornell, Columbia, Duke, and Yale—others have followed a path similar to Dartmouth's, where the groups of educational developers have remained organizationally distinct but fully integrated with their work. Integrated CTLs and cross-organizational collaboration each have strengths and weaknesses. Schools that have brought instructional design teams into existing or newly constituted CTLs have had to navigate differences in cultures, work rhythms, and outlooks. As with any organizational changes, the integration—either structurally through reorganizations or tacitly through shared cross-organizational initiatives—is not without its growing pains. Adjusting to the new demands of shared organizations and cross-organizational collaborations can be difficult for individuals with established ways of working and full portfolios of responsibilities. Merging cultures and goals within and across new groups and partnerships is always hard.

We believe that the newly integrated work of educational developers and learning designers—and the rapid growth of instructional and multimedia learning professionals on our campuses—is, on balance, an extraordinarily positive development. The growth and integration of the learning organizations at Georgetown and Dartmouth are indicative, we think, of a larger trend across higher education for institutions to prioritize investments in learning innovation.

A New Focus on Learning R&D

An emerging understanding within the fields and practices we are exploring is the need for colleges and universities to engage in learning research and development (R&D). Historically, higher education has lagged behind the investments that other industries put into research and development. Companies such as Alphabet (Google), Apple, Intel, and Microsoft spend between 10 to 20 percent of their revenues and resources on R&D.[5] Higher education, with its struggle against permanent scarcity—including trends of cost disease, public disinvestment, and unfavorable demographics—has struggled to make long-term investments in innovations to advance student learning. This is further complicated by the traditional divide between administration and faculty defined in part by the assumption that scholarship is an activity only carried out by faculty. This division tends to make the scholarly work of actually studying higher education challenging, to say the least.

At Dartmouth and Georgetown, much of the work in the new initiatives that we have invested in at DCAL and CNDLS over the past few years has been explicitly framed as investments in learning R&D. Again, we think that our institutions are not alone in conceptualizing campuswide learning initiatives within the framework of experimentation and discovery. As we will see below, this framing resonates with our colleagues at other colleges and universities. The level of pedagogical experimentation that is occurring across a diverse range of institutions in the postsecondary ecosystem is largely unappreciated, however. That much of this experimentation is being supported and funded by learning organizations has not been widely discussed, or at least discussed only inside of learning innovation communities. Part of the failure to tell this learning R&D story better is a lack of research on the R&D itself. Lacking an interdisciplinary home focused on learning innovation, cross-institutional research on learning experiments goes largely uncollected and unanalyzed.

At Georgetown and Dartmouth, learning R&D efforts focus on investing in pedagogical experiments in flipped and hybrid courses, inclusive pedagogies, social and collaborative learning, online programs, virtual and augmented reality, and experiential learning. The creation of open online courses and programs through both of our schools' participation in the edX consortium resulted in the creation of reusable digital course resources, such as videos and simulations. These materials were then utilized in credit-bearing residential courses. Where MOOCs were largely viewed in the press as efforts to replace traditional modes of instruction with low-cost online teaching, at Georgetown and Dartmouth the rationale for creating free online courses has always been to advance teaching and learning. Faculty at both Georgetown and Dartmouth who worked with instructional designers, media specialists, and multimedia developers on edX open online courses were able to transition this partnership with the learning design team to their residential courses. In this way, not only were newly developed digital learning materials (videos, simulations, etc.) brought over from the MOOCs to the face-to-face courses, so were the relationships and collaborative team dynamics.

One way to capture the shift toward an R&D mind-set for advancing learning innovation is by looking at a modified version of what was originally McKinsey's Three Horizons Model (table 1). While we argue against disruptive innovation as a necessary solution in chapter 3, the McKinsey model offers a useful heuristic for thinking about how we move from support to innovation. Successful movement from execution to continuous improvement (from horizon one to horizon two) in the teaching and learning realm reflects much of what happens in CTLs, and it should be commended. Centers for teaching and learning have been dedicated to continuous pedagogical improvement. Workshops, institutes, and ongoing consulting services have been refined over time in order to maximize incremental gains. Continuous improvement is the explicit goal of online learning units as they utilize learner data, learning science, and new technologies to continuously improve

Table 1. McKinsey's Three Horizons Model

Horizon 1: Execution	Horizon 2: Continuous Improvement	Horizon 3: R&D
Focus on maintaining the existing value to stakeholders	Incrementally improve services	Achieve nonincremental (or stepwise) advances in services
Execute and defend the core services and projects	Expand the reach of services and initiatives to new stakeholders	Invent new processes and systems
Sustain existing success	Create efficiencies in the design and delivery of services	Pilot projects with high potential impact, even with low probabilities of success
Run day-to-day operations	Develop new projects and initiatives	Celebrate failures as learning opportunities

Source: Kristen Eshleman, "Making Space for the Important," *Technology and Learning* (blog), *Inside Higher Ed*, October 14, 2015, https://www.insidehighered.com/blogs/technology-and -learning/making-space-important.

online courses. Course redesign programs, such as those described in chapter 1, can achieve incrementally better outcomes in retention, performance, and other measures of student success.

Prioritizing horizon three to advance learning via R&D is a lofty goal and unlikely to generate many conceptual objections within higher education. The challenge is that the work in horizon three is often sidelined as chronically underfunded and short-staffed departments, schools, and learning organizations manage the demands of serving current needs. Executing on the core teaching and learning mission of the university is challenging. Learning is perhaps the most complex of all human tasks. Add to that challenge the enormous variability of student preparedness for college-level work and the financial challenges faced by almost every institution, and it is predictable that most institutional efforts around teaching and learning will remain at horizon one (execution).

How the effort and time invested for execution, continuous improvement, and R&D break down for teaching and learning is not well understood (and discovering this breakdown would be an excellent research topic for a new scholarship of learning innovation that we propose in chapter 4), but we see growing commitments to increasing time spent on R&D at Georgetown, Dartmouth, and from our peers at other institutions.[6] For all of us, it's become critical to frame the activities of the learning organization within the language of experimentation and research. This sort of framing is of course familiar and comfortable for research-productive faculty, and it is one of the reasons we advocate for the interdisciplinary nature of this work in chapter 4.

A rich R&D mind-set, akin to Lockheed's infamous Skunk Works approach, in a CTL is not only challenging because of funding or internal politics but also because of the impact it can have on faculty and students. Disciplined learning experiments can fail. They often do. Promotion and tenure policies for faculty, to the extent that teaching is counted, are not built to reward experimentation and failures. And those that are tend to be far outweighed by the expectations of research and scholarship in outward-facing disciplines. Additionally, end-of-term course evaluations from students make up part of the data that go into a tenure and promotion file; failed experiments at the pedagogical level do not always lead to the best evaluations. Part of the effort to enact a learning R&D agenda at Dartmouth and Georgetown has been to find ways to increase the value and visibility of faculty learning innovation work. All new learning initiatives are undertaken with a keen awareness of the career progression gates that faculty must navigate. Teaching innovations are designed with transparency about the challenges associated with the R&D for both the faculty and students in mind.

In practice, this often means that learning innovation efforts that take the most time (such as designing and teaching a MOOC) or have the highest risk of failure (such as a large-scale course redesign) are most often undertaken with senior faculty. Faculty developers and instructional designers partnering with junior (pretenure) faculty often need to consider the risks of engaging in this work to the faculty member's career progression. Part of the role of learning innovation is to transfer the risk of engaging in educational R&D efforts from the faculty to the learning organization.

These areas in which campus learning organizations are evolving constitute only some of the shifts that we are participating in at Dartmouth and Georgetown. Other changes include a push to build capacity in learning analytics. These new capabilities are being applied both to the learning innovation initiatives that we run and with partners across campus. A focus on assessment and analytics appears to be occurring across the learning organization ecosystem. Again, there are no good data on this phenomenon—a gap that we would hope an interdisciplinary field of learning innovation could fill—but we have repeatedly heard of this investment from the learning professionals and senior leaders we interviewed for this book.

Parallel to the enhancement in assessment and analytics capabilities is a commitment by our learning organizations, and again with peers that we have queried, to prioritize research and scholarship in teaching and learning. There is a sense that campus learning organizations are poised to dramatically grow their research and scholarship footprint. Many educational developers and learning designers have long participated in original scholarship. What seems different is that research on learning is moving from the margins of the responsibilities of learning professionals to the center. It's about time. There is a great deal of scholarship to be done by learning professionals on the work of learning innovation.

Growing Academic Innovation

As we've shown, the work of traditional *and* integrated CTLs is expanding. At Dartmouth and Georgetown, this is happening in different ways. For Dartmouth, this means a particular kind of investment in digital learning that brings the CTL together with the learning design team. At Georgetown, this expansion is reflected not only in the investment in teaching, scholarship, and applied innovation already described but also in the creation in 2013 of an incubator for academic innovation called the Red House. Led by Vice Provost for Education Randy Bass, the Red House's mission is to explore structural- and institutional-level barriers for innovation, such as credit hours, seat time, semesters, time to degree, and so on. The creation of the Red House is based on a recognition that for any learning innovation to be sustainable, it needs to challenge some long-standing structural elements that limit momentum for change.

Many schools are attempting to take similar approaches by establishing local CTLs, investing in organizations for academic innovation, and finding solutions to challenges that are local to the institution's context, history, and student population. We will highlight three such approaches at Boston University, CSU Channel Islands, and Davidson College. These examples are not meant to be read as representative of how colleges and universities approach learning innovation. We could just as easily have shared a story about the development and work of Harvard's Office of the Vice Provost for Advances in Learning, the Center for Learning Innovation at the University of Minnesota Rochester, or scores of others. If the reader of this book works at a college or university, chances are reasonably good—and have improved greatly in recent years—that a center or organization devoted to learning innovation exists. In sharing the stories of Boston University, CSU Channel Islands, and Davidson, our goal is to explore some common themes around institutional learning innovation initiatives. Ultimately, we believe these frameworks can then be applied to both understand existing efforts and guide future institutional efforts.

Digital Learning & Innovation at Boston University

In 2016, Boston University (BU) created Digital Learning & Innovation, a new organization run by the Office of the Associate Provost for Digital Learning & Innovation. This new organization brought together within a single structure their existing Center for Teaching & Learning, Educational Technology Group, and Digital Education Incubator. The impetus for the realignment was BU's 2013 Digital Learning Initiative, a program that focused mainly on developing open online courses as part of the edX consortium. Prior to the creation of Digital Learning & Innovation, Boston University's Center for Teaching & Learning was quite small. Within this new structure, the CTL is growing in staff and has been successful in securing resources for instructional design, media, assessment, and communications. Digital Learning & Innovation has been able to consolidate and scale up the teaching and learning resources that had previously been disconnected at the university. Faculty and future faculty (graduate students) now have a single organization they can go to for consulting, training, and funding. Digital Learning & Innovation positions itself as "Boston University's one-stop shop for learning transformation," and the organization is committed to the purposeful cultivations of "innovative new experiments and aid in developing new residential, online, and hybrid programs."[7]

Boston University scaled up a campus-wide organization devoted to learning innovation after it initially experimented with open online courses as members of the edX consortium. In the process, BU reorganized and consolidated learning professionals from its existing CTL and ed-tech group into a single organization. Chris Dellarocas, the associate provost for Digital Learning & Innovation, has emerged as a widely respected thought leader on higher education change. The mission and strategy of Boston University's Digital Learning & Innovation is shown in figure 2.

Digital Learning & Innovation encompasses four distinct but related activities. The first is the Center for Teaching & Learning, which offers

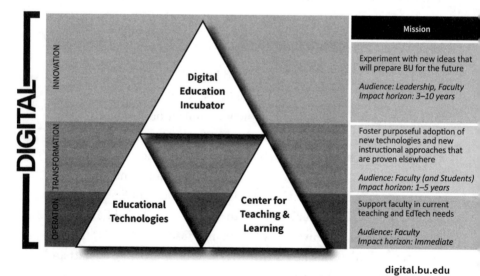

Figure 2. Boston University's Digital Learning & Innovation Mission and Strategy
Used with permission from Boston University.

faculty and graduate students training and consulting on curriculum design as well as other programming and services most closely associated with traditional campus CTLs. The Educational Technology (EdTech) Group within Digital Learning & Innovation was previously within the university's Office of Information Services & Technology. Amongst the EdTech Group's responsibilities are to manage Boston University's learning platforms, consult with faculty on integrating technology into their teaching, and evaluate new platforms and tools to advance learning. Digital Learning & Innovation works across the institution to consult on online program development, including course development, market research, and program marketing.

The Digital Education Incubator (DEI) is the experimental group within Digital Learning & Innovation, and it is led by Romy Ruukel, who was a program manager at edX before joining Boston University in 2013 as the associate director for the school's original Digital Learning Initiative. According to Ruukel, the Digital Education Incubator serves to mitigate the risk involved in institutional and faculty experiments in learning. In an interview about the incubator, she said, "There is value in these experiments for the sake of a potential big idea. The DEI absorbs some of the risk of that kind of experimentation: we go into the water and say, 'What is this like? Is this worthwhile?' If it is something with big potential, we are in a position to go further. If it is not, we've invested something in learning and discovering that it is not quite right. And that this is ok, to try it out."[8]

An analysis in October 2018 of projects in Boston University's Digital Learning & Innovation incubator reveals over forty separate learning initiatives and experiments.[9] According to Ruukel, other institutions have looked to Boston University's Digital Education Incubator as a model for catalyzing disciplined learning experiments.

While Boston University is changing the landscape of teaching and learning innovation within the school, the story of these innovation efforts is not as well known outside of the university. In many respects this is not unique to Boston University. Much of the landscape of innovation and change happening in higher education is happening in isolation at individual schools. This is due in part to the structure of higher education and in part to the local nature of many changes. They occur in the classroom first, then at the institutional level, and finally they tend to move beyond the particular institution. Boston University is a large, complex, and decentralized institution, and the various schools within BU have historically operated with high degrees of autonomy. Unlike institutions such as MIT or Stanford where similar learning organizations have been created, Boston University's had not positioned its brand as being on the cutting edge of pedagogical innovations. As Boston University's international stature as a top-ranked research and teaching institution has grown, so has the push toward prioritizing student learning. In making the large-scale investment to both reorganize learning services within a single organization and orient those services around the concept of innovation, Boston University is demonstrating its commitment to leadership in advancing student learning. The creation of Digital Learning & Innovation at Boston University should be an important story both inside higher education and for anyone interested in how the industry is changing.

Teaching and Learning Innovations at CSU Channel Islands

The Teaching and Learning Innovations organization at California State University Channel Islands operates in a very different context than that of Boston University. CSU Channel Islands (CSUCI) is the newest of the California State University system of twenty-three campuses, established in 2001. Despite having a different student profile than schools such as Boston University, CSU Channel Islands operates their center with a similar mission: "Teaching and Learning Innovations (T&LI) at CSU Channel Islands is a program designed to guide, support and inspire faculty at CSUCI to step outside of traditional boundaries of teaching to improve student learning. We are led by the CSUCI mission to put students at the center of the educational experience."[10]

In support of this mission, the T&LI team offers a range of consulting services, workshop opportunities, and resources for faculty around teaching and learning, including the Faculty Innovations in Teaching (FIT) studio. The FIT studio is a space where faculty can collaborate with learning professionals to design and create learning modules and videos for flipped, blended, and online teaching. The T&LI team has also built an online "Teaching Toolbox" for faculty that contains resources on course development and media creation. The tools and techniques developed by T&LI have the theme of "humanizing" educational technologies to offer a more personalized learning experience. Like Digital Learning & Innovation at Boston University, the educational technology approach at CSU Channel Islands is informed and driven by the research on learning.

The learning innovations that T&LI leads at CSU Channel Islands are not limited to improving teaching. The organization is also spearheading the institution's commitment to improving access to high-quality education by reducing student costs. Thirty-eight percent of CSU Channel Islands' 2017 freshman class are first-generation college students, with over half of CSU Channel Islands students receiving Pell Grants. One manifestation of this commitment is openCI, an institution-wide effort to assist faculty in discovering or creating open educational resources (OER). Across the United States, the average cost for textbooks and course materials for undergraduates is $1,200 a year.[11] In 2018, CSU Channel Islands came out with two "Z-Majors" in communications and early childhood studies that rely entirely on no-cost open educational resources.[12] T&LI is working with all the majors at the institution to replace traditional publisher textbooks with no- or low-cost OER materials.

This description of projects, services, and initiatives at CSU Channel Islands' Teaching and Learning Innovations barely scratches the surface of the impact this organization has on its institution. T&LI has its hands on the full range of activities that make up the learning mission of the university. The organization was started and is headed by Jill Leafstedt, a professor at CSU Channel Islands with a background in cognitive science, special education, disability, and risk studies.[13] Dr. Leafstedt heads a team of five instructional designers and technologists responsible for all of the traditional aspects of a CTL and an academic computing unit. Similar to Boston University, CSU Channel Islands has chosen to integrate campus learning services and professionals within a single organization and to orient that organization around innovation. T&LI, like other learning organizations with similar orientations, straddles that liminal space between an academic unit and a service unit. The scholarship of teaching and learning is integral to the work that the T&LI team undertakes in its projects and research, and in their collaborations with faculty.

What we have learned from the CSU Channel Islands Teaching and Learning Innovations is that institutional impact is not solely, or even mostly, a function of resources. The work to advance student learning need not be dependent on a large staff in a CTL or an academic computing unit. Anyone leading learning innovation efforts at an institution would welcome the ability to hire more learning professionals to collaborate with faculty and more dollars to run initiatives and programs. Resources in the absence of an institutional commitment to learning innovation, however, will almost always fail to change the teaching and learning status quo. At most institutions, tenure and promotion policies are not aligned with the goal of motivating faculty energy around learning innovation. Campus organizations such as CSU Channel Islands' T&LI are focused as much on changing the institutional culture to prioritize learning innovation as they are on providing resources and incentives. Small learning organizations such as T&LI, in which everyone in the organization works directly on learning innovation initiatives, can drive sustained learning innovation by being enmeshed in the daily teaching and learning lives of faculty and students.

Digital Innovation at Davidson College

Across higher education, learning innovation is occurring along a continuum. A college or university that lacks a learning organization such as a CTL or academic computing unit staffed by educational developers and instructional designers is likely not prioritizing learning innovation. At others, the work of learning innovation may be happening in CTLs but outside the broader strategic objectives of the institution. Learning innovation initiatives at these institutions may feel disconnected and have very little in the way of institutional structures to ensure visibility and sustainability. Davidson College stands out for their commitment to developing a systemic approach to institutional innovation that is both visible and sustainable.

The centrality of innovation in the culture that Davidson is purposefully building is evident in the name and organization of the college's technology unit, Technology & Innovation (T&I). Within the larger T&I unit is a dedicated digital innovation team. This team has put in place a process to institutionalize innovation in the form of the Davidson College Incubator. The incubator was designed to foster experimentation in areas where the outcomes of this work may not be known: "An incubator provides a transparent and collaborative system for vetting new ideas to make sure we are investing resources wisely, avoiding duplication, taking advantage of new opportunities, and inviting diverse perspectives and subject matter expertise to guide our innovations."[14] In this sense, the incubator serves to support a process of nurturing and scaling innovations that will be resilient to changes in personnel, funding, or campus developments that frequently derail these sorts of efforts. Ideas and experiments that are appropriate for inclusion in the Davidson incubator are those that:

1. Require a new financial investment from the college.
2. Include teaching material or methods that deviate from standard curriculum or delivery.
3. Require a significant, long-term commitment from the institution (more than one year).[15]

The incubator has a robust process in place for project development, too. Every idea that moves through it is associated with three groups of stakeholders. These people include the project owner, a student group supported by the T&I team, and members of an innovation council. The project owner is responsible for bringing the ideas into the pilot stage. For an incubator project, the project owner may or may not be the same person who submitted the original idea. The project owner is joined by a team of six students who are funded by the T&I group. This T&I team works closely with the project owner to provide services that include values and feasibility studies, pilot design, testing, and validation.

Both the project owner and the T&I team are complemented by a third group of stakeholders in the form of an innovation council that is made up of faculty, staff, and students from the institution as well as ad hoc members with expertise in the ideas being piloted. Each member of the innovation council agrees to commit two hours per month to the project. Decisions to attach institutional resources to innovation projects are made by the council using a process and guidelines that are well known to the community. This process contains a series of gates and stages in which a project is evaluated and can be supported for further investment or wound down.

The first gate in the process to incubate a new learning innovation is an opportunity screen. During this stage, the innovation council decides if the idea should be advanced, rejected, or put on hold. Decisions are made about the resources necessary for the project, including both dollars and people. The council evaluates learning innovation ideas based on a number of criteria. These attributes include the degree in which the idea aligns with Davidson's mission and values, the potential reward and risk of the idea, and the question of the long-term financial sustainability of the project. Particular attention is paid to an educational innovation that is credit-bearing because attaching credit to a new curricular initiative may have implications for accreditation. If the idea advances past the opportunity screen, then the idea becomes a project with a two- to four-week activity window. This second stage of the process consists of a value and feasibility assessment in which the project owner is fully onboarded and the risks and opportunities of the project are evaluated. The emphasis is on conducting a detailed investigation of the idea to identify stakeholders, define the logistics of implementation, and fully define the project's intended value and scope of impact. The costs, required resources, necessary approvals, and potential risks are fully documented. It is also at this stage where the intended beneficiaries of the learning innovation are first contacted to gauge their reaction to the idea.

Following this value and feasibility assessment is a second gate in which the innovation council again screens the value and feasibility of the project. The idea can be advanced, rejected, or put on hold. This gate is all about project feasibility. The decision criteria rest on whether the innovation offers potential value to the Davidson community, if the risks are manageable, and if the necessary resources can be found to develop and execute the project. If the required funds and approvals cannot be put in place, then the project will be stopped. This second gate ensures that any innovation projects will be aligned with the priorities of the institution. If the project makes it through the first two gates, then it moves on to the third stage of design and development. This process is designed to take no longer than a semester to complete. Its purpose is to further design, validate, and develop the idea in collaboration with key stakeholders. It is at this stage that the more traditional elements of project management are introduced, such as the development of an operational project plan, a project assessment plan, and a project timeline. Hypotheses are formed so that the intended outcomes of the initiative can be tested. It is also at this stage where any project begins to interact with established governance processes at the institution to attach credit. In this design and development stage, the background work necessary before a project is piloted is completed, with the next stage being a full pilot.

Before proceeding on to pilot stage, however, the innovation needs to pass through another gate. This third gate is a design screen. It's also the point in the process that the innovation council and the senior leadership of the institution weigh in on potential return on investment of the project. Projects that meet all the criteria for impact, feasibility, risk management, and resource sustainability can be allocated the resources necessary to proceed at this step. Alternatively, project teams may be asked to revise their project and assessment plans to garner support. Projects that have not been able to develop institutional support or that are judged to have a poor likelihood of success will be stopped. If an innovation successfully makes it through the first three gates and stages, the project will finally be ready to pilot. This methodology reverses the standard way in which most innovations are introduced in higher education. Most commonly, a new innovation starts with a pilot project. The bar is usually low to launch a pilot and involves some combination of an executive sponsor and the enthusiasm of whatever campus group or unit is doing the work. This approach is likely to water down any bold ideas that are intended to push boundaries. Davidson's innovation process, on the other hand, is designed to both bring ideas that may not traditionally be piloted to the community and increase the probability that pilot projects will eventually scale to sustainable campus initiatives.

The rigorous steps that any innovation must navigate to make it to the pilot stage may seem to inhibit creative and high-risk ideas. For the Davidson team that designed the process, however, this methodology is intended to nurture ideas that generally fail to be supported due to the limitations of budget, time, and attention that every institution faces. The goal of the Davidson digital innovation team is to bring R&D into the regular operational processes of the college. Rather than funding and resources being driven by the priorities of campus leadership or the gifts made available by donors, innovations through R&D become a standard practice baked into institutional culture and operations. Based on the results of an innovation pilot, the project then moves to the fourth and final gate. This final assessment screen includes input from the innovation council, and in cases where there is a significant risk, the board of trustees. Senior leadership then decides if the innovation should move from a pilot project to one that is formally implemented at the institution. Critically, the assumption at this gate is that most pilot projects will not move to the implementation stage. Even with the rigorous process in place to get to a pilot, Davidson is committed to only implementing innovations that can be shown to both have a large impact on the community and be economically sustainable.

This structured process to encourage and manage innovation was only being finalized at Davidson as we were researching this book. This process emerged through years of effort by Kristen Eshleman, Davidson's director of digital innovation, to institutionalize and systematize the process of innovation. This process was the outgrowth of both a recognition that the traditional methods for constructing learning were no longer adequate to the challenges faced by either Davidson students or by the institution as a whole. With an identified goal of making big shifts in Davidson's culture and operations that would move the college toward providing adaptable and student-centered experiences, the college needed a process that would drive changes in teaching and learning. Traditional organizational change processes were too slow and cumbersome to rapidly test and then support or discard ideas that had the potential to drive significant change. Innovation efforts could be killed by a small number of recalcitrant faculty or derailed by a financial shortfall or departure of a key academic leader. Davidson College has put in place a model for other institutions wishing to catalyze bold thinking. The Davidson story is also a data point in the broader higher education turn to learning as we expect this sort of intentional innovation practice to spread to other institutions.

A Road Map for Long-Term Impact

We have chosen to highlight Boston University, CSU Channel Islands, and Davidson not because they represent the only examples of institutional change enabling learning innovation. Instead, these are the sorts of examples of how colleges and universities are changing to advance learning that are becoming common across the higher education system. Schools with charismatic leaders and an appetite for risk-taking, such as Southern New Hampshire University under president Paul LeBlanc and Arizona State University under president Michael M. Crow, are the institutions that are usually profiled when institutional change and learning are discussed. Schools such as MIT and Georgia Tech are also often featured as paradigms of institutional innovation, and for good reason. MIT started its OpenCourseWare open educational material experiment all the way back in 2002 and has followed through with an institution-wide commitment to learning innovation. Georgia Tech has been a leader in creating low-cost degrees, such as the $10,000 online master's degree in cybersecurity launched in 2018. What the three schools we've explored demonstrate is that many different approaches to organizational change can be successful. Boston University and Davidson have both undertaken an entrepreneurial model that challenges institutional structures. CSU Channel Islands demonstrates that investments in learning innovation can help make college more affordable and deepen the impact of the experience for students.

Much of what we heard about organizational change to drive learning innovation from Boston University, CSU Channel Islands, and Davidson is mirrored at other universities. Each of these schools is enacting an intentional and purposeful set of structures, programs, and incentives to advance student learning. The learning innovation initiatives are fit to purpose for the culture and resources at the institution in which they were developed. Their designs are very different, but their goals are similar. Each aims to create the conditions for disciplined experiments in teaching and learning. The goals of learning innovation initiatives go beyond incremental improvements in single courses. Ideally, learning innovation efforts will result in substantial improvements in student learning that can scale across the institution.

What the Boston University, CSU Channel Islands, and Davidson initiatives also reveal is how difficult learning innovation is to achieve across different types of institutions. Large private research universities, public institutions committed to expanding educational access, and small private undergraduate liberal arts colleges all face similar challenges when it comes to making nonincremental advances in learning. Each of these schools needed to create a new organization devoted to catalyzing learning innovation. Standard higher education cultural norms do not allow for projects where the results are unknown and the risk of failure is high. The idea that advancing learning requires an R&D mind-set is foreign to most colleges and universities. Internal funding and people resources are fully committed to existing operational requirements. Investing in medium- to long-term learning projects with uncertain outcomes is often difficult to defend in a context where the funding of normal operations, such as regular classroom technology updates, are chronically underfunded.

Eshleman's description of the philosophy behind developing an organizational structure at Davidson College to catalyze innovation could apply to any organized efforts at other schools that have made this a priority:

They've taken our IT division, renamed it Technology and Innovation, and spun it into its own freestanding division of the college, which was the leadership's way of saying innovation is a priority, and we need a dedicated group that's going to manage that in the same way we have a dedicated group for, say, academic tech. As people have ideas and they want to take those ideas forward, they're not just random leads with ad hoc doing experiments all over campus. They're coming to a group that can take them through a really fragile process with all of the resources that are needed to back that up. So we'll have people who have market analysis experience, or we're going to outsource that. We'll have people who can do design thinking. We'll have all these different skill sets around innovation that are needed to help put the scaffolding around an idea and around the people who want to take this process forward. Ideally, that sets us up for success long term, and it's not dependent on one individual or the president and a couple of individuals. It's really more baked in. We're not there yet. But that's how we're adjusting it.[16]

The desire to build a durable campus structure and culture around innovation that is sustainable is a common goal among the learning professionals that we spoke to in researching this book. The goal of having learning innovation "baked in" to the normal teaching and learning operations is widely shared. Also shared is the sentiment expressed by Eshleman that "we're not quite there yet," in that nowhere does an engine for learning R&D and the initiation of disciplined learning experiments feel secure. Much depends on the ability of learning innovation units to be identified by leadership as strategic priorities and targets of fundraising campaigns or other investments.

Many learning innovation efforts seem to have gotten off the ground with a large donation or the commitment of short-term discretionary funding from university leadership. Positions in learning innovation organizations, such as instructional designers and media educators and project managers, are often on term funding lines as opposed to regular positions. As such, unless an alternative source of funding is found, the learning professionals who work with faculty on learning innovation initiatives will either need to move into more operational roles or move to another institution. The pressure is then on the learning innovation unit to find sustainable revenue models. The soft ROI for creating a "culture of innovation" at the institution has a limited shelf life. After a few years, provosts and deans will want to see a hard ROI, being unwilling to carry learning innovation projects that don't pay for themselves. At every school that we visit or speak with, our peers in learning organizations indicate there are structural efforts underway to advance learning. These structural efforts go beyond the disconnected experiments of individual faculty in their courses and encompass institution-wide learning initiatives. These learning initiatives may be focused on course redesigns for introductory/gateway courses, curriculum redesigns that integrate learning science and analytics, and new traditional and open online programs.

If there is one common denominator in all the schools we've interviewed for this book, it is that the most important enabler of institutional change to advance student learning is support from academic leadership. This leadership support can take many different forms and styles and does not necessarily need to come from the president. Provosts, deans, or other campus leaders can champion learning initiatives. In his role as the associate provost for Digital Learning & Innovation at Boston University, Chris Dellarocas recruited Romy Ruukel from edX to serve initially as the associate director of the original Digital Learning Initiative and then later as the director of the Digital Education Incubator. The outward- and institutional-facing positions of an associate provost, such as Dellarocas, help assure that the educators within the learning organization, such as Ruukel, have the resources and protection necessary to engage in disciplined learning experiments.

At CSU Channel Islands, professor of education Jill Leafstedt assumed the role of director of Teaching and Learning Innovations after being championed by Michael Berman, the vice president for technology and innovation. In 2017, Berman was appointed as the first chief innovation officer (CIO) of the California State University system, which makes us optimistic that the institutional learning innovations he championed at CSU Channel Islands will extend throughout the entire CSU system. This partnership between a faculty member and the CIO to build a structure outside of the technology organization to catalyze learning innovation may be somewhat unusual, but it was necessary at CSU

Channel Islands as the school did not have the resources to build a large learning organization with new hires. Existing people and resources had to be allocated to focus on learning innovation. For Leafstedt, the necessity of being lean and scrappy is pushing learning innovation as an asset rather than a detriment: "We feel very connected to the outcomes of the students."[17]

Kristen Eshleman has been at Davidson since 2001 and had built up substantial respect on campus as well as a national reputation as a leader in learning innovation. This reputation was necessary but not sufficient for her ability to design a process to drive institutional innovation. Her position as director of digital innovation and education has been supported by a series of other academic leaders at the institution, including then CIO Raechelle Clemmons and Davidson's president Carol Quillen. This institutional support enabled Eshleman to take the risks necessary to encourage change. At a traditional residential and highly ranked institution such as Davidson, structural change to promote innovation can be challenging. There is more downside for failure than upside for success. Schools like Davidson can feel that they have more to lose than to gain. For innovations to do more than skim the surface of an unchanging structure, they need leadership championing the process. Nor can the innovation process be the same as traditional initiatives that have outcomes that are more predictable. As Eshleman told us about the experience in developing the Davidson innovation process, "For those who want to experiment, we need a parallel process for innovation that others on campus will trust. They don't have to like the ideas, but they've got to respect the process—that people are being held accountable for the learnings, and that there is responsible and collaborative decision-making."[18]

What is essential to keep in mind about all of these stories about leadership buy-in for innovation is that this support can take different forms. The leadership support does not need always to be vocal or charismatic. Instead, academic leaders can lend their support for the development of new organizational structures and new governance processes. Academic leaders do not need to be experts on innovation or lead innovation efforts personally. As we've seen, supporting and empowering an innovation team, either in a new organization or within an existing campus learning organization, can be powerful and effective across a diverse range of institutions. Presidents, provosts, and deans can't be expected to be experts in learning innovation. What they can do, however, is apply their ability to create new organizational structures and processes at the institutions they lead in support of durable and resilient innovation initiatives.

Next Steps

In this chapter we chose to highlight institutions that have created new organizations to drive learning innovation. The very fact that these units devoted to learning innovation have only recently come into existence is noteworthy, as is the fact that there are many other centers like these that could have been included in a case study for the growing strategic role of learning organizations in advancing learning on their campuses. The work of learning innovation is also not confined to units or centers with "innovation" in their titles. We are seeing concerted institutional efforts to advance and scale learning innovation across higher education in centers for teaching and learning, academic computing departments, and schools of continuing and online education.

One illustrative example of institutional commitment to advance learning comes from the Academic Learning Transformation (ALT) Lab at Virginia Commonwealth University (VCU).[19] The ALT Lab provides faculty with a range of services. These include instructional design consulting and media creation for online, hybrid, and face-to-face classes. The ALT Lab also facilitates a community of practice around learning innovation by providing opportunities for professional development such as workshops and community networking events. The ALT Lab team includes an associate director for organizational effectiveness, five instructional designers, three members of an R&D team, and three media educators. The "About Us" section of the VCU Academic Learning Transformation website is both inspiring and illustrative of the larger trend of institutional investment to drive learning innovation:

Higher education is undergoing rapid change. We don't underestimate the challenges facing higher education. We understand how declining public investment, enrollment stagnation, and changing workforce demands have affected institutions. We understand that affordability issues are an obstacle to true equality of access and opportunity. We believe the missions of universities to expand knowledge, tackle big questions, and promote civic engagement is critical to our communities, locally and globally. We believe technology is a critical tool in meeting these challenges and preserving the value of the university.[20]

VCU's approach is also one of play and experimentation that we believe will come to characterize much of this work in higher education:

We're intrigued by other institutions' successes with large-scale and competency-based degree programs. We don't think the MOOC is dead. We're curious how artificial intelligence and virtual reality will change education in the future. We're excited about the ways technology can make our spaces more accessible and inclusive.

We're also committed to making sure best practices and strategies faculty use to cultivate knowledge and promote inquiry in the students they teach don't get swept away in all this change. We believe pedagogy should inform the use of technology, not the other way around. We make that our number one priority when developing online and technology-enhanced courses.

We are a team of educators with skills in design, development, and technology. We keep up with the current best practices in accessibility, instructional quality, student success, and faculty satisfaction. We believe in continuing to strive to deliver high-quality learning experiences with strong student outcomes at affordable and accessible rates.

We want to work with our colleagues to solve problems, create opportunities, and engage students. What problems do you see? How can we help?[21]

What will this all mean in the future? What will the work of centers at VCU, Boston University, CSU Channel Islands, and Davidson mean for student learning and the long-term future of higher education? The institutional changes to promote learning innovation that we explore in this chapter are too new to judge. Their impact on long-term student outcomes is not yet clear. The research has yet to yield conclusions. We do not know what impact these institution-wide learning initiatives will ultimately have on long-term student learning outcomes across all of higher education. We don't know if the worrying results from Arum and Roksa's *Academically Adrift* will reverse at schools that demonstrate an unusually strong commitment to institution-wide learning innovation. We believe, however, that understanding the impact of learning innovation deserves the sort of rigorous empirical investigation that we see as the appropriate domain of an interdisciplinary field dedicated to this line of scholarship, an idea that we take up in chapter 4.

THREE

Reclaiming Innovation from Disruption

THE THEORY OF DISRUPTIVE innovation holds a particular prominence within the postsecondary learning innovation community.
The core principles of disruption theory were first developed by Clayton
Christensen in *The Innovator's Dilemma* and were applied to higher
education in Christensen and Henry Eyring's 2011 book *The Innovative University: Changing the DNA of Higher Education from the Inside Out*. Arguments for the necessity of disruptive innovations in higher
education are often accompanied by claims of its imminent collapse. In
The Innovative University, Christensen and Eyring predicted that within
fifteen years as many as half of all American universities would go bank-
rupt. A prediction that Christensen reiterated as recently as 2017.[1] Many
commentators have compared the current situation in higher education
to the housing bubble of 2008, all too gleefully predicting the soon-to-
come demise of American colleges across the country.[2] The theory itself
is not perfect and has many calling into question its relevance to both the
corporate context and higher education. Still, even as disruption theory
is increasingly challenged for its explanatory or predictive value for cor-
porations,[3] the core ideas of the theory have gained currency as catalysts
for learning innovation[4] and are worth exploring further.

The central argument of *The Innovative University* is that universities are falling into the classic innovation trap. Incumbent institutions

are designed to make sustaining innovations (incremental improvements), changes that result in both higher costs and an increased vulnerability to disruption from external forces and new competitors. As described by Michael Horn, chief strategy officer for Entangled Ventures and a distinguished fellow at the Clayton Christensen Institute for Disruptive Innovation, higher education disruption has the following components:[5]

- The focus is on serving nonconsumers or nonadopters.
- The services offered tend to be simpler than existing services.
- Disruptive innovations will improve in quality over time, enabling the service to improve beyond incremental or linear improvement.
- It is impossible for legacy or incumbent organizations to adopt disruptive innovations within their core operations.

Examples of disruptive innovation practices as applied to higher education vary but generally include things such as the exclusive offering of online educational options, the move from seat-time to competency-based learning, the extension of college credit-bearing courses into high school, the offering of alternative credentials such as badges, the use of open educational course materials, and the growing impact of full-spectrum technology-based solutions for student learning.[6]

Drawing mainly on the examples of Harvard and BYU-Idaho, *The Innovative University* calls for a radical transformation in how post-secondary institutions operate in order to combat this imminent collapse. Among its recommendations is a transition from a high-cost model, where professors engage in both scholarship and teaching, to one in which teaching is prioritized. The authors warn against the tendency of schools to fall into the Harvard model, where all academic disciplines are represented and where faculty autonomy trumps learning outcomes. The disruptive innovation that BYU-Idaho followed eliminated extraneous expenses, such as the athletics program, while simultaneously investing in online education initiatives. By 2016, the online enrollment at BYU-Idaho of almost 27,000 students had surpassed the campus enrollment figure of 18,000.[7]

Disruption theory, at its core, is a description of the impacts of change and the potential hazards of maintaining a relatively consistent path. According to the theory, incumbents are at risk as they tend to prioritize sustaining improvements over radical change. For higher education, this means that traditional universities will seek to incrementally improve their offerings while building on existing structures and institutional cultures. The result may be improvements in all aspects of the university, including student learning. Campus buildings will get bigger and fancier, especially the residence halls and student centers—all those lazy rivers and climbing walls. Classrooms will evolve slowly away from fixed and tiered seating and toward flat floors and space for collaborative work. Libraries will transition from buildings that house books to spaces that invite group work and consultations with information specialists (the librarians). Learning technologies, such as learning management systems and simulations, will be introduced—but they will be layered on top of the traditional teaching and assessment methods. These improvements will inevitably come at a cost. Updates to campus buildings are not cheap. New student services incur both capital costs and salaries for the necessary experts. Learning technologies require updates to the technology infrastructure, new enterprise applications, and a growing support staff. As anyone who lived through the transition from dormitory-based phone systems to mobile phones knows, these changes may even mean reduced revenue for the institution.

According to disruption theory, the rising costs and changing revenue models associated with sustaining campus innovations will make traditional institutions vulnerable to competitors. New entrants will be able to come into the market offering lower quality alternatives to incumbents at dramatically lower costs. The disruptive innovation is not necessarily a better product, at least not initially, but one that is both *good enough* while being substantially cheaper. This new lower quality/lower priced offering will initially bring nonadopters into the market, those who have been priced out of accessing existing products or services. Eventually, the quality of the new offering will improve to the degree that even existing customers of the incumbent offering will migrate to the disrupter.

The narrative that higher education is broken[8] and the only way out of the current mess is to apply the principles of disruptive innovation is bolstered by the well-documented financial struggles and near-death experiences of a growing number of American colleges. The 2015 planned closure and reprieve (perhaps temporary) of Sweet Briar College, a private women's college in Virginia, is viewed by many as an indicator that the business model of higher education was endangered.[9] According to a widely cited 2015 study by Moody's, the number of small colleges and universities expected to close was going to triple in the following years—from an average of two per year to six.[10] The financial stress of a growing number of institutions caused publications like *Forbes* to ask "Are Small Town Liberal Arts Colleges Endangered?"[11] A report from the consultancy Parthenon concluded that "800 institutions face critical strategic challenges because of their inefficiencies or their small size."[12]

Annual gatherings, such as the ASU+GSV Educational Technology Summit, seek to accelerate higher education disruption by convening university leaders, venture capitalists, foundation officers, and start-up entrepreneurs. Sessions at the 2017 ASU+GSV conference included titles such as "DisruptED: Who Are the Real Disruptors in Higher Ed" and "The Future of Work and Industry as Educator: The Role of Enterprises in Teaching Future Skills."[13] The appeal of disruptive innovation when applied to challenges in the higher education sector is clear. The theory holds out the promise of dramatic solutions in the face of dramatic challenges. The problems of legacy higher education providers, of incumbent colleges and universities, appear so intractable that only radical change can hope to address the issues. The cure, so the thinking goes, must correspond to the disease. Incremental improvements and half measures by institutions most concerned with maintaining their place in the status hierarchy, and by higher education leaders most interested in preserving their own positions, will inevitably come up short.

Why Disruption Theory Is Attractive to Learning Innovators

In many ways, it is easy to understand why disruption theory is appealing to anyone committed to learning innovation in higher education.

Disruption theory provides a seemingly incontrovertible argument for the need to push beyond the campus status quo. No college or university wants to suffer the same fate as Kodak or Blockbuster, once highly valuable and entrenched incumbents that were made irrelevant by low-cost digital cameras and Netflix. Nor does any higher education leader want their industry to follow the path of newspapers, an industry that has been thoroughly disrupted by the internet, where revenue from print advertising has fallen from $60 billion in 2000 to $20 billion in 2015,[14] and the number of newsroom employees has shrunk from almost 70,000 to just over 40,000.[15]

It's therefore tempting to fly a disruptive innovation banner over efforts to prioritize digital learning. These efforts are often the vanguard of innovation at the institutions in which learning innovators work. Many universities are less of a command-and-control center and more like a loosely affiliated network of educational entrepreneurs (the faculty). Strategic initiatives that gain traction are those that resonate as models of change. Situating the work to innovate teaching and learning within the framework of disruption theory connects these efforts to the changing trends and pressures about which everyone on campus is aware. Comparing a university to Nokia is shorthand for arguments against the campus status quo.

As we saw in chapter 2, the approaches adopted by new centers and offices dedicated to learning innovation often take on the status of incubators and use the language of entrepreneurship. There may be many good reasons for higher education to adopt the language and models that have been successful outside of higher education. There is little disagreement that higher education needs to change, at least in part. The information economy all but demands it. If higher education has to change, then, for many it needs to do so along the lines of the start-ups and disruptive innovators that are challenging its incumbency. If we can break through the static structures and traditions that keep the body of the institution at rest, so the thinking goes, we can develop enough momentum to stay ahead of the disrupters from below.

It is also easy to see why disruption theory is appealing to those within higher education not focused primarily on learning innovation. Each year it seems that more and more services get added to the university bundle. Beyond the lazy rivers and climbing walls, many colleges and universities now offer a range of cocurricular services and amenities. The growth of nonacademic services is reflected in postsecondary staff growth. From 1993 to 2013 the number of higher education full-time staff increased by 400,000, from just under 1.4 million to just over 1.8 million. During this same period, the number of full-time faculty only increased by about 300,000, growing from about 700,000 to 1 million.[16] The growth of staff, in conjunction with a corresponding increase of part-time and adjunct faculty, have led many to conclude that teaching and learning are no longer the main priority of many colleges and universities. Disruption theory would suggest that a new entrant into the field can unbundle the postsecondary experience by stripping away nonessential services and the costs associated with their delivery. That disrupter would have a good chance of displacing traditional colleges and universities.

Problems with Disruption Theory for Higher Education

While applying disruption thinking to learning innovation is seductive, we have come to believe that the theory poorly serves higher education. We want to suggest that it's time to interrogate whether disruption theory is helpful in explaining the turn to learning or useful as a guide to leading learning innovation. For those who wish to be part of campus-wide organizational changes that promote learning, disruption theory may do more harm than good for three reasons:

1. Higher education is a complex ecosystem.
2. Learners are not products.
3. Higher education is diverse.

While we do not see this list as exhaustive by any means, we suggest it might serve as a guide for postsecondary learning innovation, and we will offer some alternatives to disruption theory to understand and drive campus learning innovation.

Higher Education Is a Complex Ecosystem

Disruption theory best explains change in zero-sum industries. Netflix killed Blockbuster as movie rentals moved from an in-store experience to a DVD-by-mail and then streaming service. Every Netflix video watched was one less Blockbuster rental. The same can be said for the loss of classified advertising in newspapers to online platforms such as Craigslist. Every free ad placed online is one less paid ad in a newspaper. Higher education, however, is not zero-sum. Improvements at one institution do not necessarily cannibalize the demand for another. While colleges and universities enthusiastically compete for top students and star faculty, the method of competition resembles little the industries in which disruption theory was built. Unlike for-profit companies, colleges and universities are committed to cross-institutional knowledge sharing and collaboration. Schools are eager to share with peer institutions the details and results of projects and initiatives. Colleges and universities across the United States and the world form a complex ecosystem that depends on the success of each institution to help educate students and to continue the pursuit of new knowledge. This information sharing is formalized in interinstitutional consortiums and associations. Georgetown University, for example, is one of twenty-eight schools that make up the Association of Jesuit Colleges and Universities.[17] Dartmouth College participates in a range of activities associated with the Ivy Plus group. Every institution is part of a larger consortium, association, or network devoted to collaboration and knowledge sharing. These associations range from the American Association of Community Colleges to the Council of Independent Colleges to the University Professional and Continuing Education Association.

Colleges and universities share so much information that it may be easier to enumerate what is not shared than what is. For example, specific data and strategies related to fundraising, marketing, and student recruitment are not necessarily broadcast to all institutions but are shared through smaller consortia, such as the Consortium on Financing Higher Education (COFHE): "The Consortium's data collection, research, and policy analysis focus on matters pertaining to access, affordability, and assessment, particularly as they relate to undergraduate education, admissions, financial aid, and the financing of higher education. All data supplied to, compiled by, and shared among the Consortium are subject to strict confidentiality guidelines."[18]

Financial information about institutional operations often will have the same level of transparency both within and across colleges and universities. Public institutions operate with different levels of mandatory disclosure and publicly available financials than private institutions (e.g., private institutions tend to keep financial information private, while public institutions share all financial information). There are no doubt aspects of the operations and activities that occur within higher education that are not shared with peers, but private operations and activities are the exception rather than the rule in higher education. Academic culture prizes openness. Disciplinary norms of scholarship demand that knowledge should be widely accessible. Even in the case of research that has commercial value, there is a strong cultural preference in academia for openness and transparency. Unlike other industries, higher education operates under the assumption that advances in one area ultimately benefit everyone in the ecosystem. Rather than fighting over a fixed number of students, colleges and universities collaborate on ways to respond to the overall demand. Being mission-driven to create economic and social opportunity for all students and communities, higher education celebrates any instance in which that overall mission advances.

Learning organizations and learning professionals within higher education are particularly committed to cross-institutional collaboration. It may be that those educators leading learning innovation initiatives and centers devoted to advancing learning are among the most networked in all of higher education. In chapter 4, we highlight the meetings that higher education learning innovation leaders attend to share ideas and plans. The extent that information—such as budgets, communications strategies, and technical know-how—is shared between learning professionals across colleges and universities would shock anyone who has spent a career in the corporate world. This cross-institutional collaboration is not because higher education learning professionals are necessarily more selfless or charitable, though that might very well be true in some cases. Instead, schools share information because getting ideas and information from other contexts is the best way to drive learning innovation efforts forward. The work of learning innovation is dependent on a cross-institutional community of practice to support the work. Any attempts at learning innovation that do not take into account the experiences and lessons of other schools are likely to fail.

Disruptive innovation theory is a framework to explain how companies and organizations rise or fall under conditions of competition. It is not a theory that predicts or explains progress. Student learning is improved not by one institution displacing another but by all institutions improving together. The goals of advancing learning within a college or university are not met if that work weakens or undermines the overall strength of the institution.

Learners Are Not Products

Disruption theory, as we have noted, predicts that incumbents will focus on incremental improvements to serve current customers, or in our case, students. These iterative improvements will respond to the current needs of some students and other stakeholders. They will also drive up the complexity and cost of the college. What is needed, according to disruption theory, are nonincumbents to develop higher education services that either bring in nonadopters or provide a somewhat inferior product for a significantly lower cost. As customers (students) move to the new inferior, but less expensive, higher education products and away from the complicated and expensive incumbent products, the former will inevitably improve. Expensive and overly complicated universities will be disrupted.

The blind spot of disruption thinking is that students are not customers, and the value that higher education provides is not analogous to a standardized service or product. If students were customers then admissions, grades, credits, and degrees could be purchased rather than earned. Not discounting the advantages of privileged students in admissions and collegiate success, grades and degrees cannot be attained by payment alone. Colleges and universities (and the professors they employ) are given the responsibility through accreditation of certifying student achievement in earning grades and credits and degrees. Higher education is a closely regulated industry. Conformity to regulations and accreditor standards is necessary for students to receive educational loans and for schools to be eligible for a range of funding and other benefits. Colleges and universities have evolved such complex structures in order to balance the needs of students with the social and legal responsibilities that their accreditation demands.

As organizations designed to fulfill missions to educate students, serve their communities, and create knowledge, colleges and universities are rightly constrained in following the disruption playbook. Changes that lower costs or improve quality must also serve a wide range of stakeholders. In the realm of learning, an innovation that results in significantly better outcomes for a segment of students will not be acceptable if the cost is worse outcomes for another segment. Students who are not served by institutional change cannot easily become customers of some other school. Professors who do not benefit from organizational changes will not support their implementation. Colleges and universities have responsibilities to the students they serve, not to those who might thrive under optimally efficient conditions. One institution's disruption might be another learner's loss of resources, support, and assistance. Or the loss of another professor's autonomy and academic freedom. Disruption theory may be a road map for continuous corporate renewal, but it is a poor road map for mission-guided organizations as complicated as our colleges and universities.

Higher Education Is Diverse

Unlike other industries, higher education in the United States is characterized primarily by its functional and historical diversity. While each degree-granting college or university offers credentials, the methods in which this credentialing occurs are vastly different across the sector. The result for the consumers of higher education in the United States is an astounding variety of options. Students can already choose to enroll in lower-cost institutions that lack the amenities of more expensive schools. Greater than 40 percent of the 18 million undergraduate students in the United States are enrolled in community colleges. This compares to 0.4 percent of undergraduates who are enrolled in one of the Ivy League schools.[19] In 2014 and 2015, the average cost for tuition and fees at a community college was $3,347.[20] While the price of community college remains out of reach for many Americans—and indeed only 62 percent of community college students can afford to attend full time without government subsidies[21]—it's difficult to imagine how higher education costs for this sector could get much lower through an alternative, disruptive for-profit model.

Community colleges already offer an excellent alternative for the majority of those students seeking an undergraduate degree. What is necessary is not more schools following the community college model of focusing mostly on delivering core instructional services but rather greater public investment in our nation's community college system. The Century Foundation reports that in 2011 the average per-pupil public funding for a student in a public research university was over $16,000. This compares to less than an average of $7,500 in per-pupil public funding for a student enrolled at a community college.[22] It strikes us as strange that those from outside of higher education who are calling most vocally for disruption within higher education do not usually accompany their pleas with recommendations for increased public investment in community colleges. Surely anyone who is interested in creating an affordable postsecondary system would also be a champion of community colleges. It is our community college system that educates a plurality of our students. These institutions are deeply embedded in the employment networks and social fabric of the communities in which they reside. Community colleges serve the critical need of providing a flexible and affordable education while also training skilled workers for local employers. Strikingly, promoters of disrupting higher education seldom mention, much less champion, community colleges.

Colleges and universities do not need to be disrupted as much as they need to be redesigned and reengineered. The same observation holds for the system as a whole. Any institutional changes that are undertaken to advance learning need to be sensitive to the context, culture, history, and structures in which these innovations are contemplated. Any theory of learning innovation in higher education that focuses on competition across or within institutions fails to describe how meaningful change occurs.

PLATO and How Technology Has Not Disrupted Learning

Despite our arguments to the contrary, it is still common today to hear that some new innovation—most often aligned with a new technology—is on the cusp of disrupting colleges and universities. Frequently mentioned as the next educational disrupters, for example, are virtual and augmented reality (VR and AR, respectively), technologies that promise to create immersive virtual learning experiences.[23] With VR and AR, the argument goes, tomorrow's students will be able to learn everything from art restoration to surgical techniques in a tactile and hands-on method, without the need to ever leave their homes. Virtual and augmented reality will substitute for physical reality, eliminating much of the need for physical campus labs and classrooms. Technologies such as these are viewed as powerful disrupters to the status quo.

The disruptive potential of technology is not a new story. Teaching and learning are often seen as most susceptible to being radically altered. But the story of the impact of tomorrow's technologies on higher education—as seen through a disruption lens—continually fails to acknowledge how change happens (and even more so that it does continually happen). As we saw in chapter 1, the last big technological advance that was supposed to disrupt higher education was MOOCs. A synthesis of the impact of the role of educational technologies on advancing learning would include stories of unwarranted hype and unmet expectations. As Audrey Watters has often pointed out, the faith that many inside and outside of higher education place on new technologies to "disrupt" the future of colleges and universities almost always ignores the history of educational technologies.[24]

In 1922, Thomas Edison famously said, "I believe that the motion picture is destined to revolutionize our educational system, and that in a few years it will supplant largely, if not entirely, the use of textbooks. I should say that on the average we get only about two percent efficiency out of textbooks as they are written today."[25] The early-twentieth-century idea that film would replace textbooks was accompanied by an equally fervent belief in the potential of radio—and later television—to revolutionize learning. In 1945, William Levenson wrote that "the time may come when a portable radio receiver will be as common in the classroom as is the blackboard. Radio instruction will be integrated into school life as an accepted educational medium."[26] Perhaps it is not surprising that Levenson believed in the transformative power of the radio for teaching and learning; at the time he made this statement he was the director of the Cleveland public schools' radio station. It is not unexpected to find the most vocal advocates of disruption theory to be the ones who might most benefit from the disruption itself. Despite some impact, neither of these technologies disrupted how students learn nor how universities and colleges operate.

The idea that the future of education was to be found in advances in technology received additional academic support in the 1950s and 1960s. B. F. Skinner, the famous psychologist and father of behaviorism, observed that "with the help of teaching machines and programmed instruction, students could learn twice as much in the same time and with the same effort as in a standard classroom."[27] In the 1960s, those teaching machines were televisions. During that decade both private foundations and the US government poured money into placing TVs in classrooms and developing programming for these "teaching machines." By 1965, the Ford Foundation had invested $70 million into televisions for classrooms in US schools, the equivalent of $544 million in today's dollars.[28] As of 1971, public and private sources had spent a total of $100 million on classroom TV, or over $600 million in 2017 dollars.[29]

While none of these technologies brought with them the full scale disruptive effects predicted by Edison or Skinner, they were not alone in attempting to change the teaching and learning dynamic. Many would be surprised to learn that the story of modern-era digital learning technologies starts in the 1960s at the University of Illinois with the invention of PLATO (Programmed Logic for Automatic Teaching Operations). The fact that PLATO is the progenitor of all subsequent digital learning platforms is not widely known even by today's most enthusiastic boosters of educational technology. There is a direct line between PLATO, the learning management system, and the emerging educational technology platforms such as data-driven adaptive learning environments.

PLATO represented both a technological and conceptual breakthrough, despite the fact that it was ultimately an unmitigated commercial failure. That PLATO is so seldom talked about in discussions of the potential of educational technology is interesting given the platform's near four-decade history. The first iteration of PLATO in 1960 was remarkably similar to today's web-based and mobile adaptive learning systems. It used a 1950s-era ILLIAC (Illinois Automatic Computer) that the school had initially utilized for post-Sputnik (1957) funded defense research. ILLIAC cost over $1 million at the time ($8.5 million in 2019 dollars) and boasted 64,000 bytes of memory, made possible by 2,800 vacuum tubes. The original PLATO terminal consisted of a screen (initially a television set) and a sixteen-button keyboard that included keys for "HELP" and "AHA!" A student would navigate sequentially through different content screens (called "frames") by inputting the correct answer on the keypad.

Throughout the 1960s and 1970s, the technology underlying PLATO became more advanced. In 1967, the TUTOR programming language was created at the University of Illinois, allowing for the creation of a wide variety of digital lessons. During that year, the PLATO III moved off the 1950s-era ILLIAC and onto a modern Control Data Corporation (CDC) 1604 mainframe system that allowed for up to twenty simultaneous users. The PLATO IV, which arrived in 1972, represented a major advance. Its plasma display supported fast vector line drawing, giving the system the ability to render graphics as well as text. The system even included a touch panel, allowing students to tap the screen to move through the lessons. The PLATO IV terminals were connected to the mainframe by phone lines, rather than the more expensive dedicated video lines of earlier systems, and could support 1,000 simultaneous students.

In 1976, the PLATO system was licensed to Control Data Corporation as part of CDC's strategy to transition to an educational technology company. Throughout the late 1970s and the early 1980s, CDC tried to market PLATO to both universities and companies as an educational training tool. The company spent over $600 million on the project but was never able to recoup this investment. In 1978, the National Science Foundation funded a $1 million evaluation of the PLATO system for its impact on student learning. This research found "no significant impact on student achievement," a devastating finding given that CDC charged $50 an hour to use the system.[30] In the 1980s, CDC tried to transition PLATO from its mainframe-terminal model to one that could run on early personal computers such as the Texas Instruments TI-99, the Radio Shack TRS-80, and the IBM Personal Computer. The company charged $5 an hour to access PLATO courses on its data centers. Unable to recoup its costs—and with the retirement of CDC CEO William Norris who had championed the vision of transitioning the company from hardware to educational technology—the PLATO business was wound down and sold in pieces to other companies.

That PLATO never succeeded as either a technology to improve education or a business does not mean that it was not important for its impact on the evolution of technology, or ultimately for its effect on the future of teaching and learning. Many technologies that are central to consumer devices, such as the plasma screen and touchscreens, were first invented for PLATO. Foundational communications tools, such as online forums and instant messaging and even email, appeared first on PLATO terminals. Even the history of multiplayer online games can be traced back to PLATO.

Understanding why PLATO ended up introducing so many long-lasting advances in technology and communications while ultimately failing as both a business and a platform to improve learning is illustrative of the limits of technology disrupting higher education. PLATO was viewed as a potential game changer for teaching and learning at a scale much larger than is currently contemplated for technologies such as virtual and augmented reality. Where VR and AR are arguably an evolutionary advance, building on established technologies such as gaming and mobile computing, PLATO was understood to be revolutionary when released. The potential for individual learners to receive adaptive instruction through a computer program and a screen, rather than an instructor, seemed at the time to predict an altogether different future of education—a future where the professor and the classroom were replaced by the terminal, the program, and the screen.

That educatorless educational future (thankfully) never arrived. PLATO, like all educational technologies that have followed, never delivered on its promise to disrupt teaching and learning, at least not in the way or to the scale perhaps hoped for by its greatest champions. At best, educational technologies that survive end up complementing rather than replacing professors. New technologies become incorporated into the existing practices of the university. This is often the most salient lesson for the theory of disruptive innovation when applied to higher education. Learning is too complex to be reduced to a technical problem amenable to technical solutions. PLATO was an authentic leap in the technology that could be applied to learning, and it laid the basis for many educational (and other) technologies that followed. Yet today, PLATO is barely remembered because the technology had little to no impact on the structure of learning in higher education. While we can perhaps imagine similarly large educational technology leaps today as PLATO was over five decades ago, it is hard to argue that these advances will be as different from today's technologies as PLATO was from what came before. The story of PLATO demonstrates that learning innovation is not a matter of technical advances alone and technologies that aim to disrupt are less likely to result in long-lasting learning innovations.

If, as we argue, disruption is not the best model to think about meaningful change in higher education, what is? We believe it's important to separate learning innovation out of the disruptive innovation framework. Innovations in learning—even the ones we describe above—have had consistent and long-term effects on the evolution of higher education. Learning innovation has been happening since the beginning of higher education (though perhaps at a pace somewhat slower than Lockheed or Xerox or Netflix). From changing modes of instruction to new ways of delivering content to enterprise technologies that simplify course-level administrative tasks, innovations have long been part of higher education.

Why Innovation?

In discussing our plan for this book with colleagues, we discovered some skepticism about the idea that learning innovation was worthy of a book-length treatment. The objection did not come from a resistance to the idea that colleges and universities were engaging in new institutional-level initiatives to advance student learning. Rather, many objected to language of "innovation" itself. That the objection is to the word "innovation" and not to how higher education is changing to advance student learning suggests a critical unpacking of the word is necessary.

In critique of our efforts to advance the idea of learning innovation as a new field of inquiry, Rolin Moe, director of the Institute for Academic Innovation at Seattle Pacific University, writes:

> Some have argued that innovation binds together disciplines such as learning technologies, leadership and change, and industrial/organizational psychology. . . . However, this cohesion assumes a "shared language of inquiry," which does not currently exist. Today's shared language around innovation is emotive rather than procedural; we use innovation to highlight the desired positive results of our efforts rather than to identify anything specific about our effort (products, processes or policies). The predominant use of innovation is to highlight the value and future-readiness of whatever the speaker supports, which is why opposite sides of issues in education (see school choice, personalized learning, etc.) use innovation in promoting their ideologies.[31]

Moe goes on in the same article to provide a brief lesson on the history of the word innovation: "The predominant usage of innovation was as a pejorative rather than a superlative, a barb to throw at opponents rather than something to aspire to. During the reign of King Charles I, both Parliament and Charles regularly cast one another as innovators in an attempt to smear the other. The innovation label came with great penalty; members of Parliament castigated as innovators were silenced by imprisonment, or in some cases physical harm; King Charles himself paid with his life."

It is only very recently, as Moe relates, that the word "innovation" has been used as a standalone descriptor. Prior to the 1970s, innovation was almost always paired with a field or a concept. For instance, political innovation, social innovation, or technological innovation. Today, innovation is, as Moe describes, "a term we all know but do not have a conceptual framework for." Innovation more often is positioned as a positive "outside-the-box" approach to solving current problems. In the world of higher education, politically oriented efforts to reduce costs—such as reducing public funding and introducing programs based on market demand rather than social goals—are billed as "learning innovation."

We think Moe is correct, at least partially, and acknowledge that the language of innovation is problematic. More on where we disagree in a moment, but it's clear that the word "innovation" may have long since passed from a useful descriptor of nonlinear change and experimentation to a jargony buzzword devoid of real meaning or content. Innovation has been captured by critics of higher education who use the concept as a club with which to beat up on slow-moving incumbent institutions. Arguments for the dawn of disruptive innovation within postsecondary education—the belief that the US postsecondary sector is as vulnerable to existential destruction as yesterday's video rental stores and makers of film cameras—are everywhere in contemporary critiques of the sector. Within higher education, the label of innovation tends to get attached to anything that is new or purported to be new, and it is more often than not used to signal any change rather than something that challenges assumptions, traditions, or common practices. In the more egregious cases, titles of programs that employ the language of innovation are often done so to advance the initiatives without fully interrogating what might be innovative about the programs themselves. Lacking any substance or allowance for ambiguity or critical dissent, innovation talk within higher education is increasingly seen as little different from empty marketing and craven sloganeering by anybody targeted by innovation messaging.

When everything is innovative, nothing is innovative. When innovation is used to advance one agenda or one group over another—for example, the direction of dollars to digital platforms over investments in security or infrastructure—then the concept suffers further devaluation. Can the language of innovation be rescued from disruption thinking and applied to the goal of designing institutional improvements to advance learning? Are there alternatives to a disruption framework for understanding and motivating learning innovation?

Our attempt to reclaim "innovation" as a useful term may simply come down to a grammatical disagreement, one of tense and perhaps one of kind. While it is very true that a "shared language of inquiry" does not yet currently exist, as Moe argues, we think it should. In fact, as we argue in the next chapter, we think it's a necessary next step for the type of evolutionary change higher education needs to make. But having a language and framework to define whether something is innovative is hardly the point and runs the risk of simply reinforcing preexisting biases against innovation. Rather, innovation is something we hope will happen, even if it does not yet exist in full. For us, any activity that purports to invest in progressive, positive change will almost by necessity be cast in a future tense. It's not important whether the work of learning innovation is currently innovative or describable, assessable, and definable as such. What *is* important is that this work attempts to be innovative. It is first and foremost an aspirational descriptor of activity, not (or not only) a set of criteria for judging success. In this sense, we agree (and see nothing wrong) with Moe's claim that "today's shared language around innovation is emotive rather than procedural." This of course does not mean that innovation cannot or should not be assessed, that we should not have a "shared language of inquiry" into what innovation is. Rather, it means that innovation encompasses a full spectrum of applied activities that need to be understood as both evocative and descriptive. We can find inspiration in our attempts to be innovative and celebrate success in those rare moments when we create something that is truly new and . . . innovative.

What about Learning Innovation?

If innovation is both aspirational and descriptive, learning innovation is about the changes we might make at an institutional or system level in order to improve student learning at the individual level. These changes might be something we aim for or something we implement with confidence. What we know, however, is that for most of the history of higher education, student learning advanced (or stagnated) as a result of the actions of individual faculty. Professors would change their approach to teaching based on experience, feedback, and examples, but there was little consistency in approach at any one school, let alone across the entire landscape of higher education. A school in which a faculty member worked might offer some incentives to improve instruction in the tenure and promotion process, but the mechanisms by which these improvements were assessed (student course reviews, infrequent classroom visits by peer faculty) were often lacking in both transparency, validity, and reliability. Non-tenure-track and adjunct faculty were even worse off, often offered almost no support, resources, or rewards for improving student learning.

Today, institutions are partnering with professors to advance learning to a much greater extent than ever before. As we discussed in chapters 1 and 2, this partnership may take the form of providing a rich set of services, workshops, resources, and communities of practice in a center for teaching and learning or an academic computing unit. At some schools, instructional designers are available to collaborate with faculty on residential and blended courses. Quality online programs almost always involve a collaboration between a professor and an instructional designer. In some instances, other experts in media or assessment are also brought on to the course team.

Institutional efforts to advance learning almost always involve intensification of inputs. Professors can rarely develop, market, run, and support online degree programs on their own. Faculty collaborate with teams at every step of a digitally mediated education. Course redesign initiatives for introductory and other large-enrollment classes usually require collaborations between faculty and other educational specialists.

Physical classrooms are being redesigned as active learning spaces, with flat floors and multiple team collaboration areas. Digital education is absorbing an ever-growing proportion of courses and programs. This, we would argue, is innovation at its best—aspirational and applied at the same time. To some, these might appear to be incremental changes only, but it is worth remembering just how much the teaching and learning dynamic has changed in the past twenty or so years. Not only have new technologies, new research about learning, and new pedagogical approaches radically altered teaching at most campuses—even if not evenly across all schools—but they've changed the expectations from students about what their participation should be. No longer passive consumers, students now expect to be partners in learning in ways that challenge long-standing assumptions about higher education. To address these challenges requires an investment in learning innovation.

It is important to note that innovation and tradition are not always at odds. They can be creative partners in driving change. The most durable and far-reaching advances in learning will occur within established colleges and universities, precisely because innovations that happen in isolation—whether within a small ed-tech start-up or a vaunted alternative approach to traditional residential education, such as Minerva Education—are less potent than ones that are shared across the entire educational ecosystem. If they fail to go to scale, they fail to have impact. This is true across all of higher education, just as it is true at any one institution. The challenge of higher education innovation is not in doing new things—it is in finding sustainable models that enable new practices to be adopted into the regular operations of colleges and universities. Unlike disruptive innovations, where the goal is to replace incumbents and eliminate traditional methods, learning innovation attempts to preserve the range of traditions and practices that have evolved at our institutions. There is too much that is good in higher education to jettison it in the name of disruption. Our existing colleges and universities serve a vital function with our communities and within our larger society. Values that promote the protection of academic freedom, discovery, and tolerance for unpopular ideas cannot be divorced from our efforts to innovate in teaching and learning. The very elements that can make change within higher education seem slow and unwieldy—such as shared governance and integration of scholarship and teaching into faculty roles—also form the basis of the strength of our collective institutions.

American postsecondary institutions enrolled over 20 million students in 2018.[32] The capacities that have been constructed to educate so many students have been built up over long periods of time. While it would be difficult to advance a plausible scenario where some other model replaces incumbent institutions, no disruptive model yet imagined, including MOOCs and other technologies, could function to carry out the mission of educating our society. New models of higher education, such as Minerva, may offer fascinating glimpses into alternative models, but this provocative boutique model enrolls (and likely could only ever enroll) a relatively small number of students. It is not that traditional higher education should not welcome these new alternative models. Rather, it is that new entrants cannot substitute for the ecosystem of colleges and universities because they have zero probability of educating students at the scale and reach of existing degree-granting and four-year institutions.[33] The cultural, operational, and organizational changes that advance student learning within established universities occur slowly at most institutions. The impact of these changes is great, owing to the scope and reach of the sector.

Despite the lack of significant alternatives, meaningful learning innovation will not occur without sustained institutional investments. Innovation efforts that purport to advance learning by eliminating resources for teaching will inevitably fail. The value of proposed university efforts to innovate how students learn should be judged against the resources committed to these initiatives. Developing a shared campus understanding that teaching and learning are complex and require significant and sustained resources is the first step in building a culture of learning innovation. Institutional investments must be directed at both professors and the structures that support their teaching. These twin investments in professors and the learning ecosystem are inseparable. The idea that the role professors play in the learning process can be substituted by technologies such as adaptive learning platforms or access to MOOCs runs counter to how students learn. Professors are the critical variable in creating an environment conducive to authentic student learning.

At the same time, professors need a range of partnerships and support from the institution for student learning outcomes to improve. These partnerships and supports come from the existing and emerging learning organizations and from campus learning professionals. Campus learning organizations will differ across schools. They will offer a diverse range of services, funding, and communities of practice. They will employ different sorts of nonfaculty learning professionals. What is important is that these learning organizations are aligned with the mission of the institution and have the resources necessary to build meaningful partnerships with faculty. Learning innovation is not a project or even a goal. Instead, learning innovation is best thought of as a culture in which learning is prioritized and resourced at all levels of an institution. The risk is that learning innovation initiatives will continue to come and go with the attention of the latest president or provost. As the average length of service of campus leaders continues to grow ever shorter,[34] the viability of top-down mandates for prioritizing learning innovation grows more tenuous. Tenured, tenure-track, non-tenure-track, visiting, and adjunct professors and instructors need to see learning innovation as aligned with their own goals and interests.

Innovation does not come without its downside. The history of the hype around every new learning technology is a history of a drive toward productivity, a goal that is at odds with many of the more laudable traditions of higher education if not downright anathema to improving access and student learning. The MOOC craze of 2012, where open online courses were positioned at least in part as potential mechanisms to save money by having the "best" professors teach millions of students, is perhaps the most egregious example of this "productivity" story. Today, artificial intelligence is touted as a technology that can reduce the demands on instructors by accomplishing tasks such as grading essays and answering common student questions. A 2017 *Quartz* article titled "Imagine How Great Universities Could Be without All Those

Human Teachers" predicted that "AI could upend the economics of teaching. . . . If you eliminate all the humdrum teaching work, universities can hire fewer professors and teaching assistants after all—and still service the same number of students (or perhaps even more of them) at a smaller budget."[35] Similarly, a 2015 *Washington Post* article, "Watch Out College Professors, The Robots Are Coming For Your Jobs," imagines a time when "some university classes can have 1,000 or 10,000 or even 100,000 students in them at any time." That article goes on to paint a picture of the future of higher education: "At some point, it's possible to imagine a scenario where the top, highest-paid human talent migrates to the nation's most elite universities, while robots take over the teaching and training of students in community colleges or vocational schools, where most of the emphasis is on learning certain very specific skills that can be used over and over again in the workplace."[36]

As George Veletsianos and Rolin Moe have pointed out, the application of technology to education is underpinned by ideology.[37] This ideology rests on the conviction that technologies have the potential to radically transform legacy industries. Just as digital technologies upended industries as diverse as music, photography, video rental, and travel—digital technology also has the potential to disrupt higher education. New technologies, according to this thinking, will be the mechanism through which intractable cost and access challenges will be solved. Teaching and learning will grow more efficient with the introduction of adaptive learning platforms and personalized learning at scale.

Next Steps

If innovation in higher education is to succeed, the language of innovation that stresses productivity needs to be replaced by an emphasis on student learning and engagement. Learning professionals need to spend more time and effort fighting against the notion that faculty can be replaced by AI or some other as yet to be invented technology. Those in the academic learning professions, and particularly those in academic technology fields, need to spend less time talking about the benefits of new technologies and more time listening to what professors need in order to have the greatest impact on their students. Any institution that wants to prioritize learning innovation needs to support and engage with their professors as they carry out the mission of teaching and learning. For learning professionals, campus learning organizations, and the professional associations that represent these groups, the most critical priority in the coming years should be to bring professors into our discussions of learning innovation. Institutional initiatives that displace educators as the most crucial factor in advancing student learning will ultimately be self-defeating. If technologies are utilized in campus learning innovation efforts, they should be positioned as complements, rather than as substitutes, for educators.

The language of learning innovation must also evolve to demonstrate benefits for both professors and students. The focus of innovation should move toward enabling educators to develop individual and personal relationships with learners. New resources that are generated by learning initiatives, such as new online degree programs, should be allocated (at least in part) to increase faculty compensation and enhance employment security. This pro-educator stand for those leading campus learning innovation efforts stands in sharp contrast to the rhetoric associated with disruptive innovation that we started with in this chapter.

Reclaiming innovation from disruption will require learning professionals to forcefully reject the technologically driven mandates of productivity and efficiency. The disruptive goal of reducing costs by diminishing the role of professors must be replaced by an insistence that learning innovation is about finding complements, not substitutes, for faculty. Champions of learning innovation should also be defenders of the values of the institutions in which their work is embedded. Commitments to leverage new methods, technologies, and structures to make nonincremental advances in learning lack meaning unless paired with an equal commitment to the values of the school in which these innovations are contemplated. By divorcing itself from the needs of the faculty and the values of the university, disruption theory has likely caused more harm than good in advancing learning innovation. A different and more values-driven framework for approaching innovation is required for learning to advance in our colleges and universities.

FOUR

The Scholarship of Learning

I N THE FIRST THREE chapters of this book, we outlined the growing investment in learning innovation that colleges and universities have been making over the past two decades, or what we've called a turn to learning. This investment accelerated in the past six years with the rise of massive open online courses and the perceived existential threat to residential colleges everywhere. The growing adoption of pedagogical models shown to have a deep impact on student learning, new digital technologies that encourage student-centered active learning, and a plethora of big (and small) data to demonstrate impact help to bolster this trend.

What would it mean for this work to continue? How will we know if learning innovation is having the desired impact? What choices should colleges and universities make as they navigate this space. In our introduction we discussed a new graduate program at Georgetown designed to help train the next generation of professionals, scholars, and teachers to undertake this work. Teaching students to become learning innovators is only part of the solution. In this and the next chapter, we outline the steps we believe are necessary not only for this work to continue but for it to have a sustainable impact on higher education into the foreseeable future.

The Professional Association

The turn to learning has driven a proliferation of professional meetings devoted to learning innovation. Professional associations and other organizations, such as consortia and even educational technology companies, have responded to the demand for information and community around learning innovation by offering an ever-expanding number of innovation-themed conferences, publications, events, webinars, and gatherings. In fact, the dominant venues in which the intersection of learning innovation and institutional change are written about and discussed today happen in professional, as opposed to scholarly, networks. The professional networks to which practitioners of learning innovation belong and contribute are robust. These networks are built through membership in professional associations and consortia, such as the Professional and Organizational Development (POD) Network, the Online Learning Consortium, EDUCAUSE, and the University Professional and Continuing Education Association, as well as the edX consortium and the Coursera partners group. Like most professional associations, the professional associations in higher education are member driven. They host annual, regional, and specialized conferences. They offer in-person and online conferences, events, and webinars. Professional associations run glossy print and online journals and community-driven forums. They collect data from member organizations and publish original reports and analysis. Some associations even have an active lobbying arm to advocate for the interests of their member institutions at the federal and state level. Other professional associations offer specialized consulting services to the colleges and universities they serve.

An emergent theme in all these professional associations, consortia, and member groups is a growing interest in parts of what we have been calling learning innovation. This is not to say that they all began with the idea of addressing an aspect of learning innovation. Some, such as the POD Network, started by bringing together folks working in newly established centers for teaching and learning. Others, like EDUCAUSE, added learning to their platform when they realized their emphasis on enterprise software and hardware in higher education needed to account for the emergence of large-scale instructional platforms like learning management systems. More recently, many of these associations that started with a different or at least tangential focus have started to adopt some aspect of learning innovation as a major part of their platforms.

In 2018, there were no fewer than thirty-four conferences, events, convenings, gatherings, and symposia devoted to the impact of digital and online learning on higher education.[1] Many of these events include both academic practitioners and corporate educational technology representatives. Discussion of innovation and of learning (though not necessarily together) tends to dominate the sessions, keynotes, and hallway conversations. This number does not even begin to account for conferences addressing the learning innovation community that are sponsored by educational technology companies, such as events hosted by Apple, Blackboard, D2L, Instructure, Pearson, and many more. Sessions at university user-group events feature updates and road maps from the sponsoring educational technology company but also speakers and general sessions that increasingly focus on learning or innovation. The large numbers of educational technology events would just about make it possible to spend the entire year circumnavigating the globe, one city at a time, attending digital learning conferences throughout the world.

If you attend one of the conferences or events, you will hear powerful success stories about how individual universities were able to leverage digital learning to improve postsecondary access, accelerate learning quality, or sometimes both. These "best practice" stories, however, are mostly devoid of theoretical frameworks that may help generalize the findings beyond specific institutions. Learning innovation as it is often explored in professional associations begins to feel like an endless series of (mostly happy) events in which improvement is a constant. But it is also true that these happy stories tend to lend themselves to the narrative that higher education is, in Clayton Christensen's terms, in need of full-scale disruption one educational technology at a time. Mostly absent in these meetings is any analysis of the larger postsecondary context in which these innovations occur. The lack of comparative data about similar initiatives across schools makes it difficult to assess the lasting impact of any particular learning innovation. The results of an ever-expanding number of professional conferences devoted to learning innovation are entirely collegial, and yet oddly unsatisfying. There is no lack of convenings, thought leaders, or reports from the field around learning innovation. If anything, the overlapping communities and domains of conversation and debate around learning innovation are too numerous to keep track of. What is almost entirely lacking from any of these digital learning convenings, conferences, and events are scholars of higher education. In almost all cases, faculty from schools or departments of education are poorly represented at these convenings. This is not the usual complaint of not enough professors (or students) attending online education, digital learning, and educational technology conferences. This is also true. What we are worried about is the absence of scholars who take a critical view of higher education and the role learning innovation is playing in its future. Academics who are immersed and enmeshed in the work of online and blended education and who are also members of a community of practice devoted to studying higher education change are often missing. This is not to say there is a complete absence of critical scholars participating in learning innovation events, but they are almost always thin on the ground.[2]

Missing from the list of professional associations and conferences devoted to educational technology and digital and online learning, then, are associations/conferences devoted to studying these activities. There is, for example, no association for the critical study of learning innovation and organizational change. The impact of all the residential and online educational programs on the universities in which they originate and the questions of the institutional conditions that give rise to these initiatives remain largely unexamined. There is a missing scholarship where the subject of study is the colleges and universities where learning innovation is prioritized, and the object is to understand the conditions in which these innovations occur. The number of colleges and universities engaged in learning innovation initiatives continues to grow, but our understanding of what these initiatives mean for higher education as a system—or even for the long-term prospects of individual schools—remains opaque.

Despite this concern, we do not want this argument to read as over-critical of the role of professional organizations and other associations in the higher education turn to learning. It is through the membership-based open online learning consortium edX that a network of colleagues enmeshed in learning innovation work first formed at Georgetown University in 2016. That network expanded through convenings such as the HAIL (Harvesting Academic Innovation for Learners) gatherings and shared presentations at conferences such as the EDUCAUSE Learning Initiative. For those in the learning innovation space, professional associations and meetings serve as platforms for networking, connecting, and relationship building. Professional meetings, hosted by associations and consortia, are the venue in which face-to-face communication can occur among colleagues who are otherwise spread across various institutions. Without the professional associations, consortiums, and other organizations and convenings, the learning innovation community would not exist.

There are, however, constraints to how research and knowledge creation can happen in these communities. Professional organizations and other associations are very good at creating professional identity and communities of practice. Their activities encourage a particular kind of exchange and sharing that has proven immensely useful. What they are less adept at is providing a framework in which knowledge and understanding can advance. Members of professional organizations seem more likely to adopt existing theories of change, such as disruptive innovation theory, than they are to develop their own. Learning about innovation efforts from peers at professional meetings or through online or print publications is important, but these peer sharing efforts are usually restricted to descriptions of best practices (or debating the validity of a phrase such as "best practices"). Even more importantly, the messy gray zone in which new ideas are proposed and debated gets relegated to the margins of professional gatherings. These ideas—the ideas that seek to see higher education as a researchable problem worth examining— are the stuff of dinner conversations and rarely of conference sessions or scholarship. If not in professional associations and at conferences, where else might this work happen?

Social Media and Learning Innovation

While conferences and professional associations play a major role in the collaborative nature of higher education, the importance today of social media to the postsecondary learning innovation community is impossible to overstate. Many practitioners working in every area of learning innovation, from online education to academic computing to centers for teaching and learning, create content and connect with one another through social media. A significant portion of the learning innovation community is fully embedded in social media networks, as social media often serves as the primary platform for knowledge exchange. As we will discuss, however, the dominance of social media as the major location of learning innovation exchange magnifies many of the shortcomings of social media as a site for extended scholarly engagement.

We define social media broadly to include web publishing platforms that are controlled by the author, as well as those digital platforms owned and run by for-profit companies that rely on user-generated content. Included in this definition would be a blog post on InsideHigherEd.com, a tweet on Twitter, and an essay published on a user-controlled WordPress site. Of these, the most important social media platform for the postsecondary learning innovation community is Twitter. More than blogs, LinkedIn, Facebook, or any other new or emerging social media platform, Twitter has evolved into the operating system of the distributed learning innovation community of practice. Each of the learning innovation conferences we have listed so far is paired with a corresponding hashtag for the event. The density of conversation in the Twitter back channel often surpasses that of the face-to-face discussions in sessions at these gatherings. The Twitter dialogue around learning innovation conferences gives these events a life outside of their physical locations. Members of the learning innovation community not in attendance gain visibility into the sessions, ideas, and debates occurring in real time within the conference. The momentum for the meeting begins to build on Twitter even before the opening sessions. Connections that were first established at conferences become solidified on Twitter once the event ends. Twitter is also the platform where learning innovation conversations on social media are amplified.

The role of social media in this exchange makes good sense. The audiences are large, often much larger than those of more traditional academic forms of publication, such as the book you are reading. A blog post or a tweet can be read by thousands of people, while an article or book might reach far fewer. The vast majority of what is written about learning innovation is also born digital. It is created for online higher education news sites or blogs, and therefore it is ideal for sharing and commentary through Twitter and elsewhere. Academics working in areas that are part of higher education's turn to learning are likely to discover content about learning innovation through their Twitter feeds. One's network recommends news and commentary through the process of tweeted links and retweets. In a very important respect, the *network* of a learning innovation practitioner—rather than a focused exchange of ideas—is what determines the flow of information. The dissemination of information and ideas about learning innovation, then, occurs more often than not through social media than in the more traditional academic channels such as peer-reviewed journals. Social media has also elevated the importance and impact of the connections between academic learning innovators across institutions. Twitter and social media as a whole have enabled the profession of postsecondary learning advancement to become more networked and better integrated, just as the number of nonfaculty academics working in these roles has been proliferating with the turn to learning. This network, while powerful, is not without its problems. The shortcomings of social media as a scholarly platform are significant and create roadblocks for a full scholarly exchange.

Here Today, Gone Tomorrow

First among our concerns about social media as a knowledge exchange platform is its ephemeral nature. Blog posts, tweets, and postings on other social media platforms have the advantages of immediacy and virality. They can be written and shared quickly. The challenge is that arguments, data, and analysis written for and published on social media platforms risk impermanence and obscurity. Even if the writing of learning innovation scholars is on platforms based on open source technologies that are not vulnerable to disappearing at the whim of its parent company, it is still not clear what will happen to that scholarship should that scholar stop contributing to the platform. Despite the common perception that anything posted online never goes away, we have a very shallow history with this medium and little evidence to know whether the ideas will outlive the person from which they were generated, an almost necessary condition of any sustained scholarship.

How social media is treated by search platforms such as Google and Bing is also opaque at best. The degree to which a blog post on learning innovation will come up in searches is dependent on proprietary algorithms designed to maximize search-related advertising revenues. Blog posts and tweets are generally not indexed by academic databases and therefore are not discoverable through databases maintained by academic libraries. Accepted measures of scholarly quality, such as the selectivity of the journal in which an article is published or the number of citations that the research receives, are absent from scholarship that is restricted to social media. The ability to optimize search engine results for particular sites notwithstanding, we don't know what we are optimizing against or why a particular blog post will show up as highly ranked in a Google search (or if they will show up at all). We don't know with any certainty if a search for topics related to learning innovation returns relevant results.

Why might this matter? Anyone teaching a course on how universities advance learning would want to include readings from learning innovation scholars. While there may be value in the "social" aspects of social media, comments, thoughts, and tweets from within a network, these posts come and go too quickly and are too easily missed. If we believe that the contributions of scholars and practitioners of learning innovation are significant, as we do, then we would want those contributions to be discoverable and sustained. We would want other scholars engaged in questions about the effectiveness of educational interventions to be able to build on the work and analysis that came before. Blog posts and tweets and other social media contributions are immediate, topical, linkable, and retweetable. But they are also fragile. Links can break. Pages can disappear. Even if URLs are somehow permanent and sites are maintained, the problem of discoverability remains.

Of course, any active contributor to social media might ask: why wait for months or years to contribute to the learning innovation conversation when blogging, commenting, and tweeting are both instant *and* enjoy wider readership (and hence impact) than publication on legacy scholarly platforms? The result is a faster metabolism of discussion but less in the way of longevity. A series of blog posts by a particular scholar may include insightful analysis and commentary on the turn to learning, but they are less likely to be placed on a syllabus to teach a potential next generation of academic leaders than a journal article or book chapter. They face a challenge of sustainability.

Sustained Scholarship

A second concern that we have with the learning innovation conversation having taken up residence on social media platforms has to do with depth and complexity. All born-digital/online content platforms privilege brevity over completeness. Even comparatively long blog posts, such as a recent piece on open educational resources by Michael Feldstein, come in at just over 3,500 words.[3] A typical blog post on InsideHigherEd.com comes in closer to 500–1,000 words. Journal articles, in comparison, range from 3,500 words on the low end to 10,000 words at the more extreme. The *Journal of Higher Education*'s instructions for authors suggest a word count of 9,000 to 10,000.[4] The *Review of Higher Education* accepts manuscripts up to 10,000 words.[5] The journal *Innovative Higher Education* puts a submission limit for authors at twenty pages.[6]

There are many advantages to the concise format of social media–based contributions to the discourse on learning innovation. Tweets can be composed quickly and scanned even faster in what amounts to an almost synchronous conversation within the learning innovation community. Blog posts may take longer to write than tweets, but the time invested in each post is only a small fraction of the time necessary to write a journal article or book chapter. Readership of blogs is migrating, like all digital content, to the phone. Blog posts of 500–1,000 words seem perfectly optimized for reading on small screens. The brevity of social media articles contributes to their impact. Not only are there no barriers regarding paywalls or subscriptions to access blog posts or tweets on learning innovation, but they also can be read in short bursts and on the go.

We lose something, however, in replacing the complicated and nuanced arguments of journal articles, chapters, or books with short bursts of social media content. A blog post works best if it contains a single big idea, provocatively asserted. Momentum and a point of view are prized in social media posts above nuance and complexity. An argument that is slowly built, with data presented to both support and to challenge the premises and assertions of the piece, is poorly fit to the standards of most social media contributions. A long article demands the sustained engagement of the reader. How teaching and learning are evolving at universities is a complicated story. There are no easy recipes that schools can follow to improve teaching and advance student learning without further driving up costs. The complex and challenging nature of learning innovation should be reflected in the scholarship about this phenomenon. Achieving a deep understanding of the drivers and inhibitors of a postsecondary turn to learning requires space to develop and explore ideas, share outcomes and data, and analyze meaning.

Style and Substance

A third concern that we have with the conversation on learning innovation living primarily on blogs and Twitter and other digital platforms is the dominant style and cultural norms of social media. Academic writing tends to be cautious, measured, and modest in its claims (this book notwithstanding). Knowledge is often built on arguments that are falsifiable or that live in contradiction. Hypotheses are never proven, only supported to a greater or lesser degree by the available evidence. Assertions must be supported with data. Ideas and concepts are always connected with those of previous publications through extensive attribution. The accretion of knowledge moves incrementally, gradually building on the literature of the scholarly field. Paradigm shifts are rare and are subject to the most intense scrutiny.

While this often glacial pace is out of date with the speed of social media, slowing down has advantages in our hyperattentive world, where ideas barely have time to find purchase before the next comes speeding by. One of the most consistent critiques of the academy is the slow pace of change, but this can also be a virtue. We know from many decades of learning science that deep learning often requires reflection, critique, and engagement. All of these things share one common feature: time. Learning takes time, whether for our students or our scholarship. Moving at the speed of Twitter rarely lends itself to deep learning.

Social media, in fact, shares none of the attributes of deep learning. Blog posts and tweets with the greatest currency are often the least equivocal. Confident assertions are read as expertise in all markets for ideas, with social media contributions around learning innovation being no different. Scholarly norms of cautious argument and modest claims for contribution do not apply to the world of social media. Journal articles and book chapters may be longer than typical blog posts, but they are standalone contributions. There is a scarcity to their existence, as barriers to publication and acceptance are high. Conversely, the market for social media influence rewards volume over quality. Successful contributors to the social media conversation, those with the highest numbers of followers and readers, tweet and post often. The overall volume of social media contributions swamps the quality of any single tweet or post in determining influence. These incentives for quantity over quality will naturally degrade the validity and reliability of the arguments.

A related drawback of locating the learning innovation conversation in social media is the performative aspect of this mode of exchange. Academic social media is not only a place to share information and to nurture professional networks but also to manage one's professional persona. There is a careerist aspect of crafting and maintaining an active social media presence. Visibility and presence on social media platforms may determine job opportunities and access to desirable professional networks. Social media participation may also carry substantial career risks for those in the learning innovation community who are not tenured. The high proportion of anonymous commenting on blogs related to learning innovation suggests that many academics do not feel safe publicly sharing their opinions and experiences.

Peer Review

Perhaps most importantly, the contributions to the conversation on learning innovation that appear on social media platforms are rarely if ever peer-reviewed. Academic scholarship has a long tradition of peer review that ensures any published work is read and reviewed by colleagues in and familiar with the field. The culture of peer review serves many vital functions. When a scholarly article or book is reviewed before publication, it is examined for its relevance to the field and, importantly, for its understanding and consideration of the research and scholarship that has come before it. A piece of writing that ignores the scholarship that precedes it will likely not be well reviewed, while an article or book that misreads or misunderstands the previous scholarship will probably be called to task. In this process of peer review, feedback is provided, and scholars in the field share in a broader and deeper understanding of the development of an idea. Additionally, peer review serves as at least one mechanism for determining the validity and stability of an argument.

Of course, social media networks can build into viable cross-institutional communities of practice. It is questionable, however, how ideologically diverse these academic social media–connected communities are in reality. Like-minded practitioners working in areas of learning innovation tend to gather in communities that align with their thinking. Academics in this field may follow tweets and blogs that conform most closely with their established views. The pervasiveness trolling through anonymous comments on blog posts, including the practice of launching personal attacks on the author rather than reasoned disagreements with the arguments being made, discourages collegial interchange between those with differing viewpoints.

As we've said, social media as a platform is not without its benefits. The erosion of barriers to publication that social media affords has opened up the academic conversation on learning innovation to more voices and perspectives. The friction-free nature of the social media learning innovation conversation has contributed to the dynamism of the field, but arguably it has also diminished any standards by which the material might be judged. An unintended consequence of the hegemony of social media in the learning innovation conversation, however, has been to deincentivize publication in traditional journals and book chapters, publications that continue to serve an important role in the vitality of scholarly exchange.

From Social Media to Scholarship

As we've described, the learning innovation community is vibrant, energized, and mission-driven. It is well connected through professional organizations and emergent social media platforms. This community is also fragmented, diffuse, and poorly served by structures that may train the next generation of learning innovation leaders or allow current practitioners to effectively lead campus and system-wide efforts. The arguments, debates, and discussions in popular nonfiction books, at conferences, and on blogs about learning innovation are invigorating and accessible, but they often lack a structure that promotes the systematic and critical investigation of institution-wide learning innovation efforts.

What is lacking is the sort of critical lens on learning innovation initiatives that scholars immersed in this world can bring to the analysis of these institutional efforts. A scholarship of postsecondary learning innovation should be able to look at individual programs and initiatives in a context both across time and institutions. Conclusions about the efficacy of learning innovation efforts from practitioners, consultants, and bloggers risk being ahistorical, noncomparative, and decontextualized. Is it possible to retain the positive aspects of the learning innovation community while addressing our concerns about professional associations, permanence, nuance, and diversity? We think that the next step forward for learning innovation is to chart a course that adopts some of the elements and expectations of an interdisciplinary academic field. We hope to retain those attributes that have made those practicing learning innovation dynamic and inclusive while also locating its work within the framework of accepted scholarship and criticism.

Interdisciplinary fields, like traditional academic disciplines, are so much a part of the academic environment that it is easy to think of these organizational classifications as somehow intrinsic to higher education. Interdisciplinary fields can feel like natural, permanent, and fixed elements of the postsecondary ecosystem rather than the very real results of fights and choices and purposeful effort. Our argument is that achieving the status of interdisciplinary field will enable the achievement of other goals, such as the ability to run graduate programs in learning innovation and at least some of the protections of academic freedom. To make this argument, and to test this idea, we need to understand what we mean when we call something an interdisciplinary field.

Interdisciplinary fields owe a great deal to traditional academic disciplines, so much so that it may be useful to understand how academic disciplines came into being before considering how interdisciplinary fields grew from these compartmentalized structures. The concept of an academic discipline can be traced as far back as Socrates (469–399 BCE). The Socratic method may not have been the first learning innovation, but it has arguably enjoyed the greatest resiliency among all pedagogical techniques.[7] In 392 BCE the first discipline-based institution of advanced learning was established by Isocrates in Athens to train students in politics. Five years later (387 BCE), Socrates's student Plato began his Academy in Athens. Topics covered at Plato's Academy ranged from geometry to jurisprudence. In 355 BCE a fifty-year-old Aristotle founded a school known as the Lyceum, an institution of learning that survived in one form or another until the Goth sacking of Athens in 267 CE. The modern conception of an academic discipline, one tied to the development of university departments in the United States offering specialized programs of study, did not emerge until around 1825. These fields of study throughout most of the nineteenth century remained limited, consisting mostly of variants of languages, mathematics, and philosophy.[8] This approach to disciplinary structure followed closely

to what French sociologist, anthropologist, and philosopher Pierre Bourdieu defined as "an academic and socially acknowledged name (that for
example can be found in a library classification system). A discipline is
inscribed in, and upheld by, the national and international networks of
research, university departments, research institutes and scientific journals that produces, certifies, rewards, and upholds that which he calls
the discipline's capital. And a discipline is characterized by a particular,
unique academic and social style."[9]

For much of the history of higher education, academic disciplines
served as commonly understood structures under which scholarly work
was undertaken. These structures, according to Janice Beyer and Thomas
Lodahl, established norms for scholarly production and exchange, but
they also indicate some of the criteria necessary for a new disciplinary
field to emerge.[10] Similarly, in arguing for strategic management as a
new academic discipline, Donald Hambrick and Ming-Jer Chen outline
the conditions in which new disciplines (or fields) are formed. They dis-
tinguish between an "informal community" and an "academic field." An
informal community "might form around a theory, a phenomenon, a
class of problems, an ideology, a methodology, or a technology,"
whereas an academic field requires greater institutional commitment,
including hiring faculty, granting tenure, seeking peer evaluations, and
training graduate students.[11]

Despite these rather clear definitions, the literature on the development and attributes of academic disciplines is contentious. There is little
consensus about what fields of scholarly study count as a distinct academic discipline, a multi- or cross-discipline, or a field of study. Not only
is there disagreement about what counts, there is no agreed upon standards of when an area of investigation graduates into an existing, combined, integrated, or new disciplinary field. An academic discipline, it
turns out, is defined much like Supreme Court Justice Potter Stewart in
1964 described obscenity: "I know it when I see it." We don't have a
clear definition of an interdisciplinary field or an academic discipline,
but we know one when we see it.

One question before us is whether learning innovation meets the "I
know it when I see it" standard for an interdisciplinary field. For some

academic disciplines and interdisciplinary fields, there is no debate. Everyone agrees. There is little need to debate the parameters of established disciplines from A (anthropology) to Z (zoology). The question gets trickier when it comes to emerging academic areas of inquiry and interdisciplinary fields. What counts as its own academic discipline, sub-discipline, sub-subdiscipline, interdisciplinary field, or simply a program of study can cause heated debates. Indeed, as we think about the move of learning innovation from a loose collection of professional associations to an interdisciplinary field, we recognize this will engender many challenges. Still, it is a debate that we think is worth having. Hambrick and Chen noted that the formation of a new discipline among an existing informal community of practitioners "entails considerable effort and risks" and therefore should only be attempted if the two following conditions are met:

A. They must view the community's agenda as permanent, or at least long-term. A group that exists to bring short-term attention to an issue or to solve a highly specific problem will not be oriented toward the establishment of a long-term entity.

B. The group must believe that it cannot achieve its objectives—either intellectually or professionally—by continuing only as an informal community. Its members must conclude that the status quo social structure will not allow them to get the funding, journal space, conference presence, or faculty positions they could get if they achieved the status of a field.[12]

Informal communities that wish to evolve into academic fields face a difficult path. Some new interdisciplinary fields, such as international business, thrive for a time, only to be reabsorbed into another more established field. Others, such as social issues in management, "survive for an extended period but in a marginal state, with limited resources, membership, and acceptance by the broader academic establishment."[13]

Why start this conversation in the first place? Couldn't professional associations, perhaps with some adjustment, serve a similar purpose? In part, our answer comes down to the advantages of defining shared problems and methodologies, and having those recognized by faculty and students as concepts worth studying. Shifting the domain of learning innovation from professional associations to an interdisciplinary field begins to acknowledge some of the very real challenges facing the field as it moves beyond the informal sharing of best practices. This can only happen when scholars are able to ask difficult questions, take risks, and challenge institutional assumptions. In short, this requires the time to do research and the academic freedom necessary to do said research freely and openly.

Academic Freedom and Learning Innovation

The learning innovators leading campus-wide initiatives are almost never protected by academic freedom. Unless the leaders of campus learning organizations came to these roles from established, tenured faculty positions, they do not have any of the protections to publish ideas that may be unpopular or controversial. Academics who work in campus learning organizations can engage in scholarship about learning innovation, but unless they have tenure they can also lose their jobs for this scholarship. The principle of academic freedom is one of the bedrocks of higher education. The American Association of University Professors' *1940 Statement of Principles on Academic Freedom and Tenure* reads, "Academic freedom is essential to these purposes and applies to both teaching and research. Freedom in research is fundamental to the advancement of truth. Academic freedom in its teaching aspect is fundamental for the protection of the rights of the teacher in teaching and of the student to freedom in learning. It carries with it duties correlative with rights."[14]

Academic freedom generally applies only to tenure-track and tenured faculty. Learning innovators, even those who teach courses and may have some faculty appointments, almost never are covered by these protections. Some measure of employment protections are particularly important if the object of the scholarship is the university. Research in learning innovation starts with the premise that change is necessary. Critiques of the current system of education, particularly as they relate to teaching and learning, may be directly applicable to the colleges and universities in which the learning innovation researcher works.

Despite the cross-institutional sharing we discussed in the previous chapter, learning innovation scholarship may run counter to the marketing message a scholar's home institution is putting forward. Writing about the need to adopt systemic changes in how the campus learning environment is structured may be interpreted by campus leaders as a critique of the current leadership practices or existing policies. Highlighting advances in learning at other institutions may run counter to the goal of universities to amplify their own advantages. Colleges and universities can be exquisitely sensitive to their public images. University communications offices work hard to highlight any positive media mentions of their institutions. This puts anyone writing critically about higher education in a precarious position. The scholarship of learning innovation should be the exact opposite of so much of the technological cheerleading that often passes as analysis in the educational technology conversation. Those working in campus learning organizations have firsthand knowledge of the limits of technologies in advancing learning. In any extensive research, a scholar of learning innovation is likely to point out the gap between the brand promise of a university around the quality of the teaching and the reality of the quality of student learning. Practitioners within this emerging interdisciplinary field are likely to be critical of the structures and incentives that are associated with advancing learning. In doing so, a scholar of learning innovation is potentially at odds with the messaging of their employers.

For example, as public funding for colleges and universities becomes scarce, and as costs continue to rise in the face of significant demographic challenges, the potential to lower instructional costs by leveraging technological platforms becomes ever more appealing. Costs can be lowered by pushing toward scale. Efficiencies can be sought by increasing the number of students that can be taught with the same number of faculty. And this productivity goal can be served by substituting technologies for educators, such as replacing professors with adaptive learning platforms. In fact, much of the initial excitement among university leaders for the MOOC craze in 2012 rested on reducing instructional costs. This was expected to happen by substituting local faculty for "superstar" faculty from other institutions, with their lectures delivered online and local educators reduced to facilitating classes. Scholars working within a learning innovation tradition might be critical of attempts to improve postsecondary productivity through technology, as we were in the previous chapter. The protections of academic freedom would benefit the mission of learning, if not the current institutional priorities.

The need for this kind of freedom may be one of the reasons why some of the most influential voices in this area work outside of academia. Independent scholars such Audrey Watters, Bryan Alexander, Phil Hill, and Michael Feldstein are among the most important thought leaders in the larger learning innovation discussion. Their status as independent scholars provides some important advantages compared to those who are dependent on academic appointments for employment. Independent scholars have the ability to think and write critically about higher education in ways that may be difficult for those dependent on a single university. In the domain of learning innovation, all four of these thinkers have been consistently insightful in critiquing the claims of educational technology boosters. Each of these scholars in different ways, through their writing, speaking, and consulting, has developed significant followings across the postsecondary marketplace of ideas. They have been effective in challenging the claims made by educational technology companies and investors around the efficacy to student learning for moving instruction to digital platforms. They have, through the platforms and channels in which their ideas are developed and spread, built up communities of professionals working within higher education who look to these scholars for context and analysis in order to evaluate claims made by those most enthusiastic about the potential of digital education.

The fact that the influence of these independent scholars in the marketplace of ideas around learning innovation is rarely matched by those working inside higher education may be traced directly back to the absence of an interdisciplinary field in this space. With the status of an interdisciplinary field comes the potential to access the protections of academic freedom. An evolution from a purely professional orientation for learning innovation to one that is more academic—or is a hybrid between the two—has the possibility of carrying with it some job protections for critical scholarship. It is impossible to know the degree to which advances in the field of learning innovation have been impeded by self-censorship among its practitioners. Of course, moving the study and teaching of learning innovation toward an interdisciplinary field will not immediately confer the protections of academic freedom. The idea that learning professionals working in learning organizations will be eligible for tenure anytime soon does not seem realistic, particularly as tenure-line positions in traditional disciplines are becoming so scarce. It is the combination of a culture of academic freedom and the employment protections of tenure that give some academics the ability to explore unpopular views. We may be able to import a culture of academic freedom, however, into our work as learning professionals. Being part of a recognized interdisciplinary field will connect established disciplinary norms, including academic freedom, with the scholarly and teaching work. It would be a start. To illustrate what we mean, it is worth looking at how another interdisciplinary field came into being.

The Interdisciplinary Field of Women's Studies

The history, trajectory, and challenges of women's studies (also called gender studies) offer instructive parallels as we seek to unpack the interdisciplinary argument for learning innovation. Women's studies began as a program at San Diego State University in 1970.[15] Today, women's studies departments and programs exist at over 650 North American institutions. These departments and programs go by different names, such as Women's, Gender & Sexuality Studies (Dartmouth) and Women's and Gender Studies (Georgetown). The vast majority of faculty teaching in women's studies departments have degrees in established academic disciplines other than women's studies even though over twenty institutions offer PhDs specifically in women's, gender, and feminist studies.[16] These institutions include top-ranked research universities such as Arizona State University, Emory University, Indiana University, Ohio State University, Oregon State University, Rutgers University, Stony Brook University, the University of Arizona, the University of Kansas, the University of Kentucky, the University of Maryland, the University of Michigan, the University of Minnesota, the University of Washington, and multiple institutions in the California public university system. Data compiled by the National Women's Study Association (NWSA, established in 1977) indicate that 90,000 students were enrolled in women's studies–related courses in 2007[17] (the latest year for which data are available). This includes over 4,300 undergraduate majors, approximately 2,700 graduate students, and over 1,000 students registered in doctoral courses.

Women's studies provides an informative window into discussions of learning innovation as a new interdisciplinary field. The political and social imperative for women's studies aside, many of the same factors that catalyzed the development and growth of women's studies as an interdisciplinary field fifty years ago exist today for learning innovation. The debates about the legitimacy of the domain of scholarship and the placement of the work within an interdisciplinary framework are present for both areas of inquiry. Entry into the interdisciplinary field of women's studies is not restricted to those with terminal degrees from programs in the discipline, although that training path is one option. Women's studies draws scholars from a range of disciplines. Perhaps the closest parallel between the history of women's studies and the possible future of learning innovation as an academic discipline is that of the purposeful intermingling of scholarship and application. From its inception, the founders of women's studies conceived their intellectual domain as an applied discipline. In a 2013 article titled "Learning from Women's Studies," Michele Tracy Berger argues that the scholars within women's studies have always sought to effect change within their institutions.[18] This advocacy includes support for new campus-based student service organizations, such as centers for diversity, multicultural affairs, LGBTQ offices, and resources for women's centers.

In 1973, Anthony Biglan proposed a disciplinary taxonomy that divides disciplines into "pure" and "applied," with distinctions between "hard" and "soft" disciplines in the life and nonlife sciences (table 2). Despite its limitations—many academics have objected to having their scholarship be defined as "soft"[19]—this disciplinary taxonomy had been surprisingly persistent. Women's studies has long adopted the approach of an applied interdisciplinary field consistent with Biglan's classification.

In addition to a commitment to integrating scholarship with positive organizational change, women's studies faculty have always navigated rigid academic institutional structures. From early on, scholars in women's studies have combined publication in peer-reviewed journals for a limited academic audience with public scholarship. Feminist scholars were early and enthusiastic adopters of op-eds, policy reports, community action projects, and institutional curriculum transformation in efforts to advance the core social justice orientation of the discipline. Later, women's studies scholars embraced—and continue to embrace—the development of networks and the diffusion of scholarship through both open access online journals and social media channels.

Table 2. Clustering of Academic Task Areas in Three Dimensions

Task area	Hard		Soft	
	Nonlife system	Life system	Nonlife system	Life system
Pure	Astronomy Chemistry Geology Math Physics	Botany Entomology Microbiology Physiology Zoology	English German History Philosophy Russian Communications	Anthropology Political science Psychology Sociology
Applied	Ceramic engineering	Agronomy	Accounting	Educational administration and supervision Secondary and continuing education
	Civil engineering Computer science	Dairy science Horticulture	Finance Economics	Special education Vocational and technical education
	Mechanical engineering	Agricultural economics		

Source: Anthony Biglan, "The Characteristics of Subject Matter in Different Academic Areas," *Journal of Applied Psychology* 57, no. 3 (1973): 207, https://psycnet.apa.org/record/1974-01798-001.

As an interdisciplinary field, women's studies is able to engage on a more equal playing field with other intellectual traditions, just as it is able to develop important cross-disciplinary and interdisciplinary lines of investigation. Women's studies may be engaged in a never-ending fight to move from the margins to the center of institutional influence and prestige, but the field is firmly established with the existence of courses, programs, and degrees. The twenty or so departments that offer PhDs in women's and gender studies are testimony to the success of the discipline in developing mechanisms for continuous renewal and resiliency. Critical to the creation of knowledge within women's studies has been the ability of the field to provide its scholars with a measure of intellectual autonomy and the protections associated with academic freedom.

Women's studies, of course, is only one of many newly formed interdisciplinary fields. We might have just as easily looked at artificial intelligence, behavioral economics, bioethics, disability studies, educational technology, information technologies,[20] library and information science, media studies, population studies, strategic management,[21] strategic security,[22] and sustainability.[23] AI (artificial intelligence) is a particularly attractive example, given that the formation of the discipline can be traced directly back to the landmark 1956 conference on "the possibility of constructing intelligent machines" at Dartmouth College.

Counterarguments to a New Interdisciplinary Field

In researching this book, we previewed our arguments for a new interdisciplinary field of learning innovation with colleagues inside and outside of higher education. The rehearsal of our interdisciplinary formation ideas took place in conference presentations, at a small gathering of higher education and learning scholars at Georgetown University in 2016,[24] and through blog posts on InsideHigherEd.com.[25] We also conducted in-depth interviews with twenty colleagues who lead learning innovation initiatives and have other leadership responsibilities at peer institutions. To our surprise, our arguments for a new interdisciplinary field of learning innovation have been controversial. The critiques that we received were collegial but often passionate.

The first major objection to our call for a new academic interdisciplinary field built around the study of learning innovation is that the discipline already exists. This research is already being done by scholars in schools and departments of education, not to mention occasionally by academics based in centers for teaching and learning (CTLs). We should note, however, that for each person who believes that the work is already happening, there were just as many who told us the field is needed precisely because the work is not being done. The differing sense of existing scholarship in this field is illustrative. It is clear that work addressing some of the questions we pose exists in the scholarly literature, but it does not necessarily mean it has the interdisciplinary framework to make it recognizable as such. In this regard, the scholarship at the intersection of learning and institutional change, both independently and in collaboration with other disciplinary partners, will only benefit from the energy devoted in an effort to establish a new interdisciplinary field.

Additionally, as both of us work at our institutions' respective CTLs and are part of the larger center for teaching and learning community, the question of where to situate this scholarship is not, well, academic. We should be clear at this point that advocating for a new interdisciplinary field does not mean we wish for or advocate for the cessation of learning innovation scholarship within CTLs. If anything, we think that a discipline that grows up in and around existing CTLs has the best chance of growing the influence and impact of the educators who work in centers for teaching and learning and our sibling learning-centric organizations on campus. In chapter 5 we present a model of how we think CTLs can evolve to give balanced weight to scholarship, the training of postsecondary learning innovators (through the development of graduate programs), and the traditional education development, assessment, programming, and consultation tasks of teaching and learning centers.

We are making an argument that the work being done by CTLs, what we think of as applied scholarship around advancing learning, needs to find a pathway toward recognition in the academy similar to established disciplines in order to have the intellectual influence on institutional practice we believe is necessary for long-term sustainability. We think that adopting some of the structure, norms, operations, and culture of established disciplines—from how the next generation is trained and socialized into the profession to the type of scholarship that is created—will be the most successful route to greater impact within higher education. In *Coming in from the Margins*, Connie Schroeder and coauthors make a similar case for upgrading the ability of learning professionals to both study and lead organizational change.[26] Through a series of case studies and analysis of the history and shifting function of centers for teaching and learning, Schroeder and her colleagues argue that organizational development is as important to the mission of CTLs as is individual faculty development. The sort of organizational development that they envision is fully aligned with our conception of learning innovation.

Another concern about our idea to build an interdisciplinary field of learning innovation that has been voiced by some of our colleagues is the worry that this field will mirror and even contribute to the worst elements of academia. These include an amplification of the academic caste system. There is a very reasonable fear that a field such as the one we are proposing will exclude those outside a narrow, elite collective of wealthy institutions or that it will marginalize scholars critical of the dominant modes and methods of academic discourse, despite our arguments for the protection provided by academic freedom. Many were concerned about the focus on scholarly publication as a method of career advancement—rather than the contribution of shareable best practices—and the competitiveness within academia for status based on research productivity and perceived impact. Relatedly, there is the concern that becoming part of a new interdisciplinary field would introduce a divide between learning innovators and traditional faculty. One of the reasons that many who were trained in traditional disciplinary fields have chosen to work for campus learning organizations is precisely because those organizations are not academic departments. These academics enjoy the status of centers for teaching and learning and academic computing units as nondiscipline based, or at least cross-disciplinary. Where training and career advancement in traditional disciplines is largely built on ever greater levels of specialization—of building on knowledge in narrow topics of scholarship and expertise—learning innovators are often generalists who revel in also having very specialized knowledge. They need to work effectively with faculty from across the university. General principles of effective pedagogy, including course design and both residential and online effective teaching practices, are applicable across academic specialties. Perhaps more than any other career in academia available to those who wish to engage in teaching and learning, a career in learning innovation provides opportunities to work across the full range of academic disciplines.

This generalist approach to academia is appealing to many in higher education learning innovation. So is the opportunity to stand outside the dominant status hierarchies that drive so much of modern university life. Learning innovators collaborate as intensively and energetically with adjunct faculty as they do with tenured full professors. What defines the collaboration between faculty and learning innovators is not research productivity or academic rank but a shared commitment to advancing student learning. The ethos of campus learning organizations is decidedly collaborative and egalitarian. The culture of these organizations is one of support and partnership for all educators across the institution. This orientation toward nonhierarchical collaboration with faculty extends to the work of learning organizations with other campus organizations. Partnerships between CTLs and academic computing units with the campus library are often strong and long-lasting. Faculty developers, instructional designers, and academic librarians work closely with each other on a range of learning initiatives. Professionals such as these may also collaborate with other nondepartmental units, such as tutoring and writing centers or programs for first-generation students, to advance teaching and learning.

This is all to say that learning organizations are very different from academic departments. Not only do they not offer courses and degrees, but they do not hire and promote based on teaching evaluations or research productivity. Their missions are to serve the institution, including the faculty and students. The professional staff of learning organizations contribute to the mission of the colleges and universities in which they work in ways that may complement, but are distinct from, faculty located in disciplinary-based academic departments or schools. The concern is that by adopting the structures and norms of academic departments—such as prioritizing scholarship and offering courses and degrees—much of what makes learning organizations so effective could be lost. What happens, for example, when a learning organization begins to compete with an established school for student enrollments? How does a learning organization that has been traditionally oriented as a service entity also act as its own academic unit? What would a blending of the traditional roles of a learning professional and an academic into a more liminal and integrated learning innovation position mean for hiring and career advancement?

Additionally, issues as fundamental as the funding models within institutions will be challenged if learning organizations expand their missions outside of the traditional service roles they have provided. Can learning organizations use funds that have been allocated to support faculty development, learning technologies, or new learning initiatives to defray the costs of hiring scholars to research learning innovation? How should any funds that come in to learning organizations through research grants or tuition dollars be allocated? Who has oversight around traditional academic decisions such as curriculum when those designing the programs and teaching the courses are faculty housed in learning organizations rather than in existing academic departments or schools?

An even more vexing set of questions for any transition to an academic orientation for learning organizations may be the whole issue of who gets excluded. Entry into almost every academic discipline requires the completion of a terminal degree. Faculty generally have PhDs.[27] The training required for entry into the ultracompetitive world of an academic career is as long and arduous as it is well established. A PhD or other terminal degree, sometimes accompanied by completion of postdoctoral fellowships, is a necessary condition for even being considered for a faculty position. In learning organizations, the situation is very different. Many people who work in these organizations do have a PhD or other terminal degree, but many do not. The pathways into a learning career in higher education are much more variable and open than those into traditional faculty careers. This is also reflected in the fields of study of the people in learning careers. Some of those who work in learning organizations have a PhD in fields such as educational technology, instructional design, or higher education. Others have terminal degrees in traditional academic disciplines, such as English or sociology. Many more have master's degrees in fields such as instructional design and education. However we look at it, a large number of professionals currently working in learning organizations have degrees in fields outside of education.

There is a legitimate worry that moving toward an interdisciplinary field of learning innovation will make access to the field narrower and more exclusive. In adopting the traditional norms of academic disciplines in order to gain some of the traditional benefits of the field, we will run the risk of losing much of what makes it so vibrant and interesting. There is little evidence that the attainment of a PhD makes a learning professional any more productive or creative in the field. Earning a terminal degree may be more of a mark of stamina than anything else. Building a career in a learning organization is one of the few ways that someone interested in teaching and learning can escape the dominant academic caste system. One's educational pedigree, the school that they went to, and the degree that they earned matter less in a learning organization than one's performance and productivity.

Rolin Moe is once again persuasive in putting forth a critique of the idea of disciplining the work of learning innovation. Moe argues that "academic disciplines signify knowledge, but they are also hierarchies embedded in power relationships."[28] Learning organizations now provide viable career paths for those who define themselves as alternative academics, or alt-acs. As we discuss in greater detail in the next chapter, alt-acs often share the values and aspirations of traditional academics to advance knowledge and create opportunity through education. Those in these roles are invested in the success of their own institutions. Alt-acs working in learning organizations strive to advance student learning by working on various initiatives and partnering closely with instructors. The risk, implicit in Moe's critique, is that by building an interdisciplinary field around learning innovation, the space that alternative academics have carved out for themselves within academia will be eliminated. Learning innovation may only have room for those deemed acceptable or credentialed enough by others already in the field. Much as a PhD in sociology is necessary to achieve the status of a sociologist, an interdisciplinary field of learning innovation is at risk of drawing equally sharp boundaries. This comes at a time when those working within learning organizations have strived to reposition themselves as educators and academics within the academy, a shift that is particularly true of the field of instructional design.

As we have argued throughout this book, this shift is occurring at many levels of higher education where faculty collaborate with a team of educators on course design and delivery. This team may include instructional designers, librarians, media professionals, and perhaps experts on assessment and evaluation. This team-based approach to teaching and learning has its origins in online learning programs and has begun to migrate to blended and residential teaching. Part of the shift in how education is designed and developed has been an upgrade in the status of instructional designers and educational technologists away from "support roles." They are now being viewed as colleagues and partners on many campuses in the midst of a turn to learning. Their expertise in student learning and effective pedagogies is being recognized along with their competencies in the workings of digital learning platforms. They are the people faculty now engage with to plan syllabi, design learning objectives, and develop active-learning exercises and meaningful formative and summative assessments. No longer are instructional designers or other professionals in learning organizations the people faculty think of as responsible for teaching them how to use the learning technologies or untangle problems in the learning management system gradebook. They are more and more seen as partners in the overall education mission.

A move to make learning organizations look more like academic departments risks leaving those who do not make that transition on the wrong side of the educator divide. Not every learning professional has the background or desire to engage in original scholarship. Not every learning organization has the interest, ability, or opportunity to offer courses and degree programs. It would be terrible if some learning professionals gained the advantages of time and protections to engage in critical scholarship and teaching at the expense of their colleagues in the field. We share the concern of our colleagues who object to a new field based on the potential constraints and hierarchy it might create.

Next Steps

Where does this leave us then? These objections are powerful and suggest any change along the lines of what we are advocating will require caution and careful attention. The CTL and digital learning communities at risk are our professional homes. The educators objecting to the formation of a new interdisciplinary field are our colleagues. Still, we think there is good reason to be optimistic about a future interdisciplinary field of learning innovation. For the work to be sustainable, it would need to recognize and reward the complex roles that are played by professionals and academics alike throughout the field. Even in a scenario where the idea of building learning innovation into an academic field were to gain traction, we think there are a great many reasons to believe the vast majority of educators in CTLs would continue working as they have been but in doing so would be understood as contributing not only to the success of their individual institutions but to the larger field.

While we are not persuaded by the arguments against an interdisciplinary field of learning innovation—we wouldn't have written this book if we were—we do think that they need to be taken seriously. The critical lens that our colleagues bring to this discussion is exactly the sort of insights we hope to unpack and share. The growing conversation about how universities adapt and change to advance learning is a conversation in which we are eager to engage. The smarter and more prescient the objections, the greater the appeal of having those objecting as colleagues. The more that arguments mounted as to why learning innovation should not be thought of as a new field, the more we wanted to bring these ideas into our scholarship. Central to our conception of an interdisciplinary field is a protected space to have sustained dialogue in order to generate new knowledge. Rather than continuing this dialogue catch-as-catch-can at professional meetings and small gatherings and through social media—we hope to create a self-funding (through tuition dollars and grants) hybrid of service and academic departments where the debate (and the subsequent scholarly output) can blossom.

FIVE

Leading the Revolution

B Y NOW YOU may have noticed that massive open online courses (MOOCs) play an important role in the story we are telling—and the argument we are making—about learning innovation. For a brief and wonderful time, at the height of the MOOC bubble, learning innovation became big news on the campuses of our most traditional colleges and universities. Task forces were formed. Guest speakers were invited. Trustees made demands. Budgets were allocated. New positions were created. New and reorganized campus organizations were formed. And like a tornado, the concentrated energy around learning innovation spawned by the MOOC bubble unwound as quickly as it formed. Within a couple of years, many of the presidents, provosts, and deans previously preoccupied with MOOCs had moved on to other pressing issues. The number of open online courses and size of the open online learning community continued to grow, but the highly visible, senior-level, campus-wide discussions about how institutions might evolve to leverage new ideas and new technologies to advance learning had largely dissipated.

The above paragraph is of course a sweeping generalization about the place of learning innovation in the academic marketplace of ideas. At almost every college and university this story will be different. The degree to which MOOCs spurred conversations on learning innovation, conversations that involved campus academic leaders, is highly variable. At our own traditional, private, selective, and predominantly residential institutions this was certainly true (and in some cases continues today). So was it also true for the other schools that joined edX and Coursera during the early years of their existence. The fact that the MOOC bubble was a catalyst for a range of broad and critical discussions about the future of every form of teaching and learning, including residential face-to-face teaching, is not necessarily well known outside of the institutions in which these discussions occurred. Even within those institutions, the excitement about learning that rapidly emerged during the years of MOOC hysteria is starting to fade from memory.

Perhaps the interest of university leadership in learning innovation—at least at a subset of institutions during the peak MOOC years—is so striking because it represented such a radical break from the past. At these schools, learning innovation had historically not been the center of the academic conversation. This does not mean that learning was not occurring, that innovation in learning was not present, or even that learning was not a stated mission and value. At some institutions—especially smaller liberal arts colleges and community colleges—a central, visible investment in teaching and learning has always existed. At these schools and many like them, the process of improvements in teaching and learning both predated the MOOC bubble and outlived its deflation. But even for the schools that found themselves at the center of the MOOC hailstorm, the turn to learning we are marking in this book has its roots not in MOOCs but in the establishment of centers for teaching and learning, the maturation of a range of educational technologies, the growth of online education, and the integration of learning professionals (such as instructional designers) into the fabric of academic life.

For many years predating the MOOC bubble, the ideas of active learning and student-centered learning environments had been moving from theory to practice. Large-scale course redesign programs to promote active learning, such as those designed by the National Center for Academic Transformation, had been going on for over a decade. Theoretical advancements and empirical findings from cognitive scientists and other learning researchers had become widely disseminated and put into practice in the methods employed by instructional designers and faculty developers in their collaborations with professors. What the MOOC bubble did was not so much create higher education's turn to learning—that had already been happening—but shine a very bright light on its existence. What was so frustrating for many in higher education learning organizations was the failure of those who built the early MOOC platforms to acknowledge the debt they owed to the work that had been happening in these centers for teaching and learning. Ironically, the centers of gravity of the MOOC world occurred at institutions—or at places within those institutions—that had perhaps contributed the least to the overall postsecondary turn to learning in recent years. Centers for teaching and learning, academic computing units, writing programs, and schools for professional and continuing education had been championing the transition from passive/instructor-focused to active/learner-centered education for many years before MOOCs hit the scene. Constructivist theories of education had been developed over decades by education researchers and learning scientists. And this disconnect was not just occurring at the loci of innovations developed for face-to-face courses. MOOC evangelists were often wholly disconnected from the broader range of online, low-residency, and blended learning programs that had done so much to introduce principles of learning science across the institutions in which they operated.

Perhaps even more disappointing for those invested in teaching and learning, MOOCs violated almost every core principle of active learning with which quality online and blended courses were designed.[1] A learning renaissance across a growing number of traditional courses and programs had begun, but this renaissance was not reflected in the affordances of the MOOC platforms. Constructivist principles, for example, posit that learning is fundamentally a social activity and that learners are not delivered knowledge but instead must create (construct) it on their own. For that to happen, models, designs, and frameworks needed to be created that enabled learning to be contextualized to the student's own experiences and worldviews. In these approaches, student initiative and autonomy are stressed over content dissemination and acquisition. The first MOOC courses to achieve massive enrollments—and that launched the formation of Coursera and edX—were instead built around video lectures and computer-graded assignments. While peer discussions did exist in the first large-enrollment MOOCs, the size of these courses—Thrun and Norgiv's 2011 Introduction to AI, for example, peaked at 160,000 enrollments—made individual mentoring by expert educators virtually impossible. The more engaged and engaging MOOCs worked around these limitations and tended to follow the principles of learning design and learning science, but these were few and far between.

With the exception of a smaller number of experimental courses, the success of MOOCs had little to do with the learning principles designed into the platform or, more often than not, the courses themselves. What MOOCs accomplished, instead, was to bring the question of how learning is changing to the center of the strategic discussions at many colleges and universities. These questions were as much about survivability, sustainability, reach, and funding as they were about learning. This was not without its benefits for teaching and learning. The space that MOOCs opened up in the strategic conversations enabled those who had been quietly working away at advancing learning to participate in institution-wide strategic discussions. Nimble campus learning innovators were able to use this MOOC excitement as a Trojan horse to engage in conversations about the need for instructional designers, media and video teams, instructional technologists, programmers, and learning analytics professionals, experts who could also work on programs and courses for traditional (matriculated) students. The energy and attention afforded by MOOCs were opportunities to address long-planned organizational changes that were necessary to keep institutions of higher education at the forefront of teaching and learning. This stealthy engagement meant increasing the staff and portfolios of centers for teaching and learning (CTLs) and academic computing units in order to do better work on campus, even as the ostensible focus was on MOOCs. At many campuses, new learning organizations were formed that aggregated previously separate teaching and learning services. These often had an explicit focus on learning innovation.

The question is why did it take something as pedagogically problematic as MOOCs to cause many in senior leadership at colleges and universities throughout the country to focus their attention on learning innovation? MOOCs were and continue to be provocative—they certainly offered new models for cost, reach, and branding—but they never were all that important in modeling or shaping how learning is changing. The real action in advancing learning is occurring in our face-to-face, blended, and online courses, including the experimental open online courses that seek to discover new platforms and learning models. Learning innovation is happening in the programs and initiatives on difference and diversity that campus learning organizations are running. Advances in learning are happening through the dissemination and adoption of concepts from educational theorists and learning scientists into course design and instructional practices of an ever-widening circle of teaching faculty. Learning innovation is happening in the introduction of data-driven teaching decisions that professors are increasingly able to make because of greater access to analytics about how their students are learning, and it's happening in the collaborative partnerships that instructional designers, faculty developers, and faculty are building as they design and teach courses. It's happening in the programs that are supporting sector-wide efforts to redesign foundational gateway courses and in the slow but steady advance of open educational resources as replacements for expensive publisher textbooks. Learning innovation is progressing in the cultural changes across campuses that are putting active and experiential education practices at the center of the student learning experience.

As we discuss later in this chapter, funding the work of learning innovation is a complex problem. Online programs have long had to find competitive advantages in marketing and learning innovations to differentiate themselves in order to attract and retain students. Advances in teaching and learning have emerged as a competitive differentiator, and MOOCs at least for a time appeared to some to represent the marriage of economics and student learning. Though MOOCs were able to attract the press, many in the learning innovation community had long attempted to leverage the return on investment that came with redesigning courses—particularly core and large introductory courses—with student-centered and active learning principles in mind. The failure to complete these courses in the early years of an undergraduate's academic career is what lies behind so much of the attrition and extended time to graduation that characterize much of American higher education.[2] Investing in learning innovation through course and program redesigns can pay for itself—both fiscally and morally—if this work results in lower proportions of students dropping out. As such, the presence of active and experiential learning programs are increasingly being used as tools to recruit new students.

These, and many more developments, lie at the center of the widespread yet mostly unrecognized postsecondary turn to learning we have been narrating. This turn has been the result of both a top-down strategy, as university leaders have supported (and found funds for) institution-wide programs and initiatives, as well as for the creation of new—or the reorganization of existing—campus learning organizations. It has also had a bottom-up push as knowledge and ideas about learning have moved out of departments and schools of education and cognitive science and into the methodologies of instructional design and faculty development. The innovations we have been marking thus far in this chapter have required an engaged group of academics and educators who not only implement large strategic, well-funded initiatives such as MOOCs, but do so in a way that merges these strategic initiatives with on-the-ground, tactical learning projects. These local projects build on the momentum of the top-down mandates to implement change across the entire landscape of learning at their institutions. This is, in the most fundamental sense, learning innovation at its best.

The rest of this chapter explores how these learning innovators are adopting and adapting this work on their campuses and for the field at large. We specifically explore the characteristics of the people engaged in this work and the challenges they encounter within the rather rigid organizational structures that define most of higher education. We argue that the faculty and administrative divide that is characteristic across all of higher education is one of the factors inhibiting learning innovation. Next, we look at economic support for learning innovation. For the work of learning innovation to continue, it needs to be funded. Waiting for the next MOOC train is likely not the best strategy (for designers and technologists or for provosts and presidents). We discuss some of the more traditional methods of funding (central funding and philanthropy) and suggest a new, alternative possibility. Finally, we look at how we sustain learning innovation into the future by creating the degree and nondegree programs needed to train students in the skills and context of learning innovation in higher education. Without a sustained investment in the next generation of learning innovators, colleges and universities will inevitably return to ad hoc approaches to improving student learning. We believe we are at an important moment in time, and the choices we make now to invest in the long-term sustainability of this work will have a significant impact on the future of teaching and learning in higher education. In each of these cases, the story of learning innovation we are telling is as much about the institutional structures that fund and enable student learning, now and into the future, as it is about the learning design and development that happens in collaboration with our faculty and in service to our students.

The New Learning Innovator

In order for the types of learning innovation we have been exploring to continue and evolve, the roles of the people imagining, designing, and supporting this work need to be better understood. This is challenging, in part, because there are so many different types of what we are calling "learning innovators." If we had to identify a common characteristic, we might say many consider themselves first and foremost to be educators, even if their primary job is not teaching. They often have a direct impact on teaching and learning by collaborating with teaching faculty on course design and development while also working to advance the institutional environment to improve student learning. Others in this category are traditional faculty who perhaps have taken a career detour into the teaching-and-learning support arena, or perhaps folks with PhDs who decided at some point in their careers that they wanted to stay in higher education by pursuing a nontraditional academic path.

For those in this line of work who hold terminal degrees, they often do so in more traditional academic disciplines. Some learning innovators are professionals trained in disciplines such as instructional design and learning technology. While still others have entered into the work through some other related field, such as information technology or student affairs. These folks tend to find themselves more and more engaged in thinking about the design of teaching and learning activities and eventually move over to do this work full time.

If the characteristics are challenging to define because of their breadth, so too are the names of categories we use to describe the folks who do this work. Individual titles such as instructional designer or learning analytics specialist aside, the category of work is so new that it has hardly been ratified within the existing structures of higher education. In this book, we use learning professional as a larger descriptive, but it is hardly without problems and it does not necessarily enjoy wide adoption. Even more of a problem is the fact that the term "professional" is often at odds with the notion of an academic. In many centers for teaching and learning, for example, there are folks who identify as professionals (graphic designers or web developers, for example) with very specific career trajectories and professional development needs. And then there are those who identify as academics, with *their* own professional development needs and (as yet to be well defined) career trajectories.

There is no clear answer here, but one increasingly popular way to describe those with PhDs who have entered this field is as alternative academics, which we briefly introduced in chapter 4. Alt-acs are those folks who were trained to join the faculty ranks but who have gone on to pursue a career outside of the traditional tenure or teaching tracks. Alternative academics capture some of the otherness and spirit of the role of the educators we are defining—they are not "mainstream" academics following traditional career paths, but they are still academics, through and through. "Alternative academic" is not the only shorthand used to describe people in these roles either, but it does avoid the problem of another popular term, the "nonfaculty educator." Even if it were not the case (as it is) that many alt-acs have faculty status, the nonfaculty educator nomenclature defines an already tenuous institutional role in terms of what it is not and not what it is. As we discuss in more detail below, the divide between faculty and administration is an already well-entrenched challenge for any learning innovation to occur. Names matter. They affect identity, success, and the well-being of the people doing this work, not to mention the degree to which they are taken seriously as colleagues and experts.

If nonfaculty educator is a problem, what about sticking with alt-acs? The problem with the language of alt-acs is that it is extremely broad. It's often used to describe a very large category of people with PhDs who work outside the teaching or tenure tracks. This can include people who have left higher education altogether (e.g., working in a museum or nonprofit) or people who have chosen paths in higher education that do not directly involve teaching and learning. Of course, many nonteaching roles can impact student learning (not to mention student growth and formation) as much as teaching roles. The growing focus on experiential, service, and co-op learning is one example of how the definition of what constitutes learning advancement is becoming more flexible. Student life, admissions, counseling, career advancement, alumni affairs, and a myriad of other campus offices and campus professionals all contribute to the teaching and learning missions of the institutions in which they are embedded. In the end, while alt-acs can be a useful category, roomy enough to encompass anyone who impacts teaching and learning, we believe it is still far too all-encompassing to serve as a useful descriptor of the category of work we are exploring. Despite their inherent limitations, both "learning professional" and "nonfaculty educators" are used in this book to describe existing roles, and "learning innovators" is used to describe those invested (now or in the future) in the kind of teaching innovation and institutional innovation we are promoting. The immediate recognizability of these terms by those in the field makes them valuable if not problematic. Perhaps someday we'll get to a place where all who work in higher education are considered educators with a common mission, even if individual work varies widely.

Why does what we call this work and the people who do it matter? Can't we simply call people by their function and leave it at that? Part of the answer comes down to how one imagines crafting a career in higher education learning outside of the traditional faculty path. If we compare the role of the learning innovator with the more well-established academic role of the professor, we see how much work is needed to help learning innovators imagine their career trajectory. The sequence of career stages in the life of a professor, for example, is well understood. If you are one of the diminishing fortunate few to land a tenure-track position, then you at least know what your career path might entail: assistant professor for five to seven years, followed by a tenure review. If successful, promotion to associate professor. Post-tenure promotion policies to full professor vary widely, but they usually constitute a narrower funnel than even that to associate professor. Academics in traditional faculty roles who transition to administrative posts (director, chair, dean, provost, etc.) talk about "coming up the hard way"—meaning they went through the tenure process.

Existing learning professionals, on the other hand, often occupy a liminal role between faculty and staff, in part because this mirrors how the learning organizations in which they work often exist at the margins between academic and administrative units. Progress along the career path of these educators tends to lack the milestones of the traditional tenure track. There is no regularized pace in which a nonfaculty educator working in a campus learning organization goes through to be promoted. With very few exceptions, there is no tenure. The challenge of defining who exactly higher education learning professionals are is one reason why we advocate in this book for the formation of learning innovation as an interdisciplinary field. We think that an academic and intellectual context needs to be created for those educators who focus their service, teaching, and scholarship on learning but who do not occupy traditional discipline-based tenure-track faculty roles.

Making things even more complicated is the fact that where one works in the university is not always the best indicator of the larger academic communities and intellectual traditions to which one is connected. A faculty developer working in a teaching and learning center, an instructional designer embedded within an information technology unit, and a director of online learning all work in distinct and separate university organizations but may all work on the same kind of learning innovations. The expert on learning analytics and the media developer, while supporting all this work, may even be in different functional units. As we explored in chapter 2, these various functions have been brought into a single organizational entity at some schools—and we expect that sort of organizational consolidation of campus learning professionals and roles to continue—while at other institutions these positions are separated across various campus organizational structures. They have different reporting lines, are housed within different campus divisions, and face different budget challenges. As we discussed in chapter 4, a new field of learning innovation has the potential to transcend existing university organizational structures and provide an intellectual home for learning innovators. Having an intellectual rather than organizational center of gravity, and an identified community of practice, will arguably enable nonfaculty educators and learning professionals to strengthen their impact across campus, regardless of the campus unit in which they sit.

Our attempts to define the characteristics of the learning innovator and their need for an intellectual home emanate from a desire to identify the full complexity of the work they are undertaking at this time. It is becoming less and less possible to be successful by siloing the work of learning off from the larger learning environment, whether at the institutional level or the broader field outside the walls of any one school. The complexity of how individuals learn requires a strategic approach if advances are going to be systemic, long-lasting, and meaningful. Investing in one area of advancing student learning must be undertaken with the perspective that any change also occurs within a larger student learning ecosystem. An institutional or strategic lens for advancing learning attempts to connect what occurs between professors and students in individual courses with the larger context in which students learn and professors teach. Part of the work of an interdisciplinary field of learning innovation, if one should emerge, is to unpack the relationship between actions taken at the organizational level (institution or school or department) and how these actions impact learning at the level of individual students.

Of course, today's learning professionals need to have a thorough grounding in the theoretical frameworks that underpin effective pedagogical practices, and they must be fluent in the language of learning science. They must be immersed in the scholarship of teaching and learning, and they should be experts in course design methodologies. They should have expertise in translating the learning objectives of the faculty with whom they partner to the medium (residential or blended or online) in which the course will be taught. This involves keeping up with the latest learning technologies and platforms and the ability to train faculty in their uses. They must also be experts in learning analytics and applying data-driven decision-making to course design and re-design efforts. These are all skills, abilities, and perspectives at the micro level of advancing learning. They operate at the level of one-to-one consultations and collaborations with professors, and sometimes with departments or schools. These are classic skills of instructional designers and faculty developers. All of these skills, however, will not be enough if the goal is to scale advances in student learning.

The next step for learning innovators is to combine their skills at the micro level of advancing learning to the meso level of department/program/school change and the macro level of institutional learning advancement. Learning innovators need to have a clear understanding of how their universities work as organizations and how colleges and universities operate within a larger postsecondary system. The level of individual student learning needs to be connected with the choices and constraints that institutions face. The larger demographic, economic, social, and political trends that impact colleges and universities must be contextualized for their impact at the level of individual learners. The research on how people learn needs to be connected with the knowledge of how universities change. The science of learning needs to expand to accommodate organizational development. The role of the campus learning professional needs to evolve to one that integrates the ground-level and hands-on work of advancing student learning with the larger institutional efforts to change our institutions.

Combining the traditional work of a learning professional with the perspective and orientation of an institutional change agent will require a different sort of training, a different set of skills, and a different community of practices. The new learning innovator will need to know as much about the history of higher education as she knows about learning theory and pedagogical best practices. She will need to have equal expertise in postsecondary financing and budgets as she has in instructional design. The knowledge of how effective leadership in the context of higher education is practiced will have to complement skills in learning platforms and learning analytics. A sense of the larger demographic, economic, and competitive forces with which the higher education system is being buffeted will go hand in hand with expertise in course design and faculty development. The twenty-first-century learning innovator will need to adopt an institutional and system-wide lens to the challenge of advancing student learning.

For the most part, learning professionals today are not trained in systems thinking. The focus of graduate programs from which many learning professionals emerge is on the methods, techniques, and theoretical foundations of learning. Case studies and theories of organizational change, particularly those related to higher education, are seldom featured in the curriculum. Some graduate programs that train learning professionals do a good job of teaching about the history of higher education, though most still focus on K–12 education. Still other programs have strengths in policy, economic, sociocultural, and demographic aspects of the modern university system, but again more likely than not they address these concerns in the context of public elementary and secondary schools. When they are part of curricula, these topics tend to exist as single courses (often electives) in the training of learning professionals. We explore an alternative model at the end of this chapter.

For those from traditional academic disciplines who want to join the ranks of learning innovators, the challenge of adopting an institutional and system-wide lens may be even more acute. Academics trained in traditional disciplines often lack coursework in learning science, pedagogy, and learning theory. They are often not exposed to any courses about the history, economics, or culture of higher education. Educators with these skill sets are not quite unicorns or yetis but they are rare. Learning innovators trained in programs of higher education come to the field better prepared to adopt an institutional and system-wide lens. Those with academic backgrounds in higher education remain a distinct minority of those working in campus learning organizations.

In whatever ways learning professionals have entered the profession, there is a need for all of us to become students of higher education. We need to complement our knowledge about advancing student learning with the skills necessary to lead change at the level of the institution. Increasingly, the work of advancing learning will occur beyond individual consulting and programming efforts and will shift to university-wide programs that seek to infuse active and experiential learning across the curriculum. These efforts may involve the development of new low-residency and online programs, both degree and nondegree, along with the diffusion of faculty training and course design methods and resources employed in online learning to face-to-face teaching. This work requires understanding the complex, adaptive system that is higher education.

The number and range of activities occurring across higher education to advance learning through innovation is startling. Visit any campus and you will find a campus-wide initiative or project, usually led by a campus learning organization, to build the school's capacity to advance student learning. All of these projects and initiatives had to be conceived of, funded, and managed. None happen without the commitment, efforts, and skills of the learning innovators who often lead these initiatives. There is very little in the way of opportunities for practice or professional development for learning innovators involved in the full spectrum to advance learning, which covers everything from small course-level design to institution-wide efforts. As we discussed in chapter 3, what does exist occurs through leadership programs, preconference workshops, webinars, and publications from professional associations. While these resources for learning innovators to lead organizational change are welcome, they are inadequate to the size of the challenge. What we hear from colleagues across the country is that learning innovators rarely get the opportunity to engage with the campus leaders they most need to collaborate with to develop sustainable institution-wide initiatives to advance learning. There is often a lack of opportunities for learning innovators to join department chairs, deans, and provosts in venues where institutional leadership and change are discussed. To do so effectively, they need to understand the micro, the meso, and the macro levels of learning innovation.

Rethinking the Faculty/Administrative Divide

As we discussed in the previous chapter, our prescription for the challenge of moving the work of learning innovation to the center of institutional priorities—and of moving learning professionals to positions of sustained institutional influence—is to nurture the work itself from a profession to an interdisciplinary academic field. Part of developing an institutional lens is the hope that we can shift how learning innovators are able to contribute to conversations about institutional strategy, particularly around teaching and learning. Institutional structures in higher education are often quite rigid, resting on many years of historical inertia. In fact, if anything is slow to change in higher education, it is the organizational structures that define governance, impact, and strategy. One of the most common elements of this structure is the divide between faculty and administration. As much of the reporting on the cost of higher education suggests, there has been a significant growth in administrative staff in the past thirty years. This growth—sometimes called bloat—has been blamed for rising costs and changing priorities.[3] Climbing walls and lazy rivers become the focus rather than maintaining a healthy portfolio of disciplinary expertise in the faculty, or so the story goes. There are many reasons to challenge this narrative, and more and more reporting is suggesting nuance is necessary.[4]

Whatever the truth is, the perception leads to a reification of a faculty and administration divide that is less than healthy. Faculty feel their roles as teachers and scholars are being undercut by overspending on administrative functions. Requests to hire faculty, either in new or replacement lines, are often refused, all while it appears that the office responsible for the climbing walls and lazy rivers keeps getting more and more staff. Staff and administrators, on the other hand, feel that their contributions to the education and formation functions of the university are rarely recognized. The increase in staff follows growing expectations by students to see their time at college as a holistic experience that involves both curricular and cocurricular activities. Don't staff play significant roles in advising, mentoring, and support for student well-being and happiness, they ask? Of course the dynamic at every institution is unique and may or may not lead to more or less tension between faculty and administration. Based on the interviews we conducted for this book, we do think it's true that this general divide has a significant impact on the contributions learning innovators are able to make at the institutional level. For example, many institutions are governed by the philosophy of faculty governance, and decisions are vetted and voted on through standing faculty committees and ad hoc task forces. These decisions are then often carried out by the staff charged with implementation. While learning innovators are sometimes included in these committees and task forces, this more often than not happens in response to a crisis or in support of a larger initiative with very limited input beyond focused problems. By arguing for a new dynamic, we hope to encourage a reconsideration of the place of learning innovators in setting institutional priorities.

The faculty/staff divide in determining institutional priorities exists, as we mentioned, across a spectrum throughout higher education. At some schools there is greater equity and inclusiveness between faculty and nonfaculty educators. At other schools, the academic caste system that places nonfaculty in "support" roles is firmly entrenched. Navigating the siloed culture of higher education is particularly difficult for learning innovators who work at the liminal intersections between traditional faculty and nontraditional academic staff. Some learning innovators who read this book and enjoy full faculty status may be surprised by the degree to which we highlight this challenge. In the research we conducted for this book, we learned that faculty status for learning innovators is unusual. It is largely concentrated in those who take leadership roles in campus learning organizations after already achieving more senior faculty or academic administrative status. These faculty sometimes come to their campus learning organization leadership roles with tenure and can return to their home academic departments should their role of learning organization leader come to an end. Even these academics who work in learning organizations tend to have difficulty navigating the faculty/administrative divide. Learning innovators who did not follow a traditional academic path of promotion and tenure, and who have built their academic career within learning organizations, may find it even more difficult.

The examples of nonfaculty educators who do enjoy the benefits of faculty status are worth studying. Building on successful models, even if rare, makes sense. Academic librarians with faculty rank come most quickly to mind. The extent to which the discipline of information science/librarianship may serve as a model for a new field of learning innovation is an intriguing question. Further research is needed to explore the history and present status of academic librarians in relation to what we may learn in our efforts to evolve learning innovation from a profession to an interdisciplinary field. We recognize, however, that the probability of learning innovators gaining academic rank across the postsecondary system is low. More likely, learning innovators will increasingly move into the role of leading learning organizations on their campuses. It may be impossible to generalize the extent to which having a dual faculty role will affect a learning innovator's ability to participate in the governance or decision-making of the departments in which they are affiliated or in cross-institution faculty committees. What these hybrid faculty titles may do is give learning innovators some greater recognition within the current institutional structures as contributing to the education of their students. Ideally this would not be necessary. There would be greater understanding of the roles that a variety of positions play in educating our students. But, until that time comes, learning innovators with some faculty role may be in a better position to contribute to institutional change.

Up to this point, we've made the case that nonfaculty learning professionals are making a significant contribution to the education of the students at their schools. What we have not discussed is whether it's also important for learning innovators to teach. The colleagues we spoke with were mixed on the answer to this question. For some, teaching experience brings with it an incredibly valuable perspective. For others, there is complete confidence in the belief that learning professionals can and are contributing to the education of their students in ways that are as necessary and as important as the faculty in the classroom. We do not want to make an argument one way or another, but we do think it is helpful for learning innovators to understand what it means to see teaching as a complex, dynamic activity. Having some experience in the classroom lends itself to a greater understanding of that full complexity. If they are going to teach, the best place for learning innovators to apply their expertise to teaching is sometimes unclear. Emerging master's programs in instructional design and educational technologies are one obvious place where learning innovators can teach. So are any programs that focus on aspects of higher education. What we have found is that many learning innovators with traditional disciplinary backgrounds end up teaching in the discipline in which they were trained. This has the advantages of allowing learning innovators to keep their hands in the academic field in which they started their careers. Unfortunately, it is challenging to keep up with the literature in the fields of learning science, higher education leadership, and other areas in which they work, let alone in their original discipline. Having to stay current in one's original academic discipline to teach and maintain a faculty appointment carries with it significant opportunity costs. There are only so many hours in the day.

Still, for many learning innovators, the idea of teaching will be daunting, and that too may be part of the growing pains of this field. Learning professionals chose to work in learning fields for learning organizations. They did not choose to follow a traditional faculty career path. Yes, they'd like equal institutional status and rights as their traditional faculty colleagues. The job security of tenure would be great, but that is a diminishing possibility for even those on traditional faculty trajectories. From this perspective, efforts to turn learning innovators into professors will not only likely fail but also run the risk of giving back many of the gains that learning professionals have made in academia. It is still a relatively new phenomenon for instructional designer roles to be created in significant numbers. Only recently has the role of instructional designer shifted from that of a technical support role—the person who helps the professor untangle the grade book in the learning management system—to an educator who is positioned to work collegially with professors. Similarly, faculty developers working in CTLs have carved out respected roles on campus as trusted colleagues, advocates, and partners for professors. They have expertise that is distinct from traditional faculty. Expertise that is recognized as valuable by their faculty colleagues. Comparable things can be said for the learning professionals working in departments of academic computing, continuing and professional education units and schools, and online learning divisions. All of these learning professionals have both distinct and valued roles on campus, and they belong to vibrant national communities of practice.

What we hope is clear from this discussion is that as higher education evolves, there should be room for a wider variety of educators on our campuses, each with their own identity and place in the higher education ecosystem. More importantly, though, we hope the faculty/staff divide that continues to characterize so much of the tension in higher education will start to break down. We believe it's important for all involved in the student learning experience to work together to deepen their collaborations and, more importantly, to deepen student learning. We have already seen this trend begin to gain momentum during the years of the turn to learning. We expect it only to accelerate in the years to come.

The Structures and Funding of Learning Innovation

We have been arguing that future success in leading institution-wide learning innovation efforts will depend as much on both knowledge of learning science and its related domains as it will on skills related to leading organizational change. Chief among these organizational skills may be the ability to develop sustainable sources of funding. Leaders of learning organizations that depend on funding allocations from the provost's office or other administrative offices will find their innovation projects vulnerable to leadership changes and financial setbacks at the institution. A strategy built around winning access to ever-scarcer institutional dollars is not the way to build a resilient and sustainable culture of learning innovation. Leaders of learning organizations are also often tasked with finding ways to bring in their own money. As we all know, creating a culture of learning innovation is a long-term endeavor. Any initiative that has the potential to deliver large-scale (nonincremental) advances to student learning also has a high chance of failure. As we argued in chapter 3, innovation is more a process than an outcome, and learning innovations require long runways and second chances. Not every learning innovation needs to be wildly expensive, but every learning innovation will require some level of resources—people and money—that will need to be sustained across budget cycles and provostal tenures. Leaders of learning organizations spend a great deal of energy and time trying to figure out how to create some margin of economic resilience for their innovation initiatives. The reality is that achieving long-term economic resilience is a constant battle. It's a battle that will require invention, fortitude, and a willingness to experiment. Until there is recognition across all of higher education of the value of learning innovation, there is likely to be no point in which financial security for these initiatives is reached. This work requires an ability to improvise, pivot, and live in the institutional gray areas.

One often undervalued aspect of leading institutional change is the need to build strong networks across institutions. Good relationships are key to institutional effectiveness everywhere. As we interviewed colleagues doing this work, we learned just how interconnected even larger universities are in this regard. It is rarely worth winning an academic battle, they argue, if that win diminishes one's campus reputation or damages any relationships. The ability of campus learning organizations to have a long-term positive impact on advancing student learning will ultimately depend on the reputation and respect that those who lead and work at the organization have with faculty, staff, and leadership. Learning organizations often need to play the long game in building their campus (and cross-institutional) networks and relationships. Still, it remains very much the case that even team-playing and respected learning organizations would be wise to work toward developing sustainable sources of funding. The greater the ambition to move the needle on student learning away from the status quo, the more acute the need is to create durable and protected sources of funding to support these initiatives. While the traditional operations of learning organizations may perhaps reliably depend on traditional funding sources—such as central budget allocations that are consistent year to year—new innovation projects and initiatives often necessitate greater financial creativity.

One way that learning organizations can develop new sources of funding to support learning innovation initiatives is to leverage their existing capabilities or core capacities. It's important to note that we are not advocating for revenue generation as much as we are suggesting how leveraging existing capabilities might save an institution the money it would spend on external services. This savings could then be used to reinforce support for the work happening on campus by learning organizations. Savings become revenue for innovation. We explore one potential example of utilizing the internal expertise of learning organizations by looking at how they can take advantage of their investments in instructional designers and faculty developers to serve as local service providers for online programs at their institutions. However learning organizations seek to develop new sources of funding, we believe strongly that any new funding for learning innovation initiatives must be seen as complements, rather than substitutes, for the traditional sources of funding that learning organizations rely on, such as (a) funding subvention from the provost or academic divisions, (b) external grant funding through foundations or government, and (c) philanthropy.

Before we discuss internal online program management, a few words on philanthropy are in order. Our conversations with colleagues across higher education suggest there is great potential for learning organizations to be featured prominently and successfully in institutional fundraising initiatives than may be broadly recognized. The focus on external fundraising for learning organizations has a long history, often concentrating on large or naming gifts for centers of teaching and learning. For example, the McGraw Center for Teaching and Learning was established at Princeton with a $5 million donation.[5] The William G. Jackson Center for Teaching and Learning at Michigan Tech was the result of a $1 million gift to establish the CTL in 2013.[6] The Joy Shechtman Mankoff Center for Teaching & Learning at Connecticut College is named after the alumni who endowed the CTL in 2008.[7] In 2016, Barnard College received $70 million from alumni to establish the 128,000-square-foot Cheryl and Philip Milstein Center for Teaching and Learning.[8]

Historically, other learning organizations—such as academic technology units—have been less likely than CTLs to receive naming gifts or to be featured in university philanthropic efforts. As more schools reorganize their teaching and learning operations to integrate previously disparate units and services, we expect the level of philanthropic focus on these integrated learning organizations to increase. One way that learning organizations are well positioned to participate in their school's philanthropic strategies is their focus and capabilities in communications and outreach. Part of the work of every learning organization is making visible the work of faculty engaging in teaching and learning experiments and innovative projects. As tenure and promotion policies often don't reward faculty investment in learning innovation, it's often up to the learning organization to showcase the efforts of faculty to advance student learning. This has led many learning organizations to develop capabilities in communications and outreach, and stories about teaching and learning innovations are shared in articles and videos. The material developed for outreach to internal institutional audiences can often be repurposed to assist institutional development offices in raising funds. We have not seen the data on how learning organizations are being included in university capital campaigns, or the average size of gifts, but from our observations of peers and colleagues it seems as if learning organizations are not highlighted enough in campus fundraising initiatives.

Internal Campus Service Provider

An area where learning organizations might develop new revenue sources to help fund learning innovation is through the provisioning of internal services that were not part of their original mandate. To be clear, centers for teaching and learning should not be charging for their services if at all possible. Faculty members should never have to decide they cannot take advantage of the resources and expertise of their colleagues in CTLs because they do not have funding. All faculty should have access to help with a teaching or design problem, just as all faculty should have access to experts who understand how the judicious use of technology can have a positive impact on student engagement and learning. Nor should any faculty member ever have to forego assessing the impact of a change in practice because they are not grant funded. Even worse, no faculty members should ever feel like the center for teaching and learning is only available to the wealthier departments on campus, however the funding is structured at that particular school. Centers for teaching and learning need stable, institutional funding to make their work part of the fabric of learning at the school. This cannot be stressed enough. We have spent a good deal of time in this book discussing innovations in learning, but innovations occur along a spectrum and are not a binary determination. To innovate, we need to learn, to assess, to experiment, to challenge ourselves, and to adapt what we learn in those activities to new experiments in learning. These are all responsibilities of institutions to support and fund.

With that caveat made (and hopefully reinforced well enough), the growth of online learning presents an interesting opportunity for learning organizations to develop new funding streams by serving as internal online program managers (OPMs) for their schools. If done well, this new source of funding can support more experimental innovations in learning. External online program managers—such as 2U, Academic Partnerships, Emeritus, Wiley Education Services, and Pearson Online Learning Services—can also partner with schools to develop and run online programs. These companies and their competitors—there are over thirty-five companies in the external OPM space at the time of writing—act as online program enablers. The standard model is for the OPM company to provide upfront capital and expertise in areas such as enrollment management and marketing to help institutions create new online programs. The programs, usually master's degrees but increasingly nondegree certificates, carry the university's brand and are delivered under the academic control and supervision of the school. In exchange for reducing the risk associated with new online programs, in part by providing the funds necessary to build a new online program, market to and recruit students, and provide the learning platforms and student support (schools provide the faculty), the OPM provider takes a share of the revenue from tuition dollars. This revenue share tends to vary between 50 and 75 percent of gross tuition, depending on the program being created and range of services that the OPM provides. Universities are generally asked to sign long-term contracts with OPM providers, ranging from three to ten years, on the assumption that the OPM will only begin to recoup its costs and start to make profits a few years into the program. It's worth noting that this model has changed some in the past five or so years. There is a slowly increasing variety of school/OPM relationships, with some moving beyond a bundled model in which the company does everything—from course design to marketing to student support—and takes a large majority of the gross tuition revenues. Noodle Partners, for example, was founded by John Katzman— founder of the Princeton Review and cofounder of 2U, then called 2tor—with the idea of creating an unbundled OPM partnership model. Under their model, schools pay either a fee for services offered, such as marketing or course design or student support, or a lower revenue share based on a more limited set of services.

However we look at it, the OPM model has grown quickly, and many colleges and universities have been able to stand up new online programs more rapidly than they would have been able to with internal resources alone. Even with the majority of revenues going to the OPM, some institutions have been able to bring in significant dollars to their institutions with new online programs. For example, Simmons University was able to bring in $56 million in new revenue through its 2U-powered online programs (after the revenue share). These funds covered the shortfalls in the university's undergraduate residential programs, allowing the school to regain financial stability.[9] In 2018, 2U and Simmons signed a fifteen-year contract extension. The OPM industry is today perhaps the hottest sector in the educational technology and for-profit education market. In 2014, 2U went public, and at the time of our writing is valued at over $4 billion. The company has partnerships with over thirty universities to offer degree (mostly master's) and non-degree online programs. In 2018, estimated revenues across all OPM providers were between $1.5 and $2.5 billion.[10] Investors continue to pour money into OPM companies. The number of schools signing up to partner with OPMs to create new degree and nondegree online programs continues to grow.

Despite the success of some online programs delivered by OPMs, more and more schools have come to realize that having an external, full-service OPM may not be in the best interest of the institution. Not only are schools signing long-term contracts in which they are giving away 50–75 percent of their gross tuition revenue—applied at times even to residential students who take an online course—but they are out-sourcing what should be core capacities in instructional design, media production, enrollment management, and platform support. Additionally, the revenue-share model means the OPM is driven by enrollment numbers, a motivation that might be at odds with the goals of the program. For example, a program that prioritizes access, equity, and quality of student engagement over larger numbers of enrolled students would find itself in a constant battle with its OPM looking to increase enrollments to increase profits, rather than to increase access or to lower the cost of a degree. The long-term contracts that OPMs demand are also coming under scrutiny as the value that the OPM partner provides drops for institutions once the program is established.

These challenges along with a host of others—quality control, generic services across many highly selective institutions served by the same OPM, encroachment on institutional expertise, the need to duplicate services with the OPM that they are now paying double for, and the reality that 40 percent of gross tuition may not be enough for a program to actually survive, to name a few—have pushed some learning organizations to ask whether they might provide similar services within the institution, and do so at a lower cost. Many of the traditional functions that bundled OPMs provide—including instructional design, faculty training, provisioning and supporting learning platforms, and student support—are already core competencies of learning organizations.

Learning organizations have also been growing their capabilities in media production, not to mention the design of simulations and other digital educational media content, in response to the MOOC wave. At schools without developed resources in instructional design, assessment, and faculty development, many leaders of campus learning organizations rightly question whether schools should be outsourcing what should be core competencies for the full spectrum of support needs on campus. New online programs can be significant revenue generators, but they can also serve as vehicles in which to build institutional capacity. The instructional design methods and educational platforms that are utilized in online programs are equally applicable to residential/face-to-face courses. Outsourcing the design and operation of an online program to an OPM company limits the diffusion of knowledge and techniques between online and residential programs. Learning organizations are also increasingly pushing back on the idea that institutions should give up half to three-quarters of all tuition revenues, when they can do the work for far less and with greater impact across the entire institution. This savings could be used to fund the full spectrum of activities of the learning organization and, even more so, support investments in learning innovation.

Despite this position, we do not wish to argue that an OPM partnership is necessarily a bad thing. Or that schools within an institution should always partner with the campus learning organization to develop new online programs. As we have seen at our own institutions, a mix of external OPM partners and internal online services can make for a healthy online education ecosystem. We have found it to also be true that partnering with various schools or programs to create new degree and nondegree online programs can result in both greater revenues to the school, high quality and economically sustainable programs, and savings that can be used to fund the campus learning organization. As the OPM industry increasingly moves toward offering an unbundled menu of services, learning organizations are well positioned to evaluate potential partners and to manage those relationships. For instance, a campus learning organization may decide to outsource noncore educational activities such as digital marketing to an OPM partner—usually on a fee-for-service basis rather than a revenue share. There is a good argument to be made that universities should not be experts in things like digital marketing and should instead invest in capabilities related to teaching, learning, and student support.

However the OPM divide plays out, learning organizations would be wise to consider what services they can provide and at what cost. If a CTL has the *capability* to do particular kinds of work, serving as an internal OPM could allow it to develop *capacity* for greater work across the institution. Providing the services that might otherwise be outsourced to an external OPM would lower overall costs of online program development for the institution and introduce savings that could enable it to support ongoing innovations on campus and online. The instructional design, analytics, and platform support created to support online courses could then be harnessed to provide greater support for the work on campus. Online education is changing. More and more schools are realizing that hybrid and online modalities will become part of the full spectrum of approaches to teaching and learning they offer. In some not too distant future, there will be no online, at least as we currently conceive of it as separate from the residential programs. There will simply be courses with different modalities. Learning organizations that can develop the capabilities and capacities to support this work now will be better positioned to help schools make this transition. As we have been arguing, understanding the intersection of learning (in this case, course delivery modalities) with the institutional dynamics at play (in this case, the cost and funding for online program management) is a fundamental part of our definition of learning innovation.

Shepherding Graduate Programs

The work we've been exploring in this book is changing rapidly. One of the most difficult aspects of it is finding people who have been trained not only as instructional designers or instructional technologists but who also understand the complex, dynamic context of higher education—its history, policies, and politics. As this work grows, the need for people trained in this work will only continue to grow. Campus learning organizations are arguably better positioned than any other school or department to design, run, and implement programs—certificate or degree—that will train the next generation of educators. To do this not only means radically rethinking how learning innovation takes place within higher education, but it also means recognizing that learning innovation is fast becoming a core function of colleges and universities in much the same way that student affairs and higher education administration did in the early twentieth century. We must imagine a model for a new learning organization that goes beyond what currently exists at most colleges and universities.

This is in part the work we are doing at Georgetown in the Learning, Design, and Technology (LDT) program we discussed in the introduction. The LDT was launched in the fall of 2017 with the first cohort of master's degree students engaged in thinking about how they might contribute to the future of higher education. They entered the program to study learning design, technology and innovation, and learning analytics within the context of critical studies in higher education. This program is not designed solely to produce expert instructional designers, instructional technologists, or learning analytics specialists. Instead, the program is designed to prepare students to contribute to (and hopefully influence) the strategic conversations that are happening across higher education about learning, whether that is a decision about moving a program online or thinking about investments in educational technology that might help the viability of the school's residential education. We are training students to contribute to these conversations not from legal, policy, or economic positions (at least not primarily) but from an understanding of learning, design, technology, analytics, and the roles these play in informing the most meaningful and effective experiences we can give our students. Starting this program at Georgetown was not easy. It was challenging to imagine building a program from within a center for teaching and learning, just as it was not easy to imagine how a program like it would navigate the institutional structures and barriers in place to make this kind of endeavor possible. But, with good partners in our Graduate School of Arts and Sciences, which houses the academic program; leadership from a provost willing to see experimentation at the institutional level as a necessary component of the future of higher education; and a dedicated and willing faculty within the our center, we've been able to forge a path we think is worth others considering.

What would it mean for other schools to adopt this approach? It would start with leveraging the work of existing campus organizations that have learning at their core. At most institutions, like Georgetown, these learning organizations are devoted mainly to service to the institution. They run faculty (and future faculty) workshops and convene campus communities around teaching and learning. In response to the MOOC wave and online programming, many of these campus learning organizations have grown over the past few years, integrating previously disparate campus functions such as instructional design, running the campus learning management system, and educational media into a single unit. This is work that is fundamental to each campus in which it is being undertaken. Making the shift to the type of learning organization we are describing means retaining the service portfolio of existing organizations but also adding some of the features of an academic department, such as teaching courses and scaffolding those courses into full-fledged degree-granting programs. There are many reasons to offer courses and develop degree programs built on the scholarly and applied work of learning professionals in learning organizations, but most important may be the need to train the next generation of higher education learning innovators.

As we discussed earlier, many learning professionals who work in learning organizations are already teaching, but that teaching is often in the traditional academic discipline in which they trained or in schools of education. Why not convert that teaching time and energy into courses and programs reflecting the field of learning innovation? Why not expand the work of campus learning professionals to embrace what is recognized as traditionally academic, integrating a teaching (and research) mission along with a service orientation? Why not leverage the growing demand for graduate programs in learning design, technology innovation, learning analytics, and higher education leadership to both grow learning innovation as a field through the creation of graduate programs and advance our campus learning organizations through the unique value a graduate program brings?

When we advanced this idea to our colleagues at learning organizations at other institutions, the response was almost always hesitant. Our colleagues would tell us that while this is an interesting and perhaps even good idea to steward a master's program in their learning organization, it would never happen on their campus. Our colleagues point out that the mission of their learning organizations is to partner and collaborate with schools, departments, and faculty to advance teaching and learning. They are not set up or designed to administer degree programs. Designing and teaching courses may be one thing, as these are tasks that learning professionals are already doing on campus. It is quite another thing to be in charge of the student experience in a graduate program addressing issues ranging from marketing, recruiting, and admissions to administering financial aid and scholarships to student advising and mentoring. Eventually the students will graduate, which means that they will be alumni, and that relationship will need to be managed. Learning organizations have lots of embedded expertise. Managing the student lifecycle is not one of them. Working with existing academic departments or schools to develop new graduate degrees is one thing. Many learning organizations have this partnership model for degree development as a core aspect of the portfolio of services that they offer. It is quite another thing to create a graduate degree program on their own.

The biggest worry of our colleagues is that time and energy spent on developing this degree program risks distracting from what they see as the core mission of the learning organization, supporting teaching and learning at their institutions. The opportunity costs for developing, teaching, and managing the degree and the students that enroll would be paid by a loss of focus and investment in the traditional learning organization functions if those organizations are unable to grow their staffs to manage a new degree program. Instead, the concern is that the work for these degree programs will be added to the already overflowing plates of existing staff. Learning innovators in campus learning organizations are already feeling stretched with the new responsibilities that they have been given during the turn to learning. Adding the work of navigating approval for a new degree program through the complexities of institutional politics and governance structures sounds daunting. And that is even before all the work to design the program, develop the courses, recruit the students, and teach the classes begins.

These are many of the reasons why campus learning organizations, and the learning professionals who run these units, may shy away from attempting to steward new graduate programs in learning innovation. Still, we think that this is an idea that learning organizations should consider. At schools that do not have a school or department of education, developing a graduate program for future higher education learning professionals may be an easier lift. Many universities have education schools/departments and education faculty, but their focus is usually heavily if not exclusively on K–12. For these institutions, creating a graduate program that is explicitly aimed at higher education may be more possible. At universities that have faculty already engaged in studying and teaching about higher education, there may be opportunities to collaborate with these faculty to develop graduate degree and nondegree certificate programs that have yet to be offered.

In the end, it is less important where these graduate programs aimed at training nonfaculty educators sit in the campus organizational structure and more critical that these programs exist. It is essential, in our estimation, that graduate training in instructional design or learning analytics or higher education leadership is designed and taught in collaboration and partnership with those currently working in the learning organizations wherein graduates of these programs are likely to find jobs. Instructional designers should be involved in teaching instructional design. Those leading learning analytics projects should be part of teaching about learning analytics. And those who are leading campus-wide learning initiatives should be part of teaching about higher education leadership. At every school, any new graduate degree to train learning professionals will need to have faculty teaching courses from around the institution. Even the largest campus learning organizations will not have staff with the expertise and backgrounds required to develop and teach graduate-level courses across the full range of areas necessary for a degree program. Any graduate program offered by a campus learning organization will be by necessity interdisciplinary. This is one of the strengths of the learning organizations offering graduate degrees. The development of the program and the teaching of courses will further bind the organization with the faculty. Professors brought in from around campus to help develop and teach in the program will contribute to the vibrancy and depth of the learning organization's communities of practice. A degree program done in close collaboration with faculty from traditional disciplines could help close the gap between the abstract, theoretical work on learning and the hands-on, applied activities of learning organizations.

Learning organizations may be able to bridge to a full master's by offering online nondegree/alternative credential programs in areas of their design and innovation core competencies. Many learning organizations, such as our own, have provided leadership for their institutional forays into open online learning. Online certificate programs in instructional design, learning analytics, and higher education leadership are experiencing a surge in demand, as universities seek to recruit more nonfaculty learning professionals in response to the turn to learning. Because of these programs, there may be fewer institutional governance hoops to jump through for campus learning organizations to create nondegree, as opposed to degree, programs. Those who follow the educational credentialing market closely are seeing signs that employers are willing to accept alternative credentials as signals for employment readiness. The skills that learning professionals need to work in academic environments, including instructional design and analytics and media skills, can be learned and assessed effectively through online platforms. Alternative credential programs are labor intensive to produce, but less so to run, as they are often designed to scale to hundreds, and sometimes thousands, of learners. The line between nondegree and degree programs is starting to erode, as programs such as edX's MicroMasters program provide a path for learners to matriculate into full master's programs. In either case, certificate or master's degree, there may be a place for learning organizations to enter into the role of helping to train the next generation of learning innovators.

Next Steps

In this chapter, we've proposed a number of ways learning organizations can adopt practices that invest in learning innovation, from clearly defining the roles of learning professionals to breaking down barriers between faculty and administrators to finding alternative sources of funding to shepherding a new degree program in the field. Our hope is that each of these suggestions will give leaders of learning organizations a place to start a discussion about how to create sustainable interventions in learning innovation. Not all of these may be possible or even desirable at any one institution, and some, like redefining the role of learning professionals, may need broader conversations than any one learning organization is able to begin on its own. We also hope that engaging in these conversations will help give real weight and stability to the growing interdisciplinary field of learning innovation.

If learning innovation is to evolve into a field with its own questions, methods, and models, however, one outstanding question worth asking is whether a master's degree in this field is enough. Stewarding a graduate degree in partnership and collaboration with other departments, schools, and faculty from a learning organization is appealing in many ways. The demand for master's degrees for professionals wishing to go into some aspect of education and learning in higher education is strong. A master's program can be designed to be completed in a year for full-time students, or over a couple of years for students who are juggling work and family commitments. The formats of master's programs are increasingly moving toward either fully online or low-residency degrees. These programs can enroll students who don't live near the campus, increasing the potential demand for the program and the quality of applicants.

Developing master's programs for aspiring higher education learning innovators is probably the right place to start, but the work of learning innovation will likely not continue building momentum until new PhD programs are developed to train the next generation of scholars and teachers in this field. The PhD program is the logical enabler and perhaps outcome of the creation of a new interdisciplinary field in learning innovation. A PhD in learning innovation could serve as the degree of future higher education learning innovation leaders, while graduates with a PhD in this emerging discipline would be more likely to engage in scholarship and knowledge creation needed to sustain the field. The idea of a PhD program in learning innovation stewarded by a campus learning organization is aligned with the idea that this work is evolving from a professional activity to a broad academic space in need of applied scholarship. The field will not move forward unless it gains the momentum of structures specifically designed to create new knowledge—and train new scholars—in the field.

The challenges of developing PhD programs in learning innovation from within campus learning organizations are even more striking than stewarding master's programs. Where master's programs can generate revenue for a school, PhD programs represent a challenging financial proposition. Students in master's programs pay tuition. PhD students usually have their tuition costs funded. Full-time doctoral students in traditional academic disciplines typically receive a stipend. The cost to support PhD students in traditional disciplines is offset by external research funding and by the assignment of doctoral students to teaching responsibilities. The tuition dollars from master's students also help offset the cost of funded doctoral students. Doctoral students are high quality and low-cost labor for teaching assistants and course sections, and perhaps in this field growing experts in learning innovation. Perhaps a PhD in learning innovation would catch the attention of some deep-pocketed educational foundation. Much of the support from foundations for higher education is in service of nonincremental academic innovations. The building of new knowledge around learning innovation, and the training of the next generation of learning organization leaders, may conform with the strategic goals of a philanthropic foundation. Or perhaps some entrepreneurial university president will read this book and grasp the opportunity for their school to differentiate itself as a leader in learning innovation. She will champion the creation of a new PhD program within a campus learning organization. This effort would garner national attention since, as far as we know, it has never been attempted. Or maybe some particularly resourceful leader of an existing campus learning organization will find a way to make this happen, despite all the obstacles. For this to happen, however, the idea of a PhD in learning innovation based in a campus learning organization needs to be discussed and debated. We hope that this book helps bring about that conversation.

How precisely a campus learning organization might overcome all these challenges to build PhD programs in learning innovation is an open question. The barriers to build doctoral programs in learning innovation seem as daunting to us as to everybody else. But for this work to continue to grow, we need sustained institutional investment. This investment needs to come not only in the form of internal support for learning professionals (and their professional development) and learning organizations (and the scaffolding necessary for them to generate new sources of revenue) but also as an ongoing recognition of the place of learning innovation in the success of higher education. The future of higher education depends in part on our understanding how learning happens at both the individual and institutional levels, and to imagine, design, and implement new, innovative approaches to learning within and across this landscape.

The Future of Learning Innovation

IN 2018, the Georgia Tech Commission on Creating the Next in Education released a report titled *Deliberate Innovation, Lifetime Education*.[1] In that report, the Georgia Tech authors made an argument for a new kind of university, one that offers a low-cost, high-quality experiential education by leveraging digital platforms and artificial intelligence. The report followed on the success of the university's low-cost online master of science in computer science, which at a tuition of $6,630 was priced at a sixth of the cost of the comparable on-campus degree program.[2] That year also saw the closure of the University of Texas System's high-profile Institute for Transformational Learning (ITL).[3] Begun in 2012 with an investment of $100 million, ITL's mission was to create new digital learning platforms and transformative online programs. Among the reasons cited for closing the institute were its inability to develop a self-sustaining business model, as it was bringing in only $1 million a year after having spent $77 million of the initial investment.

The initiatives at Georgia Tech and the Texas System are examples of a broader movement across higher education to invest in learning innovation. These efforts, which have grown substantially over the past few years, are part of a larger story of the efforts of individual institutions and state systems to leverage digital technologies to improve learning, increase access, and lower costs. What the apparent success of the Georgia Tech initiative and the evident failure of the ITL initiative tell us about the future of learning innovation across higher education is unclear. Without the sort of detailed comparative and historical context that a scholarly approach can provide, we are left to rely on news accounts, blog posts, and internal university reports, when available, to evaluate these efforts.

The pressure on colleges and universities to make fundamental changes in response to demographic and economic headwinds is incredibly strong. The confluence of public disinvestment, rising costs (cost disease), and declining numbers of high school graduates in many areas (particularly the Northeast and the Midwest) have all brought into question the long-term economic sustainability of many institutions. Add those fiscal and organizational challenges to the persistence of low graduation rates at many schools—not to mention research such as Arum and Roksa's *Academically Adrift: Limited Learning on College Campuses*—then questions of the efficacy of learning innovation initiatives take on a greater strategic import.

There are many things we do not yet know about learning innovation. We don't know if the aims of learning innovation efforts are having significantly positive impacts on the institutions in which they are emerging. We don't yet know if the learning innovation efforts of the early twenty-first century will end up being substantial or strategic. We don't know if the impact of these learning innovation efforts will be long-lasting and consequential. It may be that future scholars will look back on the learning innovation efforts as institutional fads and failed organizational experiments. But we think it's important to find out. It's crucial to understand the impact of these investments and this work, not only to demonstrate success or failure but to plan a path forward for new investments in learning innovation.

We trace the challenge to make sense of the success and failure of institutional initiatives such as those of Georgia Tech and the University of Texas as part of a broader systemic gap in how learning innovation is studied. The problem, as we see it, is not that higher education is unable to make big changes when it comes to advancing how students learn. The core educational practices of faculty are changing rapidly and for the better. Colleges and universities are in the midst of numerous experiments and initiatives designed to improve student learning. The challenge is that higher education as an industry has not developed the right methods to analyze, evaluate, and diffuse learning innovations. For all its emphasis on research, higher education fails more often than not to study itself.

Why is this so? How is it possible for postsecondary learning innovation to be so widely discussed and yet so little understood? The conversations about learning innovation are mainly occurring among learning professionals engaged in learning initiatives. As we discussed in chapter 4, we worry that the conversation on learning innovation is not occurring in the durable medium of scholarly books and peer-reviewed articles. Instead, this learning innovation conversation happens across professional gatherings and on social media screens.

A scholar of learning innovation could visit almost any college or university and find something to study. Every school that we know about through our own academic professional networks has something exciting going on with teaching and learning. Wherever we go we see new active learning classrooms and hear talk about introductory course redesigns. It seems as if every school is working to make traditionally large lecture courses into active learning experiences. Where our experience of college in the late 1980s and early 1990s was in classrooms with fixed, tiered seating and high-stakes exams, today's undergraduates are likely to enjoy moveable classroom furniture and opportunities for low-stakes formative assessment. But even with something as evolutionary as these changes, there is very little good cross-institutional data on postsecondary learning innovation. There are very few ways to track national trends about course redesign, active-learning classroom renovations, or the introduction of instructional designers as faculty collaborators. These data remain largely invisible within individual colleges and universities, much less across the entire post-secondary sector. In this epilogue, we endeavour to offer advice to those on our campuses interested in contributing to a more resilient strategy—one not dependent on the next educational fad—to promote and study learning innovation.

Advice to Presidents, Provosts, and Deans

This book has made a case that higher education is in the midst of an unrecognized but consequential turn to learning and that a new multi-disciplinary field of learning innovation is coalescing around this trend. If these claims are accurate, what then should the response be from academic leaders? What actions should those championing learning innovation now be contemplating? Our advice to presidents, provosts, and deans is to not wait for the next educational fad to come around to put learning innovation at the top of your agendas.

More than likely, there is already an enormous amount of learning innovation occurring at your school. The challenge is that this learning innovation is likely to be atomized, siloed, and disconnected. It will be occurring in the advances in teaching and learning being made by individual faculty members, often in ways that are out of step with the departments in which these professors are based. These professors are likely departmental outliers in their approach to teaching and learning by taking risks and investing time that is outside the normative expectations for faculty at most institutions. The work to innovate one's teaching is time and energy intensive. Doing new things in one's classroom brings the risk of poor student evaluations. Students often balk at the demands of active learning. Passively absorbing lectures is easier than actively constructing one's learning. Students may be entertained by a charismatic professor giving a performative lecture. There is little correlation, however, between student reports of course quality in course reviews and the degree to which they learn. Significant time investments and the risk of poor student course evaluations will inhibit professors from investing in learning innovation. Tenure and promotion policies that do not recognize the introduction of active learning techniques into teaching will also discourage faculty from working with learning organizations to redesign their courses and experimenting with new teaching methodologies. Academic leaders should be aware of, and honest about, the disincentives for faculty to invest their time in learning innovation. They should not shy away from articulating the challenges that professors face in treating their teaching as a disciplined experiment. Presidents, provosts, and deans should take every opportunity to increase the status of the work of faculty engaged in learning innovation.

Too often, academic leaders believe themselves limited in setting institutional priorities due to funding constraints. When it comes to learning, however, money is only one of the tools available to drive change. What may be just as important as dollars are ideas. Academic leaders have the power to advance an agenda through the messages that they deliver. Presidents, provosts, and deans have the power to convene. Their presence at campus meetings and events can lend gravitas to the agenda. Developing—and sticking to—a clear set of talking points on where learning innovation aligns with institutional mission is among the most powerful options that university leaders can exercise. A willingness to bring up at every opportunity the areas where learning innovation is occurring can ensure that this work is recognized. The more visible projects and initiatives that advance learning are, the more other constituents on campus will want to join. University leaders who are genuinely interested in how postsecondary learning is changing, and who stay on top of trends on campus and across higher education, can catalyze learning innovation at their institutions. Part of the shift that academic leaders must make is to reconceptualize existing university operations within a learning innovation framework. The best example of this shift would be to contextualize existing online educational programs as part of an institution-wide research and development effort. This shift will require the foresight to change the focus of online programs away from a predominantly revenue-generating objective and toward one designed to improve teaching and learning across the institution. This goal to leverage online learning initiatives to advance student learning, especially in traditional face-to-face courses, runs counter to how these distance programs are often implemented. Too often, online education programs and the staff that run them are segregated from residential courses.

For university leaders, the cause of supporting learning innovation efforts need not be dependent on the ability to allocate new resources toward these initiatives. Of course, we'd be overjoyed if this book convinced a president, provost, or dean to place learning innovation at the center of their strategic fundraising and investment priorities. By all means, please feel free to steer dollars toward your centers for teaching and learning (CTLs), academic computing units, online learning divisions, and schools of professional education. We think that those investments will pay off in greater access and equity, lower rates of attrition for existing students, the ability to grow the student body through online education, and through improved student learning. We are acutely aware, however, that every campus stakeholder is clamoring for scarce resources. Learning professionals—and the learning organizations in which they work—are no different. While budgets are constrained, one asset that campus leaders do have are platforms to promote ideas. We ask that presidents, provosts, and deans use their platforms to promote the idea of learning innovation.

Our other advice for university leaders is to find opportunities to make a place for campus learning professionals at strategic institutional tables. The core work of every college and university is advancing student learning. Learning professionals, outside of traditional faculty leaders, are only sometimes invited to play a role in setting long-term institutional directions. Many of the learning innovators we spoke with in preparation for writing this book indicated how rare it was to find the director of a CTL, or a dean of an online learning unit, enjoying membership in a president's cabinet. How frequently are campus learning professionals included in search committees for high-level academic appointments? Those who have find the experience and the connections incredibly valuable to their work. The visibility and influence of the leadership of campus learning organizations is often mediated by the provost or dean to whom they report. In the best case, these academic leaders are also knowledgeable champions of learning innovation. In all cases, the long-term efforts to place innovation and learning R&D into the DNA of institutional practices can be set two steps back should the related provost or dean end up moving on. Careful thought should be given to how campus leaders who focus on learning innovation, and the organizations that they lead, can be integrated into the durable and visible governance structures of the institution.

Reinforcing Learning Innovation

Throughout this book we have argued that we are in the midst of a turn to learning. This turn is the result of no single event or trend but rather of the confluence of many factors that came to an inflection point in 2012 to create something new across the higher education ecosystem. This confluence rose from the diffusion of learning science across and within universities—with a particular focus on active learning and student-centered design principles—and the maturation of educational technologies, as represented primarily by the ubiquity of the learning management system. The growth of online education and the impact of the MOOC bubble in coalescing new conversations about learning science helped continue this turn. Finally, widespread efforts to reorganize campus learning organizations, either through the development of integrated CTLs or through close collaborations of learning professionals across institutional organizational boundaries, confirmed the importance of this emphasis on learning throughout the higher education ecosystem.

We believe this turn to learning marks a moment in higher education that is important to reinforce. We can do so by investing in learning innovators and the organizations they support. We can do so with research and scholarship, with open discussions about the problems, challenges, and opportunities that drive higher education, and with a full understanding and critical engagement of the history of learning in higher education. This turn to learning should be considered more of a hypothesis than a definitive description of higher education change. It may be that the new institutional focus on learning innovation that we observe is a mirage, the product more of wishful thinking than an actual event. Or it could be that a focus on learning innovation exists at a few schools—particularly well-resourced institutions—and therefore does not add up to a meaningful trend. It may be that we are right about the turn to learning but wrong in our judgement of its impact and durability. It could be argued that describing the institutional inputs to student learning is a misguided approach and that a better lens to understanding learning in higher education is to look at student learning outcomes.

Or it may be that we are in a time of fundamental change in how teaching and learning is constructed in higher education, a legitimate turn to learning, but that we have identified the wrong factors in describing and explaining this trend. We believe these potential understandings of this turn to learning are all worth exploring further.

One place to begin, we've argued, is with the learning organizations that are supporting this work. The organizational changes that are happening at our home institutions of Dartmouth and Georgetown as well as those at Boston University, CSU Channel Islands, Davidson, Duke, Michigan, Yale, and many others reflect this momentum. Our hypothesis—derived both from research conducted for this book and our experience being embedded in a network of higher education learning professionals—is that change in learning organizations is more widespread across the higher education ecosystem than is commonly recognized. Many colleges and universities have experienced or are planning significant organizational changes in support of learning innovation. These changes include an emphasis on learning R&D, a commitment to integrate the research on learning into teaching practices, and efforts to connect advances in online and residential education with each other. Much is happening around blended learning, classroom redesign, and the desire to bring active and experiential learning opportunities to introductory and gateway courses. At some schools there is a focus on learning analytics with the goal of making data-driven teaching decisions. While at others, the focus is on evolving traditional educational practices to better align with a commitment to inclusive pedagogy and a goal to educate the whole person.

There is no single template that colleges and universities are following to prioritize learning innovation, and this speaks to the strength and potential of this work. One challenge in getting a handle on this trend is that the choices and actions within individual schools around learning innovation vary so widely. With the exception of a few schools, such as Duke, learning innovation initiatives seldom fly under the banner of "Learning Innovation." These initiatives sometimes occur within CTLs but are as likely to occur in other learning organizations such as academic computing units, distance learning departments, continuing and professional education schools, the academic library, academic incubators, or other places. Traditionally, each of these learning organizations mentioned had its own professional organization and community of practice. Members of learning organizations have developed identities—as educational developers and instructional designers and assessment experts and librarians—that are professionally distinct. More and more, however, the professional and organizational boundaries of learning professionals and the organizations in which they work no longer reflect how teaching and learning play out on our campuses. To a degree that is greater than at any time in higher education history, teaching is becoming a team sport. Professors partner with a wide range of nonfaculty learning professionals in the development of their blended and online courses. Even professors who still design, run, and evaluate their own courses do so in a teaching environment—both physical classrooms and digital learning platforms—that has been designed, implemented, and supported by learning professionals. Teaching and learning in higher education is becoming more complex and resource intensive. The changes in the makeup and activities of learning organizations are both a response to and driver for this intensification. We think that this trend deserves much more attention, debate, and critical scholarship. We believe colleges and universities must fully commit to the turn to learning, and a strategy of prioritizing learning innovation is higher education's best defense against disruption.

Theories of Higher Education Change

In this book we also argue that the theory of disruptive innovation, as developed by Clayton Christensen, is a poor framework from which to understand or guide change in higher education. When it comes to understanding how learning is changing, the theory of disruptive innovation is particularly unsuited to the task. The need to address and then unpack disruption theory as it relates to learning innovation is particularly important because this framework has become the dominant lens in which this phenomenon is viewed. In many instances, ideas around innovation and disruption have merged so that the two concepts are utilized almost interchangeably. This is unfortunate, as a disruption orientation toward advancing learning innovation is likely to be ineffective. Arguments around the impact of new learning technologies in "disrupting" higher education are commonly made without reference to the long history of educational innovation. In chapter 3 we highlighted perhaps the most "revolutionary" educational technology of them all, the now little remembered 1960s-era PLATO system. We wonder if a technology as truly different and advanced for its time as PLATO could fail to do much to disrupt learning; shouldn't we be more circumspect in making claims about future technologically driven disruptions in higher education?

In rejecting disruption theory as a framework to understand and guide learning innovation, we make the argument that we need to replace it with something better. This theoretical framework to make sense of learning innovation must be homegrown from within higher education. The days when we can import a theory from other industries and then retrofit it to make sense of how learning is changing within our colleges and universities should be over. A theory of learning innovation should start from an understanding that dynamic change has been a feature of higher education since the development of the earliest colleges and universities. To characterize higher education as static is to fundamentally misread its history and to undervalue the contributions of all those who have given so much to make our institutions places of opportunity and knowledge creation. As we argue in this book, there is too much that is good about higher education to think that "disrupting" our colleges and universities is how we should think about innovation.

When it comes to learning, theories of innovation also must account for the sheer scale and diversity of the learners that the system serves. The plurality of all undergraduates now attend community colleges. Public institutions operate under conditions of endemic underfunding combined with ever-increasing levels of demand. How community colleges, and other institutions that are similarly resource constrained, will both drive and benefit from learning innovations are among the most important questions facing our community. This is also one of the areas that is the least well explored in this book. Despite our own blind spots when it comes to understanding and describing learning innovation at community colleges and similar institutions—a deficiency we hope to address in subsequent scholarship—we are acutely aware that any theories about learning change that fail to integrate this sector will be incomplete. Theories to explain and guide higher education learning innovation should start from where most students are educated, and today those places are community colleges and other public institutions. Theories of learning innovation based on the experiences of a small number of disproportionately wealthy private institutions can't be generalized to the higher education sector as a whole. Just as disruption theory left community colleges and their students bereft of any helpful framework to advance learning (or really anything else), alternative theories of learning innovation will need to avoid this outcome.

The Next Learning Innovation Conversation

Centering learning innovation discussions within events sponsored by professional organizations has done much to bring visibility to the turn to learning within professional circles but little to extend this visibility to the larger higher education community. Most professors remain wary of the ideas and practices espoused by administrators. In large part this is a rational and perhaps justified response among faculty given the dominance of disruption talk among the boosters of learning innovation. Seldom are larger institutional issues such as financing and demographics brought deeply into conversations about learning innovation. The efficacy of learning innovation will depend heavily on pulling the conversations out of social media and professional associations. The social media back channel has emerged as an indispensable complement to professional conferences, but it does little to change the larger conversations on campuses. The cross-institutional networks that were once mostly nurtured at annual meetings have been extended and amplified through social media. The various groups within the larger learning community are highly networked, tied closely together through common values and a willingness to share information. Social media enables cross-institutional connections between learning innovators to persist and strengthen between professional gatherings. However, the conversations about learning innovation within professional organizations most often occur between learning professionals occupying similar campus roles. Educational developers and instructional designers and online learning managers speak with each other. It is rarer for them to have the opportunity to speak with professors, much less deans or provosts, from other institutions as colleagues and collaborators. Learning innovation conversations are too often restricted to areas of pedagogy and technology or program design and pilot projects. We have made the case that the dividing line between academics who study higher education and nonfaculty educators who work on learning initiatives should be more often crossed. Schools could reclassify instructional designers and faculty developers as educators (or learning innovators) rather than staff. Campus learning professionals could be asked to participate more in the strategic governance of the schools where they work. Presidents, provosts, and deans could stress the centrality of learning innovation when relating their visions for the future of their institutions.

What can higher education learning innovators do to ensure that the turn to learning of the last few years does not end up being an anomaly in the larger story of higher education transformation? Waiting for academic leaders to recognize the strategic importance of learning innovation to their institutions—and to direct commensurate resources and attention to these efforts—does not seem like the wisest course of action. Academic leaders are under enormous pressures to navigate their schools through the existential challenges of funding erosion, demographic change, and cost disease. Giving the attention to advancing learning that it needs to succeed is unlikely. While fully committing to working with academic leaders and professors to elevate learning innovation on our campuses, learning innovators can do much to drive change even as the slow process of institutional change plays out. Learning professionals can evolve their perspectives to encompass an organizational, and even system-wide, perspective. They can complement their knowledge of how learning works at an individual level with expertise about the institutional structures that mediate the advancement of learning. They can become as much students of the history and economics and culture of higher education as they are of learning science.

Does a solution to this intersection of learning, organizational change, and learning professions exist in a rethinking of the academic nature of this work? Could a new interdisciplinary field of learning innovation be created? As we discussed in chapter 4, the argument that we should create a new interdisciplinary field of learning innovation is among the most actively disputed claims that we have made. We are certain there will be many counterarguments to this idea in whatever reactions this book generates, and we think this debate is important to have. If we are to move forward with a deep investment in learning innovation, we need to do so with an open conversation about the field and its impact on higher education. We are rarely, however, in control of these kinds of intellectual shifts. One of the unavoidable ironies of the turn to learning, and the cross-institutional focus on learning innovation that we believe we are in the midst of, is that this trend was accelerated by MOOCs. The irony is that MOOCs, while interesting and important for many reasons, are also antithetical to so much of what actually matters in learning innovation. Recognizing the importance of MOOCs in energizing a different conversation about learning innovation on our campuses and across the larger higher education ecosystem, does not then directly lead to a plan to build on this conversation once everyone has moved on to the next educational fad.

As we argue throughout this book, building a theory and a set of practices to advance learning innovation around the next technological disruption is a direct path to irrelevance. Technology, on its own, does not advance learning. Technology can play a complementary role to every other element in the construction of student learning, but technology is never an effective substitute for either the work of the educator or the commitment of the institution. Unfortunately, too many who self-identify with the language of learning innovation have advanced a "technology-first" outlook, having failed to listen to educators and learners about what they really need or want. This has given the practice of learning innovation a mixed, if not outright negative, reputation among the constituents (the professors and the students) that it should be serving.

Leaders of learning innovation need to own up to this mixed track record. We need to discover how to have a different sort of conversation (we argue for a more critical and scholarly conversation) with our faculty partners.

As we have said, many of the ideas that we have explored in this book are incomplete. While we believe we are living through a postsecondary turn to learning, we cannot claim this turn is stable or ubiquitous. Where we see indications of colleges and universities reorganizing their operations and evolving their cultures to prioritize advancing student learning, we are unable to ground these observations in data. The experiences with learning innovation at our institutions, and among our community of practice in which our ideas have been nurtured, may not be representative of the larger postsecondary ecosystem. The critique that we are overly influenced by the recent history of the selective and well-resourced institutions that are similar to our own is fair, as is the recognition that our ideas about a higher education turn to learning are US-centric. We submit, however, that putting forth the idea of a turn to learning as an observation to be challenged is aligned with our larger argument that a new interdisciplinary field needs to be created. This field would take as one of its core questions that of how colleges and universities are changing to advance student learning. Practitioners in this discipline would broaden their investigations to encompass all institutions. They would aim to achieve what we have only gestured at, that is definitive and evidence-based conclusions about learning changes across higher education.

The Future of Learning Innovation

If a new field of learning innovation is a path worth exploring, the investigation of how institutions change to advance learning should not wait for its creation. We have most of the pieces in place today to engage in that scholarship and to teach that research to students of higher education. The integration of learning science and the study of organizational change can occur as part of the ongoing scholarship of teaching and learning work of CTLs, academic computing units, and other campus learning organizations. Professors of higher education can be brought more deeply into the work of learning innovation that is occurring wherever new online programs are being built or where new technologies and methods are being introduced into face-to-face courses.

Teaching and learning have never been static activities. They have evolved and changed as our institutions have also gone through massive shifts. The recent turn to learning across the higher education sector has been so consequential because it has been at a system-wide scale. It has occurred within the incumbent institutions that educate millions of students, and not within the small start-ups that seek to disrupt the higher education sector. When it comes to learning innovation, the ideas that have been advanced to explain change in higher education have often obscured as much as they have enlightened. We're afraid that learning innovation will fail to gain a firm footing in higher education or live up to its potential to significantly improve the quality of student learning, unless those leading institutional efforts evolve their work from a professional practice to a scholarly pursuit. Learning innovation needs to develop a set of ideas, and a collection of research and scholarship, to match its methods.

The future of learning innovation by definition needs to be contextualized within the structural challenges that higher education faces. How learning advances in the face of challenging economic, demographic, and competitive headwinds is among the most important of questions that anyone studying the future of higher education should seek to answer. The case we are making about why colleges and universities should invest in learning innovation needs to be shared. This case gets more challenging to make as colleges fight to discover a path toward economic sustainability in the face of public disinvestment, a drop in the number of traditional college-age students in many regions, and new competitors for student enrollments. Long-term investments in advancing learning should not be limited to a few wealthy and high-profile institutions. Learning innovation should be broad-based, showing up as a strategic priority for academic leaders across the higher education ecosystem.

The work of higher education learning innovation will never reach its potential unless the ideas of learning innovation take firm root and spread rhizomatically.[4] All the activity around new forms and methods of teaching and learning in recent years has been vastly exciting. As we have tried to demonstrate in this book, we are in the midst of a higher education teaching and learning renaissance, albeit a fragile one. The nonfaculty educators who have partnered with professors to bring about this turn to learning, as well as the faculty developers in CTLs and instructional designers in academic computing and online learning units, are often too busy doing the work of learning innovation to study learning innovation. Professors of higher education remain largely disconnected from the hands-on on-the-ground work of running the organizations and initiatives most responsible for higher education's turn to learning. The work of campus learning professionals is at times too applied, and the scholarship of higher education professors is too abstract. Ideas about learning innovation will not emerge until the practice and scholarship of learning innovation come together.

Those of us immersed in learning innovation projects and initiatives need to develop the space, time, and freedom to think and write about this work in the context in which the work is done. Campus learning organizations in which learning innovation operations, projects, and initiatives are based need to expand their missions to incorporate scholarship—and we believe teaching—as coequal priorities with service. The ideas of learning innovators should be widely circulating across the broader debates about the future of higher education. It is time for the story of the institutional changes that are catalyzing learning innovations across higher education to receive the attention and scholarly investigation it deserves.

Introduction. A Turn to Learning

1. See, for example, Harvard University's Technology, Innovation, and Education Program; Stanford University's Learning, Design, and Technology Program; and Penn State's Learning Sciences and Technologies Program.

2. Steven Leckart, "The Stanford Education Experiment Could Change Higher Learning Forever," *Wired*, March 20, 2012, https://www.wired.com /2012/03/ff_aiclass/.

3. "Countries Arranged by Number of Universities in Top Ranks," Ranking Web of Universities, July 2018 edition, accessed March 25, 2019, http://www .webometrics.info/en/node/54.

Chapter 1. Foundations of the Learning Revolution

1. Academic Innovation: University of Michigan (website), Regents of the University of Michigan, accessed July 30, 2018, http://ai.umich.edu/.

2. University of Michigan, "Office of Academic Innovation Increases Experimentation and Leads Presidential Initiative," press release, accessed August 1, 2018, http://ai.umich.edu/blog/office-of-academic-innovation -increases-experimentation-and-leads-presidential-initiative/.

3. Quoted in University of Michigan, "Office of Academic Innovation Increases Experimentation and Leads Presidential Initiative."

4. Nancy Chick, "A Scholarly Approach to Teaching," *Scholarship of Teaching and Learning Guide* (online), Vanderbilt University Center for Teaching, accessed July 30, 2018, https://my.vanderbilt.edu/sotl/understanding -sotl/a-scholarly-approach-to-teaching/.

5. John D. Bransford, Ann L. Brown, and Rodney R. Cocking, eds., *How People Learn: Brain, Mind, Experience, and School* (Washington, DC: National Academies Press, 2000).

6. Bransford, Brown, and Cocking, *How People Learn*, 2.

7. This account of the history, contours, and impact of SoTL draws heavily on the Vanderbilt Center for Teaching's *Scholarship of Teaching and Learning Guide*. See Nancy Chick, *Scholarship of Teaching and Learning Guide* (online) (Nashville, TN: Vanderbilt University Center for Teaching, n.d.), https://my .vanderbilt.edu/sotl/.

8. Ernest L. Boyer, *Scholarship Reconsidered: Priorities of the Professoriate* (Princeton, NJ: Carnegie Foundation for the Advancement of Teaching, 1990).

9. Charles E. Glassick, Mary Taylor Huber, and Gene I. Maeroff, *Scholarship Assessed: Evaluation of the Professoriate*. An Ernest L. Boyer Project of the Carnegie Foundation for the Advancement of Teaching (San Francisco: Jossey-Bass, 1997).

10. "ISSOTL: History," International Society for the Scholarship of Teaching and Learning, accessed December 18, 2018, http://www.indiana.edu/~issotl /history.html.

11. "*Teaching and Learning Inquiry*: The ISSOTL Journal," International Society for the Scholarship of Teaching and Learning, accessed December 15, 2018, http://www.indiana.edu/~issotl/TLI.html.

12. Rhea Kelly, "Survey: Blended Learning on the Rise," *Campus Technology*, September 20, 2017, https://campustechnology.com/articles/2017/09/20 /survey-blended-learning-on-the-rise.aspx.

13. Nicole Dudenhoefer, "UCF Now Manages Course Redesign Resources from Online Learning Pioneer NCAT," *UCF Today*, February 13, 2019, https://today.ucf.edu/ucf-now-manages-course-redesign-resources-online -learning-pioneer-ncat/.

14. Carol A. Twigg, "Improving Learning and Reducing Costs: Fifteen Years of Course Redesign," *Change: The Magazine of Higher Learning* 47, no. 6 (2015): 4, https://doi.org/10.1080/00091383.2015.1089753.

15. Kim Kankiewicz, "There's No Erasing the Chalkboard," *Atlantic*, October 13, 2016, https://www.theatlantic.com/technology/archive/2016/10 /theres-no-erasing-the-chalkboard/503975/.

16. Phil Hill, "LMS Is the Minivan of Education (and Other Thoughts from #LILI15)," *E-Literate*, May 7, 2015, http://mfeldstein.com/lms-is-the-minivan-of -education-and-other-thoughts-from-lili15/.

17. Audrey Watters, "Beyond the LMS (Beyond the VLE)," *Hack Education* (blog), September 5, 2014, http://hackeducation.com/2014/09/05/beyond-the -lms-newcastle-university.

18. "Top 6 Vendors in the Global Higher Education Market from 2017 to 2021: Technavio," *Business Wire*, March 09, 2017, http://www.businesswire.com /news/home/20170309005784/en/Top-6-Vendors-Global-Higher-Education -Market.

19. I. Elaine Allen and Jeff Seaman, *Digital Learning Compass: Distance Education Enrollment Report 2017* (Oakland, CA: Babson Survey Research Group, 2017), 18, https://onlinelearningsurvey.com/reports/digtiallearningcomp assenrollment2017.pdf.

20. Allen and Seaman, *Digital Learning Compass,* 20.

21. Ron Legon and Richard Garrett, *CHLOE: The Changing Landscape of Higher Education* (Quality Matters and Eduventures, 2017), 18, https://www .qualitymatters.org/sites/default/files/research-docs-pdfs/CHLOE-First-Survey -Report.pdf.

22. Robert Ubell, "Why Faculty Still Don't Want to Teach Online," *Inside Higher Ed*, December 13, 2016, https://www.insidehighered.com/advice/2016/12/13/advice-faculty-members-about-overcoming-resistance-teaching-online-essay.

23. Scott Jaschik and Doug Lederman, *2016 Inside Higher Ed Survey of Faculty Attitudes on Technology* (Washington, DC: Gallup and Inside Higher Ed, 2016), 20, https://www.insidehighered.com/booklet/2016-survey-faculty-attitudes-technology.

24. Jaschik and Lederman, *2016 Inside Higher Ed Survey of Faculty Attitudes on Technology*, 19.

25. Barbara Means, Yukie Toyama, Robert Murphy, Marianne Bakia, and Karla Jones, *Evaluation of Evidence-Based Practices in Online Learning: A Meta-Analysis and Review of Online Learning Studies* (Washington, DC: US Department of Education, 2009), https://eric.ed.gov/?id=ED505824.

26. Tuan Nguyen, "The Effectiveness of Online Learning: Beyond No Significant Difference and Future Horizons," *MERLOT Journal of Online Learning and Teaching* 11, no. 2 (June 2015): 315, http://jolt.merlot.org/Vol11no2/Nguyen_0615.pdf.

27. Thomas L. Friedman, "Opinion: Come the Revolution," *New York Times*, May 15, 2017, https://nyti.ms/2wacH2y.

28. Laura Pappano, "The Year of the MOOC," *New York Times*, November 2, 2012, https://nyti.ms/2kBM8OV.

29. To understand how Gartner Research's hype cycle relates to MOOCs, see Joshua Kim, "How a MOOC Could Be a Faculty's Best Friend," *EdSurge*, May 22, 2013, https://www.edsurge.com/news/2013-05-21-opinion-how-a-mooc-could-be-a-faculty-s-best-friend and Wikipedia, s.v. "Massive Open Online Course," accessed December 18, 2018, https://en.wikipedia.org/wiki/Massive_open_online_course.

30. Even this origin is contested. Diversity University offered open online courses at scale in a modified multiplayer virtual reality world starting in 1993 (see Wikipedia, s.v. "Diversity University," last modified December 14, 2018, https://en.wikipedia.org/wiki/Diversity_University), and James O'Donnell claims the first MOOC in 1994 via Gopher and email (see Wikipedia, s.v. "James J. O'Donnell, last modified April 3, 2019, https://en.wikipedia.org/wiki/James_J._O%27Donnell).

31. Rolin Moe, "The Brief & Expansive History (and Future) of the MOOC: Why Two Divergent Models Share the Same Name," *Current Issues in Emerging eLearning* 2, no. 1 (2015), https://scholarworks.umb.edu/cgi/viewcontent.cgi?referer=&httpsredir=1&article=1009&context=ciee.

32. Wikipedia, s.v. "Massive Open Online Course."

33. Steven Leckart, "The Stanford Education Experiment Could Change Higher Learning Forever," *Wired*, March 20, 2012, https://www.wired.com/2012/03/ff_aiclass/.

34. Jeremy Hsu, "Professor Leaving Stanford for Online Education Startup," *NBCNews*, January 25, 2012, http://www.nbcnews.com/id/46138856/ns /technology_and_science-innovation/t/professor-leaving-stanford-online -education-startup.

35. Thomas L. Friedman, "Opinion: Revolution Hits the Universities," *New York Times*, January 26, 2013, https://nyti.ms/2jNJRwd.

36. Anh Nguyen, "Breaking through the Barriers to Postsecondary Education," *Impatient Optimists*, June 21, 2012, https://www.impatient optimists.org/Posts/2012/06/Breaking-Through-the-Barriers-to-Postsecondary -Education.

37. Amie Newman, "What Are 'MOOC's and Why Are Education Leaders Interested in Them?," *Huffington Post*, updated January 13, 2013, https://www .huffingtonpost.com/impatient-optimists/what-are-moocs-and-why-ar_b _2123399.html.

38. Andrew Rice, "Anatomy of a Campus Coup," *New York Times Magazine*, September 11, 2012, https://nyti.ms/2jRxVcV.

39. William J. Baumol and William G. Bowen, "On the Performing Arts: The Anatomy of Their Economic Problems," *American Economic Review* 55, no. 1/2, (1965): 495–502.

40. Max Chafkin, "Udacity's Sebastian Thrun, Godfather of Free Online Education, Changes Course," *Fast Company*, November 14, 2013, https://www .fastcompany.com/3021473/udacity-sebastian-thrun-uphill-climb.

41. Will Oremus, "University Suspends Online Classes after More Than Half the Students Fail," *Slate*, July 19, 2013, http://www.slate.com/blogs/future_tense /2013/07/19/san_jose_state_suspends_udacity_online_classes_after_students_fail _final.html.

42. Google Trends, s.v. "MOOCs," accessed October 5, 2017, https://trends .google.com.

43. See Phil Hill, "MOOCs Are Dead. Long Live Online Higher Education," *Chronicle of Higher Education*, August 26, 2016, https://www.chronicle .com/article/MOOCs-Are-Dead-Long-Live/237569 and John Warner, "MOOCs Are 'Dead.' What's Next? Uh-oh," *Inside Higher Ed*, October 11, 2017, https://www.insidehighered.com/blogs/just-visiting/moocs-are-dead -whats-next-uh-oh.

44. Dhawal Shah, "By the Numbers: MOOCS in 2016," *Class Central MOOC Report*, December 25, 2016, https://www.class-central.com/report /mooc-stats-2016/.

45. Courtney Lockemer, "CIT and Online Duke Are Now Duke Learning Innovation," Duke Learning Innovation blog, October 30, 2017, https:// learninginnovation.duke.edu/blog/2017/10/cit-online-duke-now-duke-learning -innovation/.

46. Bulleted list paraphrased from Lockemer, "CIT and Online Duke Are Now Duke Learning Innovation."

47. MJ Bishop and Anne Keehn, *Leading Academic Change: An Early Market Scan of Leading-Edge Postsecondary Academic Innovation Centers* (Adelphi, MD: William E. Kirwan Center for Academic Innovation, 2015), https://www.usmd.edu/cai/sites/default/files/LeadingAcademicChangeProjectRe port.pdf.

48. Bishop and Keehn, *Leading Academic Change*, 13.

49. "College Profiles," Colleges That Change Lives, accessed August 3, 2018, http://ctcl.org/category/college-profiles/.

50. See table 326.10 in "2016 Tables and Figures," *Digest of Education Statistics*, National Center for Education Statistics (NCES), US Department of Education, accessed July 30, 2018, https://nces.ed.gov/programs/digest/d16 /tables/dt16_326.10.asp.

51. Doug Lederman, "Study Raises Questions about Popular Assessment Tool," *Inside Higher Ed*, June 2, 2010, https://www.insidehighered.com /quicktakes/2010/06/02/study-raises-questions-about-popular-assessment-tool.

52. Doug Lederman, "Studies Challenge the Findings of 'Academically Adrift,'" *Inside Higher Ed*, May 20, 2013, https://www.insidehighered.com /news/2013/05/20/studies-challenge-findings-academically-adrift.

Chapter 2. Institutional Change

1. Roger L. Geiger, "The Ten Generations of American Higher Education," in *American Higher Education in the Twenty-First Century*, 4th ed., edited by Michael N. Bastedo, Philip G. Altbach, and Patricia J. Gumport (Baltimore, MD: Johns Hopkins University Press, 2016), 17–18.

2. Christopher J. Phillips, "An Officer and a Scholar: Nineteenth-Century West Point and the Invention of the Blackboard," *History of Education Quarterly* 55, no. 1 (2015): 82–108, https://doi.org/10.1111/hoeq.12093.

3. Libraries, of course, have long played a vital role in the success of teaching and learning in colleges and universities. This role has varied from passive repository of books and journals to active research partners to support spaces for dynamic teaching and research activities.

4. "Learning design" and "learning designers" are terms often used synonymously with "instructional design" and "instructional designer," while some programs intentionally focus on learning design to place the emphasis on learning rather than instruction.

5. Joshua Kim, "How Much Should We Be Spending on Learning R&D?," *Technology and Learning* (blog), *Inside Higher Ed*, March 1, 2017, https://www .insidehighered.com/blogs/technology-and-learning/how-much-should-we-be -spending-learning-rd.

6. Joshua Kim, "5 Questions for the Director of the Kirwan Center for Academic Innovation," *Technology and Learning* (blog), *Inside Higher Ed*, February 15, 2017, https://www.insidehighered.com/blogs/technology-and -learning/5-questions-director-kirwan-center-academic-innovation.

7. Digital Learning & Innovation (website), Boston University, https://digital
.bu.edu/.

8. Romy Ruukel (director, Digital Education Incubator, Boston University) in
discussion with the authors, December 2017.

9. "Projects," Digital Learning & Innovation, Boston University, accessed
December 19, 2018, https://digital.bu.edu/projects/.

10. Teaching and Learning Innovations (website), California State University
Channel Islands, https://www.csuci.edu/tli/.

11. Jacob Jenkins, "Channel Islands Blazes a Trail to Cut Textbook Costs,"
Ventura County Star, March 10, 2018, https://www.vcstar.com/story/opinion
/columnists/2018/03/10/channel-islands-blazes-trail-cut-textbook-costs
/412324002/.

12. Alexa D'Angelo, "CSU Channel Islands to Offer Two Textbook-Free
Majors and Has Plans for More," *Ventura County Star*, July 7, 2018, https://
www.vcstar.com/story/news/education/2018/07/07/csu-channel-islands-offer
-textbook-free-majors-fall/738949002/.

13. "Faculty Biographies: Jill M. Leafstedt," California State University
Channel Islands, accessed August 2, 2018, http://ciapps.csuci.edu/Faculty
Biographies/jill.leafstedt.

14. Kristen Eshleman, "Davidson College Incubator" (internal PowerPoint
presentation shared with the authors on October, 5, 2018).

15. Eshleman, "Davidson College Incubator."

16. Kristen Eshleman (director of digital innovation and education, Technology & Innovation, Davidson College) in discussion with the authors,
December 2017.

17. Jill Leafstedt, (director, Teaching and Learning Innovations, CSU
Channel Islands) in discussion with the authors, December 2017.

18. Kristen Eshleman (director of digital innovation and education,
Technology & Innovation, Davidson College) in discussion with the authors,
December 2017.

19. Academic Learning Transformation Lab (website), Virginia Commonwealth University, accessed December 20, 2018, https://altlab.vcu.edu/.

20. "About Us," Academic Learning Transformation Lab, Virginia Commonwealth University, accessed December 20, 2018, https://altlab.vcu.edu/about-us/.

21. "About Us," Academic Learning Transformation Lab.

Chapter 3. Reclaiming Innovation from Disruption

1. Doug Lederman, "Clay Christensen, Doubling Down," *Inside Higher Ed*,
April 28, 2017, https://www.insidehighered.com/digital-learning/article/2017/04
/28/clay-christensen-sticks-predictions-massive-college-closures.

2. Jim Rogers, "American Higher Education Is One of the Greatest Bubbles
of Our Time," *Business Insider*, January 13, 2015, http://www.businessinsider
.com/jim-rogers-higher-education-is-a-bubble-2015-1.

3. Jill Lepore, "What the Gospel of Innovation Gets Wrong," *New Yorker*, June 19, 2017, https://www.newyorker.com/magazine/2014/06/23/the -disruption-machine.

4. Doug Lederman, "Scenes from Ed-Tech Heaven (or Hell)," *Inside Higher Ed*, April 22, 2016, https://www.insidehighered.com/news/2016/04/22/modest -shifts-attendees-and-perspective-big-ed-tech-summit.

5. Michael Horn, "Disruptive Innovations in Higher Ed Emerging from Outside Mainstream," *Forbes*, July 23, 2015, https://www.forbes.com/sites /michaelhorn/2015/07/23/disruptive-innovations-in-higher-ed-emerging-from -outside-mainstream/.

6. Stuart M. Butler, "Rethinking College: Disruptive Innovation, Not Reform, Is Needed," *Social Mobility Memos* (blog), Brookings, October 23, 2015, https://www.brookings.edu/blog/social-mobility-memos/2015/10/23 /rethinking-college-disruptive-innovation-not-reform-is-needed/.

7. Brett Crandall, "Idaho Releases Fall 2016 Enrollment Figures," *BYU- Idaho Newsroom*, October 12, 2016, http://www.byui.edu/newsroom/10-12-16 -enrollment-fall-2016.

8. Matt Morava, "Higher Education Is Broken, but Not How You Imagine," *Medium*, May 23, 2016, https://medium.com/manager-mint/higher-education-is -broken-but-not-how-you-imagine-ee8cde68d92.

9. Mark Toner, "The Highly Endangered Higher Education Business Model (and How to Fix It)," *American Council on Education*, June 12, 2015, http:// www.acenet.edu/the-presidency/columns-and-features/Pages/The-Highly -Endangered-Higher-Education-Business-Model.aspx.

10. Kellie Woodhouse, "Closures to Triple," *Inside Higher Ed*, September 28, 2015, https://www.insidehighered.com/news/2015/09/28/moodys-predicts -college-closures-triple-2017.

11. Richard Vedder, "Are Small Town Liberal Arts Colleges Endangered?," *Forbes*, December 23, 2016, https://www.forbes.com/sites/ccap/2016/12/23 /small-town-liberal-arts-college-r-i-p/.

12. Parthenon-EY Education practice, *Strength in Numbers: Strategies for Collaborating in a New Era for Higher Education* (Ernst & Young, 2016), http://cdn.ey.com/parthenon/pdf/perspectives/P-EY_Strength-in-Numbers -Collaboration-Strategies_Paper_Final_082016.pdf.

13. ASU+GSV Summit (website), accessed December 5, 2017, https://www .asugsvsummit.com/.

14. Derek Thompson, "The Print Apocalypse and How to Survive It," *Atlantic*, November 3, 2016, https://www.theatlantic.com/business/archive/2016 /11/the-print-apocalypse-and-how-to-survive-it/506429/.

15. "Newspapers Fact Sheet," State of the News Media, Pew Research Center, June 13, 2018, http://www.journalism.org/fact-sheet/newspapers/.

16. See table 314.10 in "2015 Tables and Figures," *Digest of Education Statistics*, National Center for Education Statistics (NCES), US Department of

Education, accessed July 30, 2018, https://nces.ed.gov/programs/digest/d15 /tables/dt15_314.10.asp.

17. Association of Jesuit Colleges and Universities (website), accessed July 30, 2018, http://www.ajcunet.edu/.

18. Consortium on Financing Higher Education (website), accessed July 30, 2018, http://web.mit.edu/cofhe/.

19. Gail O. Mellow, "The Biggest Misconception about Today's College Students," *New York Times*, August 28, 2017, https://nyti.ms/2vCozUz.

20. Danielle Douglas-Gabriel, "There's a Big Catch in Obama's Plan for Free Community College," *Washington Post*, January 9, 2015, https://www .washingtonpost.com/news/wonk/wp/2015/01/09/the-big-thing-missing-in -president-obamas-plan-for-free-community-college.

21. Mellow, "The Biggest Misconception about Today's College Students."

22. Richard D. Kahlenberg, *How Higher Education Funding Shortchanges Community Colleges* (Century Foundation, 2015), 4, https://tcf.org/assets /downloads/Kahlenberg_FundingShortchanges.pdf.

23. Matthew Lynch, "5 Trends Disrupting Higher Education," *Edvocate*, January 3, 2018, https://www.theedadvocate.org/5-trends-disrupting-higher -education/.

24. Audrey Watters, *Teaching Machines: A Hack Education Project* (blog), accessed July 30, 2018, http://teachingmachin.es/.

25. Todd Oppenheimer, "The Flickering Mind," *New York Times*, January 4, 2004, https://nyti.ms/2MK9znT.

26. William Levenson, *Teaching through Radio* (New York: Farrar & Rinehart, 1945), 457.

27. Todd Oppenheimer, "The Computer Delusion," *Atlantic*, July 1997, http://www.tnellen.com/ted/tc/computer.htm.

28. Audrey Watters, "The Flying Classroom: The Midwest Program on Airborne Television Instruction," *Hack Education* (blog), May 14, 2015, http://hackeducation.com/2015/05/14/mpati.

29. Oppenheimer, "The Flickering Mind."

30. Bill Ferster, *Teaching Machines: Learning from the Intersection of Education and Technology* (Baltimore, MD: Johns Hopkins University Press, 2014), 101.

31. Rolin Moe, "Making 'Academic Innovation' Meaningful," *Inside Higher Ed*, May 16, 2018, https://www.insidehighered.com/digital-learning/views/2018 /05/16/risks-treating-academic-innovation-discipline-opinion.

32. "Fast Facts: Back to School Statistics, Elementary and Secondary Education," National Center for Education Statistics, accessed July 30, 2018, https://nces.ed.gov/fastfacts/display.asp?id=372.

33. For a snapshot of the scale and reach of existing educational institutions, see "Fast Facts: Educational Institutions," National Center for Education Statistics, accessed July 31, 2018, https://nces.ed.gov/fastfacts/display.asp?id=84.

34. "Higher Ed Presidents Are Serving Shorter Tenures. New Research Shows Why," *EAB Daily Briefing*, November 16, 2016, https://www.eab.com/daily-briefing/2016/11/16/higher-ed-presidents-are-serving-shorter-tenures-new-research-shows-why.

35. Allison Schrager and Amy X. Wang, "Imagine How Great Universities Could Be without All Those Human Teachers," *Quartz*, September 20, 2017, https://qz.com/1065818/ai-university/.

36. Dominic Basulto, "Watch Out College Professors, the Robots Are Coming for Your Jobs," *Washington Post*, June 2, 2015, https://www.washingtonpost.com/news/innovations/wp/2015/06/02/watch-out-college-professors-the-robots-are-coming-for-your-jobs/.

37. George Veletsianos and Rolin Moe, "The Rise of Educational Technology as a Sociocultural and Ideological Phenomenon," *EDUCAUSE Review*, April 10, 2017, https://er.educause.edu/articles/2017/4/the-rise-of-educational-technology-as-a-sociocultural-and-ideological-phenomenon.

Chapter 4. The Scholarship of Learning

1. "US Higher Education Technology Conferences 2018," EdSurge, accessed December 19, 2018, https://go.edsurge.com/US-Higher-Education-Technology-Conference-Calendar-2018.html.

2. A notable exception may be at the Digital Pedagogy Lab gatherings, which have developed a reputation of approaching learning innovation work from a critical scholarly perspective.

3. Michael Feldstein, "Some Thoughts on OER," *ELiterate*, June 7, 2018, https://mfeldstein.com/some-thoughts-on-oer/.

4. "Instructions for Authors," *Journal of Higher Education*, accessed July 31, 2018, https://www.tandfonline.com/action/authorSubmission.

5. "Author Guidelines," Johns Hopkins University Press, accessed July 31, 2018, https://www.press.jhu.edu/journals/review-higher-education/author-guidelines.

6. "*Innovative Higher Education*: Instructions for Authors," accessed June 10, 2019, https://www.springer.com/cda/content/document/cda_downloaddocument/instruction+for+authors+ihie.pdf?sgwid=0-0-45-428798-p35612147.

7. Eli Cohen and Scott J. Lloyd, "Disciplinary Evolution and the Rise of the Transdiscipline," *Informing Science: The International Journal of an Emerging Transdiscipline* 17 (2014): 189–215, http://www.inform.nu/Articles/Vol17/ISJv17p189-215Cohen0702.pdf.

8. Arti, "Development of Education as a Discipline: An Analytical Study" (PhD thesis, University of Lucknow, 2014), 74, http://hdl.handle.net/10603/70652.

9. Arti, "Development of Education as a Discipline: An Analytical Study," 74.

10. Janice M. Beyer and Thomas M. Lodahl, "A Comparative Study of Patterns of Influence in United States and English Universities," *Administrative Science Quarterly* 21, no. 1 (1976): 104–29, doi:10.2307/2391882.

11. Donald Hambrick and Ming-Jer Chen, "New Academic Fields as Admittance-Seeking Social Movements: The Case of Strategic Management," *Academy of Management Review* 33, no. 1 (2008): 34, https://www.jstor.org /stable/20159375.

12. Hambrick and Chen, "New Academic Fields as Admittance-Seeking Social Movements," 34–35.

13. Hambrick and Chen, "New Academic Fields as Admittance-Seeking Social Movements," 35.

14. "1940 Statement of Principles on Academic Freedom and Tenure," American Association of University Professors, accessed August 2, 2018, https:// www.aaup.org/report/1940-statement-principles-academic-freedom-and-tenure.

15. Elizabeth L. Spaid, "Women's Studies Matures as an Academic Discipline," *Christian Science Monitor*, March 22, 1993, https://www.csmonitor.com /1993/0322/22121.html.

16. "Study of Women & Gender," Smith College, accessed August 2, 2018, https://www.smith.edu/swg/graduate.php.

17. Michael Reynolds, Shobha Shagle, and Lekha Venkataraman, *A National Census of Women's and Gender Studies Programs in U.S. Institutions of Higher Education* (Chicago: National Opinion Research Center, 2007), https://www.nwsa.org/Files/Resources/NWSA_CensusonWSProgs.pdf.

18. Michele Tracy Berger, "Learning from Women's Studies," *Contexts* 12, no. 2 (2013): 76–79, https://journals.sagepub.com/doi/pdf/10.1177 /1536504213487706.

19. Adrian Simpson, "The Surprising Persistence of Biglan's Classification Scheme," *Studies in Higher Education* 42, no. 8 (2015): 1520–31, https://www .tandfonline.com/doi/abs/10.1080/03075079.2015.1111323.

20. *Information Technology—An Academic Discipline* (Association for Computing Machinery, 2011), http://www.sigite.org/wp-content/uploads/2011 /03/IT-Discipline-Summary.pdf.

21. Hambrick and Chen, "New Academic Fields as Admittance-Seeking Social Movements."

22. Sheldon Greaves, "Strategic Security as a New Academic Discipline," *Journal of Strategic Security* 1, no. 1 (2008): 7–20, https://scholarcommons.usf .edu/jss/vol1/iss1/2/.

23. William C. Clark, "Sustainability Science: A Room of Its Own," *Proceedings of the National Academy of Sciences* 104, no. 6 (2007): 1737–38, https:// www.pnas.org/content/104/6/1737.

24. Carl Straumsheim, "Contours of a New Discipline," *Inside Higher Ed*, May 16, 2016, https://www.insidehighered.com/news/2016/05/16/train-future -ed-tech-leaders-higher-ed-needs-new-discipline-some-say.

25. Joshua Kim, "Learning Innovation Is Evolving into an Academic Discipline," *Inside Higher Ed*, April 26, 2018, https://www.insidehighered.com/blogs/technology-and-learning/learning-innovation-evolving-academic-discipline.

26. Connie Schroeder, *Coming in from the Margins: Faculty Development's Emerging Organizational Development Role in Institutional Change* (Sterling, VA: Stylus, 2011).

27. For some departments, such as Creative Writing, the terminal degree may be an MFA rather than a PhD.

28. Rolin Moe, "Making 'Academic Innovation' Meaningful," *Inside Higher Ed*, May 16, 2018, https://www.insidehighered.com/digital-learning/views/2018/05/16/risks-treating-academic-innovation-discipline-opinion.

Chapter 5. Leading the Revolution

1. Tony Bates, "Comparing xMOOCs and cMOOCs: Philosophy and Practice," *Online Learning and Distance Education Resources*, October 13, 2014, https://www.tonybates.ca/2014/10/13/comparing-xmoocs-and-cmoocs-philosophy-and-practice/.

2. "U.S. College Dropout Statistics," CollegeAtlas.org, last updated June 29, 2018, https://www.collegeatlas.org/college-dropout.html.

3. Caroline Simon, "Bureaucrats and Buildings: The Case for Why College Is So Expensive," *Forbes*, September 5, 2017, https://www.forbes.com/sites/carolinesimon/2017/09/05/bureaucrats-and-buildings-the-case-for-why-college-is-so-expensive/.

4. Robert Kelchen, "Is Administrative Bloat Really a Big Problem?," May 10, 2018, https://robertkelchen.com/2018/05/10/is-administrative-bloat-a-problem/.

5. "About Harold McGraw Jr.," McGraw Center for Teaching and Learning, Princeton University, accessed August 1, 2018, https://mcgraw.princeton.edu/about/about-harold-mcgraw-jr.

6. "William Jackson: Transforming the Student Learning Experience," Michigan Technological University, accessed August 1, 2018, https://www.mtu.edu/giving/donor/recognition/lifetime/major/jackson.html.

7. "CTL History," Connecticut College, accessed August 1, 2018, https://www.conncoll.edu/offices/center-for-teaching--learning/ctl-history/.

8. "Barnard College Receives Largest Combined Gift in 126-Year History," Barnard College News, January 28, 2016, https://barnard.edu/news/barnard-college-receives-largest-combined-gift-126-year-history.

9. Jon Marcus, "Graduate Programs Have Become a Cash Cow for Struggling Colleges. What Does that Mean for Students?," *PBS*, September 18, 2017, https://www.pbs.org/newshour/education/graduate-programs-become-cash-cow-struggling-colleges-mean-students.

10. Phil Hill, "OPM Market May Be Growing, but It's Not without Chaos," *Eliterate*, May 7, 2018, https://mfeldstein.com/opm-market-may-be-growing-but-its-not-without-chaos/.

Epilogue. The Future of Learning Innovation

1. "Commission on Creating the Next in Education: Report Home," Office of the Provost, Georgia Institute of Technology, accessed March 27, 2018, http://www.provost.gatech.edu/cne-home.

2. Lindsay McKenzie, "Online, Cheap—and Elite," *Inside Higher Ed*, March 20, 2018, https://www.insidehighered.com/digital-learning/article/2018/03/20/analysis-shows-georgia-tech's-online-masters-computer-science.

3. Doug Lederman, "Lessons Learned from a $75 Million Failed Experiment," *Inside Higher Ed*, February 21, 2018, https://www.insidehighered.com/digital-learning/article/2018/02/21/lessons-learned-shuttering-universitys-internal-digital-learning.

4. Dave Cormier, "Rhizomatic Learning—Why We Teach?," *Dave's Educational Blog*, DaveCormier.com, November 5, 2011, http://davecormier.com/edblog/2011/11/05/rhizomatic-learning-why-learn/.

Academically Adrift: Limited Learning on College Campuses (Arum and Roksa), 50–51, 84, 177
academic computing units, 71, 135, 143, 183–84
academic departments, comparison with learning organizations, 135–36
academic disciplines: definition, 123–24; faculty's accountability to, 12, 17–18; historical development of, 123; new, 124, 125; taxonomy of, 130–31. *See also* interdisciplinary academic field, learning innovation as
academic freedom: administrative staff's lack of, 12; autonomy of, 54; learning innovation scholarship and, 105–6, 126–29, 191
academic incubators, 183–84
academic units, 72; relationship to administrative units, 11
accreditation, 74, 94
active learning, 23–24, 31; in core/introductory courses, 145–46, 178, 183; development of, 142–43; efficacy of, 26; MOOCs and, 36, 145–46; research-based practices for, 33–34; students' resistance to, 179
adaptive learning platforms, 48, 98, 107, 127
administrative staff: increase in, 90; institutional service responsibility of, 12; relationship with faculty, 155–59
administrative units: learning innovation, involvement in, 13; relationship to academic units, 11
AJCU. *See* Association of Jesuit Colleges and Universities
Alexander, Bryan, 38, 128

alternative academics (alt-acs), 17, 137–38, 148–49
American Association of University Professors, 1940 *Statement of Principles on Academic Freedom and Tenure,* 126
Aoun, Joseph, 5, 24, 47
Aristotle, 123
Arizona State University (ASU), 77, 130
artificial intelligence (AI), 39, 42, 48, 83, 107–8, 132, 176
Association of Jesuit Colleges and Universities (AJCU), 19–20, 91
ASU+GSV Educational Technology Summit, 88
augmented reality (AR), 63, 96, 99–100
autonomy: of faculty, 17, 54, 86, 94, 132; interinstitutional, 70; of students, 143–44

banking model, of higher education, 4
Bass, Randy, 66
Berman, Michael, 80–81
best practices, 112, 114
Bill and Melinda Gates Foundation, 39; *Leading Academic Change* study, 46
Bishop, MJ, 46
blended learning, 5, 14, 29–30, 33, 34, 36, 55, 59–61, 71, 104, 113, 138, 143, 145, 152, 183, 184
blogs, 115, 116, 117–19, 122
board members, as learning innovation proponents, 17
Boston University (BU), 58, 183; Center for Teaching and Learning, 58, 61, 67, 68–69; Digital Education Incubator (DEI), 67, 69, 80; Digital Learning and Innovation (DLI), 67–70, 71, 80;

Boston University (*cont.*)
Educational Technology Group (ELG), 67, 69
Bourdieu, Pierre, 123–24
Brigham Young University (BYU)-Idaho, disruptive innovation at, 86
business model, of higher education, 88, 176

California State University (CSU) Channel Islands (CSUCI), 58, 183; Faculty Innovations in Teaching (FIT) studio, 70–71; Teaching and Learning Innovations (T&LI), 70–72, 77, 80–81; Teaching Toolbox, 71; "Z-Majors," 71
campus learning organizations: comparison with academic departments, 135–36; leadership's influence on, 146, 181; new, 43–46; reorganization of, 182; research and scholarship focus of, 66, 191
career paths, in learning innovation, 134–35, 136–39, 150; social media and, 120–21
CDC. *See* Control Data Corporation
centers for teaching and learning (CTLs), 1–3, 56–59, 183–84; access to, 162–63; at Boston University, 61, 67, 68–69; core activities of, 57–58; growth of, 50, 57; integrated model of, 59–62, 182; learning innovation scholarship within, 133–34; roles of, 29, 44–45, 57; trends within, 46
change, institutional, 10, 20, 53–84, 183; during 1950s, 54–55; academic innovation and, 66–77; entrepreneurial model of, 77; integrated organizational structure of, 59–62, 182; learning innovators' role in, 187–88; learning R&D focus of, 62–66; long-term impact of, 77–82; scholarly investigations into, 191
Changing Landscape of Online Education (CHLOE) report, 35
chief innovation officers (CIOs), 80–81
Christensen, Clayton, 85–86, 112, 184
classroom redesign, 183
Clemmons, Raechelle, 81

closure, of colleges, 88
collaboration, in teaching and learning, 55; interinstitutional, 2, 91–93, 182; between learning innovators and faculty, 135, 138; in online course design, 104; team-based, 138
Colleges That Change Lives (CTCL), 49
Collegiate Learning Assessment, 50–51
Columbia University, 45, 61
Coming in from the Margins (Schroeder et al.), 134
community colleges, 91, 95, 108, 142, 185–86
competency-based education (CBE), 47, 83
competition, 91, 93
conferences, 111, 112–13, 115–16
Connectivism and Connective Knowledge (course), 38
connectivist pedagogy, 38
consortia, 91–92, 111
Consortium on Financing Higher Education (COFHE), 91–92
constructivist theories, 31, 143–44
continuous improvement, 63–64
Control Data Corporation (CDC), 98–99
core/introductory courses, active learning in, 145–46, 178, 183
Cormier, Dave, 38
Cornell University, 61
costs, of higher education: administrative, 13; of community colleges, 95; cost disease, 40, 49, 174; of disruptive innovation, 87, 93; increase in, 48; instructional, 127–28; of learning-based education, 176; of nonacademic services, 86, 89–90; of textbooks and course materials, 71. *See also* tuition
course dropout rates, 31. *See also* graduation rates
course evaluations, 54, 179–80
Coursera, 38, 39–40, 41–42, 142, 144
course redesign, 30–31, 145–46, 178
credentialing, 1–2, 94, 172. *See also* graduate programs, in learning innovation
Crow, Michael, 5, 77

CTCL (Colleges That Change Lives), 49
CTLs. *See* centers for teaching and
    learning
cybersecurity, 77

Dartmouth College: academic innovation
    initiative at, 21, 183; artificial
    intelligence conference, 132; Center
    for the Advancement of Learning
    (DCAL), 9, 31, 56–57, 58, 60–61, 62,
    66; Digital Learning Initiative (DLI),
    60; Experiential Learning Initiative
    (ELI), 60; interinstitutional consortia
    membership, 91; learning R&D efforts
    at, 63, 64–65; women's studies, 129
Davidson College, 58, 183; digital
    innovation at, 72–77; Incubator, 73;
    Technology and Innovation division,
    72, 73–74, 78–79, 81
deans, role in learning innovation, 17,
    179–81, 187
*Deliberate Innovation, Lifetime
    Education* (report), 176–77
Designing the New American University
    (Crow), 5
Dewey, John, 28
digital technologies, 4. *See also* technology,
    educational
disruptive innovation theory, 85–109,
    112, 114; appeal of, 88–90; cost
    aspects, 87, 93; critique of, 90–96,
    184–85; MOOCs and, 19, 37–38,
    44–45
distance learning departments, 183–84
doctoral degree, as academic qualification,
    136–37
doctoral programs, in learning innovation,
    173–75
Downes, Stephen, 38
Duke University, 61, 183; Learning
    Innovation unit, 43–44

ecosystem, of higher education, 91–93,
    106, 182, 183
Edison, Thomas, 96–97
educational developers, 59–62, 187
educational technologists, 138
educational technology companies, 111,
    112

EDUCAUSE, 59, 111–12; Learning
    Initiative, 19, 114
edX, 19, 63, 80, 111, 142; Boston
    University's membership with, 67, 68;
    content and approach of, 41–42;
    founding of, 38, 144; growth of, 39–40;
    JusticeX, 40; MicroMasters program,
    172; networking through, 114
Eliot, Charles William, 22, 53
End of College, The (Carey), 5
enrollment, 40–41, 106, 144
entrepreneurial model, of organizational
    change, 77
Eshleman, Kristen, 64, 76, 78–79, 81
experiential learning, 24, 26, 47, 146, 183
Eyring, Henry, 85–86

faculty: autonomy, 17, 54, 94; collabora-
    tion with nonfaculty learning
    professionals, 184; increase in number,
    90; learning innovation role of, 1–2,
    17, 108–9, 179; loyalty to academic
    disciplines, 12, 17–18; student
    evaluations of, 54, 179–80; student
    learning role of, 104, 106–7; tradi-
    tional responsibilities, 54
faculty / administrative staff divide,
    155–59
Feldstein, Michael, 118, 128
financial information, transparency, 92
financial stress, in higher education,
    13–14, 177, 185–86
Freire, Paulo, 4, 28
Friedman, Thomas, 37, 39
funding, for learning innovation,
    146–47, 159–62, 180–81; allocation
    of funds, 136; central funding, 136,
    161; factors affecting, 13–14; internal
    campus services–based, 162–67; new
    methods of, 161–67; philanthropy-
    based, 136, 161–62; for public higher
    education institutions, 185–86; return
    on investment, 79–80

generalist approach, to academia,
    134–35
Georgetown University, 183; academic
    innovation initiative, 21; Center for
    New Designs in Learning and

Georgetown University (*cont.*)
Scholarship (CNDLS), 1–2, 9, 31, 45–46, 56–57, 58–60, 62, 66; Harvesting Academic Innovation for Learners, 19, 23, 114; Initiative on Technology-Enhanced Learning (ITEL), 60; interinstitutional consortia membership, 91; Leadership Round-table on Academic Transformation, Digital Learning, and Design, 19; Learning, Design, and Technology program, 1–2, 9, 45–46, 168–69; learning R&D efforts, 63, 64–65; Red House, 9, 45–46, 66; women's studies, 129
Georgia Institute of Technology, 77; Commission on Creating the Next in Education, 176–77
GI Bill, 54
governance: faculty, 156; learning professionals' involvement in, 181, 187. *See also* shared governance
graduate programs, in learning innovation, 167–75; and Learning, Design, and Technology program, 1–2, 9, 145–46, 168–69
graduate students, learning science training, 29
graduation rates: higher education, 50, 51, 55, 146, 177; high school, 177
Groom, Jim, 38

HAIL. *See* Harvesting Academic Innovation for Learners
Harvard University, 22, 38, 41; disruptive innovation at, 86; Office of the Vice Provost for Advances in Learning, 67
Harvesting Academic Innovation for Learners (HAIL), 19, 23, 114
higher education: banking model, 4; business model, 88, 176; challenges to, 13, 187; crisis in, 21–22, 48–49; diversity, 94–96; economic sustain-ability, 177, 190; enrollment, 40–42, 106, 144; financial stress in, 13–14, 177, 185–86; graduation rate, 50, 51, 55, 146, 177; radical changes in, 23; traditional format of, 53–54; turning

point in, 3–4, 20, 182; turn to learning in, 3–4, 7–8, 146, 179, 182
high schools, graduation rate, 177
Hill, Phil, 32, 128
Horn, Michael, 86
How People Learn: Brain, Mind, Experience, and School (Bransford, Brown, and Cocking), 26
How We Learn: The Surprising Truth about When, Where, and Why It Happens (Carey), 5

innovation, language of, 101–3, 109
Innovative Higher Education (journal), 118
Innovative University, The (Christensen and Eyring), 85–86
Innovator's Dilemma, The (Chris-tensen), 85
InsideHigherEd.com (IHE), 115, 118, 132
instructional design, graduate program, 1–2, 168, 172
instructional designers: collaboration with faculty, 104, 138, 158–59; educator status of, 187; organ-izational integration of, 59–62
intellectual property, 12
interdisciplinary academic field, learning innovation as, 10–11, 15–16, 122–40, 151, 155; academic freedom and, 126–29; counterarguments to, 131–39, 188; historical perspective, 123–24; research role in, 189
internal campus service providers, 162–67
International Society for the Scholarship of Teaching and Learning (ISSOTL), 27–28
investments, in learning innovation, 106–7, 176–77. *See also* funding, for learning innovation
Isocrates, 123
ISSOTL. *See* International Society for the Scholarship of Teaching and Learning
Ivy Plus consortium, 19–20, 91

Journal of Higher Education, 118
Journal of the Learning Sciences, 27

Katzman, John, 164
Keehn, Anne, 46
Khan Academy, 42
knowledge sharing, cross-institutional, 91–93, 127
knowledge transfer, 54
Koller, Daphne, 38

leadership, in learning innovation, 17, 79, 80–82, 107, 142, 179–81
Leadership Roundtable on Academic Transformation, Digital Learning, and Design, 19
Leafstedt, Jill, 71, 80–81
learner-centric institutions, 49
learning: new models of, 4–5; turn to, 3–4, 7–8, 146, 179, 182
Learning, Design, and Technology (LDT) program, 1–2, 9, 45–46, 168–69
learning activities, 154
learning analytics, 47, 48, 65–66, 152, 183; training in, 1–2, 168, 172
learning innovation: challenges to, 9–14, 22–23; definition, 6–7; educational theories of, 184–86; future of, 82–84, 108–9, 189–91; growth of, 66–67; introduction process for, 74–76; language of, 101–3, 109; long-term impact of, 77–82; obstacles to, 177–78; prioritization of, 19, 107, 109, 155, 180–81, 183, 184; re-inforcement of, 182–84; sustainability of, 7–9; traditional educational approaches in, 105–6
learning innovation community, 18–20, 104, 111–14; fragmentation of, 10, 122; social media use of, 115–22; 186–87; thought leaders of, 128–29
learning innovation events, 111–14, 115–16
learning innovators, 147–55; academic rank of, 155–59; characteristics of, 147–51; qualifications and skills, 151–54; resources of, 154; titles of, 148–50; training, 153–54, 167–72
learning management systems (LMSs), 31–34
learning professionals, 16–17, 148, 150; governance participation of,

181, 187; multiple roles of, 12–13; organizational boundaries of, 184. *See also* alternative academics
learning research and development (R&D), 62–66, 76, 78, 79, 181, 183; McKinsey's Three Horizon Model of, 63–64
learning science, 4–5; diffusion of, 25–31; training in, 29
LeBlanc, Paul, 77
lectures, traditional *versus* redesigned, 29–31
Levenson, William, 97
librarians: academic rank of, 157; learning initiative involvement of, 135
libraries, 183–84
LMSs. *See* learning management systems

Make It Stick: The Science of Successful Learning (Brown), 5
Massachusetts Institute of Technology (MIT), 38, 39; OpenCourseWare, 42, 77
massive open online courses (MOOCs), 3, 19, 36–38, 188; active learning *versus*, 36, 145–46; bubble, 58, 127–28, 141–45, 182, 197; cMOOCs, 38–39; disillusionment with, 40–41, 141; disruptive effect, 19, 37–38, 44–45; enrollment, 40–41, 144; purpose, 63; xMOOCs, 38. *See also* Coursera; edX
McKinsey's Three Horizon Model, 63–64
Minerva Education, 105, 106
Moe, Rolin, 101–2, 103, 108, 137–38
Montessori, Maria, 28
MOOCs. *See* massive open online courses
multimedia learning professionals, 59–60, 61–62

National Center for Academic Transformation (NCAT), 142–43; Progress in Course Redesign, 30–31
National Women's Study Association (NWSA), 130
NCAT. *See* National Center for Academic Transformation

networking, 18–20, 111–14; for institutional change, 160; through social media, 115–22; in women's studies, 131

New Education, The (Davidson), 5

Ng, Andrew, 38

niche programs, 47

nonfaculty educators, 148–49

Northeastern University, competency-based education, 47

Norvig, Peter, 39, 144

online education: focus of, 180; growth of, 34–36; impact of, 24; as percentage of all coursework, 29–30

Online Learning Consortium (OLC), 19, 59, 111

online program managers (OPMs), 162–67

OpenCourseWare (OCW), 42, 77

open educational resources (OER), 71, 77

organizational development, 134

organizational structure, 151; faculty/administration division in, 155–59; learning professionals' integration into, 59–62

partnerships, in learning innovation, 107. *See also* collaboration, in teaching and learning

peer review, 28, 121–22

Pell Grants, 71

Pew Charitable Trusts, 30

philanthropy, 161–62

Piaget, Jean, 28

Plato, 123

PLATO. *See* Programmed Logic for Automatic Teaching Operations

POD. *See* Professional and Organizational Development (POD) Network in Higher Education

Pollack, Martha, 21

Pope, Loren, 49

presidents, role in learning innovation, 17, 179–81, 187

prioritization, of learning innovation, 19, 107, 155, 180–81, 183, 184

private colleges, financial stress of, 48

Professional and Organizational Development (POD) Network in Higher Education, 19, 59, 111

professional associations and organizations, 10; interdisciplinary approach and, 125–26; learning innovation focus of, 19–20, 111–14, 115

Programmed Logic for Automatic Teaching Operations (PLATO), 97–100, 185

promotion, 72, 179; post-tenure, 150

provosts, role in learning innovation, 8–9, 17, 179–81, 187

public colleges, financial stress of, 48, 185–86

Quillen, Carol, 81

R&D. *See* learning research and development

Rascoff, Matthew, 43

research universities, origin of, 22, 53

residential learning, transition to online learning, 34–37

retention rates, 55

Review of Higher Education, 118

Robot-Proof: Higher Education in the Age of Artificial Intelligence (Aoun), 5, 24

Rogers, Carl, 28

Ruukel, Romy, 69, 80

Sandel, Michael, 40

San José State University, 40

Schlissel, Mark, 21

scholar-practitioners, 12–13, 15

Scholarship Assessed: Evaluation of the Professoriate (Glassick, Huber, and Maeroff), 27–28

scholarship of teaching and learning (SoTL), 11–14, 26–28, 110–40; academic freedom in, 105–6, 126–29, 191; deficits, 178; interdisciplinary approach of, 122–26; need for, 189–91; peer review in, 28, 121–22; social media and, 115–22; thought leaders of, 128–29

shared governance, 17, 54, 106

Siemens, George, 38

Simon, Herbert, 28
Skinner, B. F., 97
Skunk Works approach, 65
Small Teaching: Everyday Lessons from the Science of Learning (Lang), 5
social media, 131; cross-institutional networking on, 186–87; as learning innovation discussion platform, 115–22, 178
Socrates, 123
Southern New Hampshire University, 43, 47, 77
specialist approach, to academia, 134–35
Stanford University, 38, 39, 41
student-centered learning, 28, 31, 145–46, 182
student course evaluations, 54, 179–80
student debt, 48
student learning outcomes, 13, 14, 35–36, 40, 50–51
Sullivan, Teresa, 39
sustainability, of learning innovation, 7–9
Sweet Briar College, closure of, 88
Syracuse University, Writing Program, 29

teaching: alignment with learning science, 26, 28–29; digitalization of, 13; as learning innovators' role, 157–59, 169–72; new models of, 4–5; traditional format of, 53–54
Teaching & Learning Inquiry (journal), 28
technology, educational, 31–32, 55–56, 176; disruptive effect of, 96–101, 185, 188; ideology of, 108; role in learning advancement, 188; traditional, 53–54
tenure, 17–18, 72, 150, 179
textbooks, 54, 96–97; cost, 71; replacement with open educational resources, 71

thought leaders, 128–29
Thrun, Sebastian, 3, 39, 40, 42, 144
transparency, 92
tuition, 48, 55, 164, 165, 166, 176
Twigg, Carol, 30–31
Twitter, 115–19, 120

Udacity, 3–4, 39, 40, 41
universities, new model of, 176
University of Illinois, Programmed Logic for Automatic Teaching Operations, 97–100, 185
University of Manitoba, 38
University of Maryland, use of learning analytics, 47
University of Michigan, 183; Center for Research on Learning and Teaching, 50, 56, 67; Office of Academic Innovation, 21, 43
University of Minnesota Rochester, Center for Learning Innovation, 67
University of Texas, Institute for Transformational Learning (ITL), 176–77
University of Virginia, 39
University Professional and Continuing Education Association (UPCEA), 19, 111

Virginia Commonwealth University (VCU), Academic Learning Transformation (ALT) Lab, 82–83
virtual reality (VR), 96, 99–100

Watters, Audrey, 32, 33, 96, 128
What the Best College Teachers Do (Bain), 5
women's studies, 129–32

Yale University, 61, 183; Poorvu Center for Teaching and Learning, 45

"Z-Majors," 71